The 50/50 Solution

The Surprisingly Simple Choice that Makes Moms, Dads, and Kids Happier and Healthier after a Split

EMMA JOHNSON

sourcebooks

Published by Sourcebooks
P.O. Box 4410, Naperville, Illinois 60567-4410
(630) 961-3900
sourcebooks.com

Library of Congress Cataloging-in-Publication Data is on file with the publisher.

Printed and bound in the United States of America.
SB 10 9 8 7 6 5 4 3 2 1

*For my mom
and my dad*

CONTENTS

INTRODUCTION

Equal Rights, Equal Responsibility

I grew up in a world that blamed divorced, separated, or never-together parents for the dissolution of society in general and viewed single parenthood as a scourge and women as the victims of it all.

That's not how I see it today.

I see the ballooning number of separated families—of which one in four U.S. kids aged twenty-one and younger are a member—as potential leaders of massive culture change that stands to make parents, our kids, and our very society better.

Imagine a world where the time, expense, and emotional labor of parenting is automatically shared equally between men and women, undoing millennia of sexism to the benefit of every parent and—most importantly—every child.

I argue for a rebuttable presumption of equal parenting times—what I call 50/50 parenting throughout this book—when parents live separately. That means that when parents do not live together—whether they divorce, move apart, or never lived together in the first place—it is assumed that parenting rights, time, and responsibility are shared equally. That default, of course, is not appropriate when a parent is abusive, living with severe mental illness, or genuinely absent. This approach is already taking root in a handful of states with new laws, and it is supported by scores of excellent studies that find compelling benefits of equal parenting for children, men, and women. Organically, quickly growing pockets of parents around the United States and beyond are starting their two-home journeys equally through their own agreements, influenced by their peers and advice from lawyers and family therapists and perhaps inspired by celebrities' Instagram accounts of their own equal, co-parenting harmony.

Despite these advances, we are still far from a society-wide norm of children enjoying equal time and care from both their dad and mom. Instead, the federal government documents that 80 percent of custodial parents are mothers, and at least a quarter of kids grow up without an actively involved father.

Undoing sexist gender norms has been a monumental undertaking for the general population, and separated families are no exception. When it comes to separated families, the outdated norms mimic the 1950s mother as housewife/father as breadwinner model: kids stay with the mother, who becomes the primary caregiver, with visits from the father, who pays child support as the primary breadwinner. This model is the root of the pay, wealth, and power gaps that plague women and the gaps in mental, physical, and spiritual health that plague men, who as a group struggle with astonishingly high rates of suicide, unemployment, and isolation.

These norms, most of all, do a disservice to children. Marginalized dads, we know, check out of their kids' lives, and when they do, children suffer by every known metric: poverty, poor academic performance and future job prospects, early pregnancy, drug use, incarceration, and emotional underdevelopment and related lifetime relationship struggles.

Meanwhile, the science is clear: the closer parenting schedules are to 50/50, the better the kids fare. In fact, outcomes for these children are nearly identical to families in which their parents are married and live together.

Nonetheless, policies and laws, especially welfare and child support laws that mostly apply to poor families, drive co-parents apart and dads away from their children. Our culture reflects these laws and vice versa. *Unequal* parenting is the status quo.

If you ask women, including mainstream feminists, why it so often happens that moms are the primary parent, the answers include the following:

+ "Dads just don't want to step up and do their share."
+ "Moms are biologically predisposed to be better parents."
+ "Men are often violent so we can't assume children's safety alone with them."

Ask men why parenting schedules are so unequal, and you'll hear answers like these:

+ "It's just easier for the kids to stay primarily at one home."

+ "Feminism has given women all the power in family court, so dads rarely get equal time."
+ "I want to be more involved with my kids, but it is just so hard to co-parent and navigate the system."

The reality, as I argue throughout these pages, is that we are all victims of old systems and dated misunderstandings about child development that have colored the roles we play in partnership and parenting inside and outside relationships. And it's on us to assume the responsibility of making decisions for our families based not on outdated scripts but out of love, understanding, and compassion, with the best information available.

If you are reading this introduction in an online book vendor's preview feature or at your local bookstore and you never actually buy the book, here are the things I need you to know:

+ Scores of studies over the past couple of decades have drawn a remarkable conclusion: fathers and mothers are equally important to the development of children. In fact, children have the capacity to equally bond with men and women, and moms and dads have equal capacity to bond with children—*from birth*. Babies can and do bond with more than one caregiver. Most of all, in all the research on shared parenting, it is the **kids who have an even split of 50/50 time with each parent who fare the best throughout childhood and for the rest of their lives.** No study has found negative outcomes associated with 50/50 parenting schedules.

+ Equal parenting schedules do not compromise child-mother bonds.
+ Parents who share parenting time equally fight less, and equal parenting is connected with lower rates of domestic violence and child abuse.
+ Moms with 50/50 parenting schedules earn more money.
+ Dads who are actively involved with their children are happier, healthier, and more professionally successful and may even live longer.
+ The phenomenon of 50/50 parenting is sweeping the country and the world in new laws and dramatic cultural shifts. If you do not get on board today, you will be a relic judged by future generations, including your kids.

The big takeaway is that even when conflict is high, even when there are periods in time when a 50/50 schedule is not appropriate, equal parenting time can and should be the presumption.

Why I Wrote This Book

In publishing, they say you write the book you need.

In my case, this is the book I needed to write to work through all the mistakes I made in my own divorce and single-parent journey. It is the book I needed to write to forgive *my* parents for the mistakes they made in their divorce and single parenting. And it is the book I needed to write to help other moms and dads do it better—not only for themselves but also for their kids (who are really all our kids, our future) and a better, less gendered, more inclusive, and healthier world.

This book, though, is not about me. This is the one part of *The 50/50 Solution* where I tell you about my own journey, because you likely want to know and because I am here to tell you: if my kids' dad and I got to 50/50, you likely can too. First, I'll spoil the ending: I'm not someone who vacations with my ex-husband or who has boozy brunches with my kids' stepmom. We are not all best friends. However, after fifteen years of co-parenting, we are doing better than ever, hang out at the kids' events, and are welcome in one another's homes. Our claim to fame is that our two households—my kids' dad and his wife, my boyfriend and I—all successfully and happily relocated to a new city a couple of years ago.

However, over the years, my kids' dad and I have had a rough go of getting to a 50/50 schedule.

The short version: we were married, living in New York City. I had taken time off from my career when our daughter was born. Shortly after, my then husband suffered a traumatic brain injury that would have killed most people, but miraculously, he survived. But not without setbacks.

Within a year of my husband coming home from the hospital, I'd given birth to another baby, and my husband had moved out. Here is where I skip over the details for the sake of my family's privacy and co-parenting harmony. But I need you to know that our first years after separation included the following:

family court appearances, a temporary restraining order with police station custody exchanges, and me arguing for majority parenting time with no immediate overnight visits. The latter was motivated by a very legitimate concern, considering my ex's brain injury, and colored by my own sexism.

I was a mess—so ready to get away from this man while also loving him very much and worrying about him. I would find myself enraged at him while also sympathetic to his recovery and rooting for him—for us—to be better than our own upbringings, which were largely devoid of our fathers. We both wanted him to be an involved, present dad.

But we hadn't set up our relationship for equality when we were married, and neither of us sought it when we divorced. Early on, it never occurred to me to have a 50/50 schedule—I didn't know any families that did and had never seen them in the media, and none of the attorneys or mediators or therapists that I consulted even suggested it as a possibility. Now, perhaps they were looking at our tragic brain injury reality and saw that 50/50 would not be an appropriate structure for our family, but here is what I wish I had at that time and what I propose that we set forth for families, including those facing difficult situations:

+ Laws on the books throughout the land that presume my kids' dad and I have both equal rights to and equal responsibility for our children
+ Expectations that both parents be equally responsible in time, logistics, and dollars

+ Support systems in place for the myriad issues that can and do come up with human parents, including physical and mental illness, addiction, and more

In my case, since our family was going through a very difficult situation, either of us would have been able to reach out to a court mediator, or my attorneys would have diplomatically counseled me that I could make my case for a majority-time parenting schedule, and if that was granted, we'd work with court professionals to help us move toward an equal parenting schedule. Everyone in this ecosystem would reiterate that equal parenting schedules are known to be what is best for kids. This model would communicate to my kids' dad that he was safe to take some extra time to heal and not be at risk of permanently losing his time or relationship with his children. This model would have communicated to me that I would have to be flexible in the spirit of being a good mom. Perhaps we'd have fought less. We'd certainly have spent less money on lawyers and felt less anxiety over what our futures would look like, because we would be guided by a road map that looked pretty compelling and fair. And these counselors would remind me, *you may think you want your kids with you all the time, but trust me: in a few years, you will need a break. Thank me later.*

Instead, I hired an attorney who set me up for the standard-issue divorce package. The "basic plan," if you will:

The kids and I stayed in the nice home we owned.

I got majority time with the kids—a newborn and a toddler.

My ex moved into an apartment.

He paid child support.

He visited the children on weekends.

And like many women, I got standard-issue "support" along with my standard-issue divorce: unsolicited advice, astonished rage, and loaded rhetorical questions—all from family and friends who had recently been so supportive of my marriage but who now wanted me to win not only the war of divorce but the war of women vs. men:

+ "Take him for all he's worth! He owes you."
+ "Are you going to allow him to see the kids?"
+ "You'll relocate to be near your family, obviously."
+ "If you moved, he would fade out of the picture. Then you can raise your kids like you want and not have to deal with him."
+ "Whatever you do, don't let him off the hook."

Much of this advice was shocking to me, even if on some level, it did appeal to my divorce rage at the time. I mean, he'd been a good dad. We both loved the kids. Why would I want him out of their lives just because my feelings were hurt or he was so difficult?

Still, I bought into most of it. If divorce is a battle, I won. And if divorce is a feminist battle, I really won. After all, I was now being compensated for the unpaid labor I provided by taking care of the kids that benefited his career, right?

Except that over the next couple of years, my victory soured.

In the early years, despite my earlier insistence that the kids belonged primarily with me, I found myself *living* for the kids' eventual Saturday overnights with their dad and the Wednesdays when he'd pick them up from school for their weekly dinner visit.

Beyond the time imbalance, I was in charge of the emotional labor: making and keeping appointments, schlepping to soccer/ theater/chess/dance/trumpet, arranging and attending meetings with teachers and counselors at their school, managing and paying for health, dental, and eye care. Basically, everything fell to me—even as he returned to his career and generally recovered from his injury.

I desperately craved a break from parenthood. I reveled in those Wednesday afternoons when I could work uninterrupted. I hungrily used these hours to book meetings and attend networking events. I eagerly anticipated evenings when I could go for dinner with girlfriends, enjoy a date without the expense of a babysitter or stress about coordinating time out of the house.

From where I sat, fatherhood appeared to be an optional, choose-your-own-parenting-adventure, while motherhood was an expected duty. Men insisted on their rights as fathers, but there was no sense of equal responsibility. I would come to see that women often insist on our right to be the dominant parent but eschew our financial responsibilities. Equal rights must mean equal rights *and* equal responsibility in a civilized society—including civilized families.

For years, I kept a mental tally of what I did for our children and what my ex didn't. The list mushroomed, and so did my resentment. Tension morphed into conflict. I was bitter. My rage grew as, eventually, nearly all the financial responsibility fell to me and especially as the inequity affected the kids, who wanted to spend more time with their dad.

Even though we were usually pretty pissed at each other, my ex and I do have a deep connection, forged by knowing each other for twenty years. I could see—when my ego and rage would deflate for long enough—that not being the involved dad he always dreamed of being was destroying him too. Eventually, over the years, we chipped away at that delta in our schedule: I'd approach him with the suggestion he take one more overnight, then two, then eventually, we agreed to split the schedule and expenses down the middle—regardless of what had been filed in the courthouse. One week his house, one week my house. Holidays and summers 50/50.

That one move improved the dynamics of our whole family, including for the kids, who by now were in middle school.

This experience compounded that of my own childhood, when I very deeply connected with my father despite the fact that he struggled with depression and addiction and was an every-other-weekend dad. Our connection ended up faltering for lots of reasons: his struggles, ensuing conflict with my mom, and some adultification that gave me, a child, the power to veto visits. By the time I was ten, he had largely slipped out of my life—a loss that also fuels the work I do to advocate for 50/50 parenting.

The undercurrent of my own passion for this work is my WWE-level internal wrestling match with my lifelong relationship with mainstream feminism. One of my early acts of defying gender norms was as a high school senior in my rural Illinois hometown in 1994, writing a term paper that argued for legalized prostitution. "Is she allowed to do that?!" one of my classmates asked the teacher in hushed horror. Before that, I joined a pro-choice rally with four other women in front of the local courthouse where we waved wire coat hangers in defiance of threats to *Roe v. Wade*. There were unshaved armpits and Take Back the Night marches in college. And in this century, my kids and I campaigned hard for Hillary—and even harder against Trump/for Biden.

For the past decade, I have been devoted—professionally and personally—to closing gender gaps through my work as a journalist, on my blog, Wealthysinglemommy.com, in my books, by speaking about equal parenting at a United Nations gender summit, and through various media projects. The more I peeled away the layers of gender, especially through the lens of parents who live separately, the more it became clear that in my own divorce, I had bought blindly into a lot of cultural-normative assumptions about men and women and what is fair. In sorting out the aftermath of my divorce, I unearthed what would come to be a deep cynicism about my beloved feminists.

In researching this book, I interviewed Harvard economist Claudia Goldin, considered the grandmother of gender economics and who has since been named the first female to win the Nobel Prize for Economics. I was thrilled that she quickly responded to my email request for an interview and nervously prepared to jump on a call with her. I spent an hour or so typing notes that detailed her insights about how limited government data is in regard to father involvement, braved her bristling responses to my reporter-y prompts for tidy quotes, and joined her in a good laugh when she quipped that Bill Gates, who'd recently announced his divorce, "will be a noncustodial dad—which anyone can be in an eighty thousand-square-foot house."

But when the subject of father equality and child support arose, Goldin's response stopped me in my tracks, mouth agape. "If a parent isn't paying child support, we probably don't want him around the children," she said.

For real?

"I'm not saying he can't be a good dad, but if an individual isn't working, disproportionately he is going to be on something—and that is not the sort of person we want with kids."

In sum, this Harvard grandmother of gender economics believes poor men are dangerous to their children. Never mind the mounds of quality research that give voice to the reality that men, nearly universally, want to financially support their kids but often simply can't afford to—they're not deadbeat but *dead broke*. Forget about the sweeping changes to federal and state programs that address unaffordable child support and its impact on families, because we know that the best thing we can do for children and their parents (and the state) is to support relationships between children and their dads. Goldin seemed to be blind to the facts and stuck with vintage narratives about men, especially poor men, being worthless losers unworthy of parenthood.

As I conducted the research to write this book, I ran into that mentality from older feminists time and again: *Equal parenting is nice if it works but should not be the presumed norm since men are so dangerous.*

Increasingly, I find myself dismayed, angered, and puzzled by headlines in my news mainstays like the *New York Times*, the *Atlantic*, and NPR that stick to the narrative that I bought into when I was fifteen years old, thirty years ago, waving my coat hanger in front of the Sycamore, Illinois, courthouse: *Men have all the power. The patriarchy is unilaterally evil and omnipotent. Men are abusive. Women are victims. Dads are incompetent fools at best, with a high probability of being dangerous. Children don't need fathers.*

After years of hearing from so many single, divorced, and separated fathers and mothers, my early assumptions about gender and parenting could no longer stand up to the facts. If women are so powerless, why was it so easy for me to attain primary care of my children? And if primary care of children is a feminist coup, why was it so overwhelming and miserable? If the patriarchy was beating us all down, why were so many of my peers and I enjoying so much professional success (albeit while also feeling so burned out by taking care of kids and home at the same time)? And why have so many headlines over the past half century screamed about the very real need for more equality in household labor and childcare but failed to put forward the obvious answer for separated parents: equal time sharing?

Those mainstream media headlines increasingly rang to me as simplistic, reductive, and myopic at best—not to mention sexist.

But as I dug into the research, I found that they were also often filled with lies. The facts and science are readily at hand, and yet there is one dominant narrative that blatantly dismisses and/or vilifies men. Even lazy caveats that qualify claims with "most" and "often" ("most men don't want to be equal parents") are still firmly sexist, marginalizing *half* of the population as inherently flawed—including my own darling son. As time went on, my rage at mainstream feminism heightened and left me feeling marooned.

Which is why a flippant comment by a Harvard feminist about the basic inability of poor dads to even be around their children left me feeling like my feminist, progressive tribe had jumped the proverbial feminist shark. The day of that interview, I hung my head in shame, dismay, and self-hatred. I could see how our feminist rhetoric was actually hurting all of humanity.

That was September 1, 2021. The evening of that day, after dinner with my feminist children and my feminist boyfriend, I checked the day's headlines on my Apple feed, and dominating every news outlet, local, state and even international, was this: Texas had banned every abortion after six weeks, and the U.S. Supreme Court voted not to block it. *Roe v. Wade* was soon to be overturned.

Feminist whiplash smacked me right across my feminist face. The patriarchy had struck once again. "We are fucked," I said aloud.

I would like to say that I have reconciled my conflicting feelings about gender, equality, family, and divorce, but I have not. I have only distilled two things that I know to be true:

1. Gender is messy, complicated, and evolving and devolving

simultaneously, and equality will not magically present itself, especially if we do not unpack how complex it is and acknowledge our own blind spots.

2. Separated families provide a unique opportunity to address gender inequality. After all, it is impossible to legislate equal childcare for married couples, but it is absolutely possible—and very effective—to legislate gender-neutral, equal parenting for the fourteen million U.S. families who live separately.

The 50/50 solution is possible for nearly all separated families, what I wish I had known from the start, and what I want for you.

A Note about Lexicon

I am living in the real world, and I one hundred percent acknowledge and respect that many families are not heteronormative. However, one of my top goals for this book is to make what can easily be wonky and academic information easy to understand to a broad audience. As such, I have stuck to referring to families as having moms and dads. This is also because so much of the sexist norms at the root of this issue are, indeed, entrenched in mom-dad families. You will notice that I also defer to stereotypical gender norms when describing things like child support and custody—referring to primary custody parents and child support recipients as moms only, though about 20 percent are dads. Again, this is for the sake of ease for the reader as well as to focus on the inequalities at the root of this issue.

1

The Cult of Motherhood and Gender Gaps

"This is a mere and subtle form of anti-feminism by which men—under the guise of exalting the importance of maternity—are tying women more tightly to their children than has been thought necessary since the invention of bottle feeding and baby carriages."

—Margaret Mead

"Mothers don't want to give up the self-esteem, the status, and the power that comes from being told, 'You're so special as a parent, you're superior as a parent.' Who wants to give that up? That's a good feeling. What price are you paying in your relationship? What price are your children paying for you being mother superior? What price are you paying economically for that?"

—Linda Nielsen, PhD, Wake Forest University professor

When parents live separately, the majority of moms have the kids with them the majority of the time. The reasons are many:

+ If the parents lived together, the mom was probably the primary caregiver, and couples tend to replicate their married dynamic postdivorce.
+ The father's job is more demanding, so it is easier for her to take on the child-rearing.
+ Most parents adhere to the idea that kids fare best when they live primarily in one home and that home should be the mother's, as another common notion is that women are biologically better suited to parenting than men. We also fall into assumptions that men simply are uninterested in or are incapable of daily parenting and thus grant the child-rearing domain to women.
+ "Winning" majority custody is often motivated by money, as more custodial time equals more child support and more control overall and is considered a triumph in a contentious breakup.

Yet all these perceived advantages to "getting the kids" come at a steep price for women. In reality, an equal parenting schedule is best for women, for our children, for the men we co-parent with (and the men we love, who may or may not be the same person!), and for gender equality.

Today, now that structural sexism like laws barring women from schools, jobs, and banks has largely been removed, the core variable in gender equality is time. If moms and dads each have equal time to invest in their careers, educations, and businesses—which also means they spend equal amounts of time taking care of the kids and keeping the household running—women can earn equally. That leads to equal buying power, equal investing power, and eventually equal influence in business, politics, and the world. In the United States, women have made remarkable strides in these public spheres, with women now being either equal or in the majority across all levels of education and early professional life. Yet gender pay and leadership gaps persist—mostly because of family demands on women's time.

While we cannot legislate what happens inside a marriage and require husbands and wives to equalize childcare and housekeeping and therefore equalize earning power, we *can* legislate what happens after parents divorce. There is a unique and powerful opportunity for legislation and family courts as well as our culture to support separated parents in creating truly gender-equal families where each parent takes equal responsibility for the children in time, care, and money.

But first women have to acknowledge that we are not perpetual victims and own the fact that we hold tremendous power over domestic life in our culture. Popular opinion supports women being primary caregivers and assumes, erroneously, that we are biologically superior to men in this regard. As a result, when we split with our partners, single moms get primary custody nearly all the time while also receiving child support—even, sometimes, when she earns more and even when she can financially support her household. If we buy the narrative that parenthood (motherhood) is our most meaningful work, then women are masters of the private realm.

As I will elaborate on in the next chapter, public programs have been successful in curbing poverty rates for women and children, while men increasingly struggle financially. All around us, we see scholarships, grants, programs, conferences, and opportunities of all kinds that specifically target women—women who already have an upper hand when it comes to family, children, and home and now, more and more, degrees and jobs and financial security in larger numbers than men.

It's time for women to recognize that we have the ability to change our lives, our families' lives, and the whole world for the better—if we can share this power. But first we must understand what gaining this power has cost us.

Consider Elizabeth. When Elizabeth and Sean met in their late twenties, she was working in marketing for a media company, and like all her friends, she was passionate about her career. That was one of the things that drew Sean to her and her to him—he was also very ambitious and focused on building his career in sales. "From our first date, we loved talking about our work. As the relationship grew, we discovered that we both like setting goals, and I always felt like we supported each other in that way," Elizabeth said. "We were on the same team. Whenever I got ahead at work, Sean was the first person I told, and he was always rooting for me. We earned about the same back then, and all our bills were paid from the same joint account. I hardly remember how we divvied up the household chores—we both just took care of what was needed, and it always seemed fair."

Fast-forward a few years and the couple married and left the city for the suburbs, and today have three children under age ten. Elizabeth quit her six-figure marketing job after their first baby was born, and since then, Sean has earned the family's income as a sales executive for a pharma company, often traveling while Elizabeth manages the house and kids. "Everything I read and everyone around me told me that it is best for kids when they have a parent at home, and it just made sense that parent would be me—just like it was my mom and her mom before her," said Elizabeth. "Even though I loved my career and had worked hard for my degrees and promotions, being home with the kids just seemed so important. I believed that kids need their mom home. Most of the other moms in the neighborhood also stayed home. Plus, I really loved being with them. I didn't want to feel like I was missing out."

Nonetheless, the arrangement left her feeling like she had no breaks, no appreciation for her work as wife and mother, and a sense of being stuck—especially compared to Sean, whose career was skyrocketing. "I'd be so exhausted from the kids and resentful that he got to leave the house and be part of the world every day. When he walked in the door in the evening, I'd practically throw the baby at him." Yet whenever fights escalated and Elizabeth fantasized about leaving the marriage, she stopped cold at the fact that she had no income of her own. "I'd think, 'There is no way I could get divorced and afford to stay in this house.' I really wanted to give the kids that stability. That is what we set out to do as a couple."

Sean, meanwhile, resented the fact that the house was often a mess and that he was expected to do half of the childcare and housekeeping when he got home on top of the long hours required to keep his career progressing. It all made Sean feel unappreciated in his role as the breadwinner. "I am expected to do half the housekeeping and childcare when I am home but have no choice but to earn 100 percent of the income. It's really overwhelming," he told me. "I'd always assumed that she would go back to work when the kids started elementary school, but that just isn't happening. And I can't do anything about it."

Sean also felt stuck. "I'd think, 'If we divorced, I'd have to pay so much in alimony and child support, lose a chunk of my retirement—and barely get to see my kids.' And that is pretty much what happened."

Tensions between the couple led to constant fighting, and while the story is not entirely clear, Elizabeth blamed Sean for having an affair, while Sean says he has his own suspicions about Elizabeth's conduct. No matter the reason, Elizabeth and Sean have divorced. She has the kids the majority of the time, and he pays her more than $6,000 per month in alimony and child support, even though she now works full-time as support staff for a real estate agency. Just as she'd hoped, Elizabeth stayed in the house they had bought together.

While they were married, Elizabeth and Sean were a

modern-day June and Ward Cleaver (plus a generous dollop of bitter acrimony): he worked and earned money and depended on her to care for house and home. She cared for the kids and home and depended on his income.

Now, divorced, that dynamic is exactly recreated—and then some. With an every other weekend and Wednesday night dinner schedule for Sean to see his kids, Elizabeth is clearly the primary parent.

Elizabeth spends afternoons running to hockey practice and piano lessons. She is the one who schedules pediatrician visits, researches summer camps, and runs interference with home-work. When the kids get sick on a Friday when Sean is tech-nically on the parenting clock or a blizzard closes schools for a week in their New Jersey town, it's Elizabeth who takes time off from her job to care for the children. "Even if I get fired, my job is less critical," she told me. "Sean makes so much more than me."

Sean is still stuck as the breadwinner, and because he has twenty-four-seven standby childcare—thanks to Elizabeth—he never has a reason to figure out how to care for the kids in a pinch or contemplate taking a professional hit to prioritize family. And Elizabeth is still stuck as the full-time caretaker despite her full-time job. She is often burnt out and resentful that Sean doesn't do his share—which isn't helped by the fact that she is still finan-cially dependent on him. Meanwhile, Sean and Elizabeth's kids are growing up entrenched with gender-typical role models, which studies find time and again are a powerful predictor in whether boys grow up to participate in childcare and girls' future professional success. Gender gaps persist, and no one wins. "I love that my kids see me as the main parent, the one who is there for them after school, but I hate that my girls mainly see me as a mom—not as a professional," Elizabeth says. "That bothers me."

Sean and Elizabeth didn't set out to be relics. Like most parents, they went with what they knew—moms take care of kids, dads work—even though it wasn't working well for either of them when they were married.

While there are so many stories of men being the unavailable primary providers and women being the unappreciated primary caregivers—and trust me, as the founder of a website and a Facebook group for single mothers, I have heard tens of thousands of them—there are also always extenuating circumstances that make each situation feel unique:

+ "He starts drinking after the kids are in bed."
+ "He works the night shift."
+ "He cheated—he doesn't deserve them."
+ "He stays up all night playing video games."
+ "He moved in with his girlfriend after two months. I don't want the kids to be around her."
+ "He doesn't put them to bed on time, and they are exhausted."
+ "He doesn't *want* to take them more than every other weekend."

Underlying all these urgent arguments against equal time with the dad is the notion that the mom is within her right to decide how many hours each week her children's father is allowed to see them—a blind sense of power so pervasive we rarely question it.

Today, while women have fought and won on many fronts of the gender revolution, the majority of families are still rooted firmly in 1950s nuclear family values prototypes: woman as caretaker, man as breadwinner. Man has power in the world, and woman has power at home. Time-use studies by the Pew Research Center and the Bureau of Labor Statistics from the last two decades report that mothers who work outside the home shoulder 65 percent of childcare responsibilities versus 35 percent for men—an imbalance that has remained consistent since the year 2000 and been reported on ad nauseam in *New York Times*, Slate, *Washington Post*, and *Atlantic* articles about how women do it all and are about to break!

According to some study findings, these figures are hardly poised to improve. While survey after survey finds that the majority of young people believe that women and men should be treated equally in the workplace, a startling (to me at least) percentage of millennials believe that a woman's place is in the home. A National Institutes of Health poll of American high school seniors found that in 1994, 58 percent disagreed with the notion that families work best when the man is the breadwinner and the mother is focused on taking care of the home and family, but by 2014, only 42 percent of high school seniors disagreed. More recently, a 2019 Gallup poll found that men aged eighteen to thirty-four were the least likely age group to perform daily childcare instead of their female partners—5 percent versus 7 percent of men aged thirty-five to fifty-four and 10 percent of men fifty-five and up. One glimmer of hope is that the youngest group of men was more likely than their older counterparts to wash dishes, clean the house, cook, and do laundry, although the 2021 American Time Use Survey shows that women still do an hour more each day of housework and childcare than men, a gap that gets bigger the younger the kids in the household are. Survey findings published by Pew in 2023 found that of parents who live together—married or cohabiting—mothers overwhelmingly say they do the majority of childcare tasks like scheduling, homework help, and providing emotional support, while dads say either *they* do the majority or the couple shares those tasks equally.

In her book *All the Rage: Mothers, Fathers, and the Myth of Equal Partnership*, Darcy Lockman summed up these trends: "The rising status of women outside the home has actually increased our inclination to reinforce male dominance inside it." That may be true, but there is evidence that men are actually working just as hard at household tasks, though they may be outdoors with yard work, doing more of the driving, especially during dangerous weather, and taking care of the family's vehicles. Also, there looms the question as to whether all that housework actually needs to be done. Can't the mom just relax her standards a little?

In fact, research finds this perceived labor gap is indeed complicated. One study found that the more professionally successful a woman is, the larger her share of housework at home, suggesting that she overcompensates for emasculating her husband by doing more "feminine" vacuuming and cooking, while he may do less "women's work" to underscore the idea that his masculinity is being encroached on by his wife's growing paycheck. Actually, married mothers overall do more housework than single moms. The single moms I know have plenty of theories on this: *I'm no longer picking up after his slobby ass! I can finally relax in my own home!*

I aim to extend grace to all parties involved here. I don't think most of these struggling couples intentionally malign one another's gender or professional success, but we are all complicated products of our cultures, policies, and families of origin while also being annoying and human.

Even those of us who are astonished by these attitudes also hold our own unconscious, deeply gendered attitudes. We are all guilty of sexist behaviors that hold ourselves and our families back—including hovering over our kids all the time.

It is often reported that U.S. moms spend far more hours, including far more intensive parenting hours, than past generations, with working moms today investing at least as many hours with our kids as stay-at-home moms did in the 1970s. Meanwhile, thanks to technology (dishwashers, Swiffers, easy-to-clean kitchen floors, snowblowers, leaf blowers, and air fryers that will lickety-split heat your vegan Trader Joe's samosas) and perhaps more lax expectations of sparkling clean homes, we now spend on average far fewer hours on housework than our grandmothers and mothers did—hours we shifted to intense parenting. Americans, after all, have powerful work ethics.

The irony of all the fighting for more parenting time in divorce is that as a whole, parents today seem to enjoy parenting less—especially higher-income, white parents. More than ever before, parents across social classes feel more pressure to be constantly teaching and nurturing our children, engaging in high-intensity parenting that can include an exhausting schedule of running kids around to multiple extracurricular activities, tutors, and therapists; coordinating playdates; intently playing with our children; and listening to their feelings—all tasks that are taken on disproportionately by mothers, regardless of whether all this intensive parenting actually helps our kids or whether our co-parents agree that all that parenting is actually a good idea. That same 2023 Pew survey found that almost a third of us find parenting stressful some or most of the time, with three times as many lower-income moms than upper-income moms finding parenting enjoyable (38 percent versus 14 percent). Far more mothers than fathers say being a parent is stressful, yet we perpetually argue to maintain the power and responsibility over the home front.

Why? Why do so many of us assume such gendered parenting and household roles in the first place? Especially when many of us apparently do not even enjoy caring for these kids who are making us stressed and broke and breaking up our relationships?

Could it be that women are spending more time on childcare because they are doing extraneous activities while men focus more on what truly needs to be done at the same time as giving the kids the gift of free play and independence?

If we aren't enjoying our parenting duties, why do we accept—even fight for—these gendered stereotypes after our marriages end? Even when we resented how unsupported we felt in this women's work during the relationship?

This chapter is not an exercise in victim blaming. Instead, I aim to illuminate how societal expectations to be the primary parent have held women back in the working world but also granted us dominance at home. And this is a power we abuse at the expense of the very children we aim to nurture—and ourselves.

Custody Started Off as a Win for Women

Today, unequal parenting time holds women back financially and professionally, but the norm of primary custody being awarded to divorced mothers actually has its roots in nineteenth-century feminist activism. At that time in Britain, children were valuable primarily for their ability to generate income—as wage earners in lower-class families and inheritors of property and titles for the rich. Meanwhile, married women were considered property of their husbands rather than autonomous beings of inherent worth. Women's assets, their income, and even their children were the legal property of their husbands. In the event of divorce, children were treated as a financial asset and as such remained with the father, and the mother had no rights whatsoever to see her children.

That is until British novelist and socialite Caroline Norton lost her young children when she filed for divorce from her violent husband, George Norton. When she left George after yet another physical fight, he sent their three children—the youngest of whom was still only two years old—to his sister's house and denied Caroline any right to see them. Caroline fought fiercely and publicly to keep her children, writing pamphlets and articles and lobbying for the favor of friends and politicians all the way to Parliament. In 1839, in direct response to Caroline's campaign, Parliament passed the Custody of Infants Act, granting custody of children up to the age of seven to their mothers and guaranteeing mothers the right to visit with their children up to the age of sixteen. Queen Victoria signed the bill into law and extended a personal invitation for a visit from Caroline, curious about this fierce female advocate.

Interestingly, the biggest pushback against the bill by parliamentarians was that giving women dominant rights over children would lead to an increase in divorce—which history has proven to be quite true.

Norton's case was part of a shift in Western culture, which was beginning to move away from thinking of children as miniature adults with financial potential and toward an increased embrace of the emotional and psychological development of young humans, including how that development is tied to their parents—especially their mothers. Laws governing child labor and compulsory education swept Europe and North America, and Victorian mothers were expected to both breastfeed and bond with their babies—even though bottles and nannies were common. During this time, the "cult of motherhood" started to emerge. Women were gaining legal rights, industrialization meant fathers increasingly worked outside the home for long stretches, and advances in home technology meant women had more time on their hands to invest in their children—an effort that was increasingly concentrated as families had fewer children. At the same time, a new surge of popular women's magazines started to standardize a family culture that put a Christian mother at the center of the home, according to University of California, Berkeley, professor Mary Ann Mason. "The cult of motherhood, portrayed as a romantic, even spiritual ideal, worked to women's favor in obtaining custody of their children after separation, divorce, or death of a husband," Mason wrote in her 1994 book *From Father's Property to Children's Rights: The History of Child Custody in the United States.* "Judges' decisions increasingly noted the superior role of mothers in their decisions, thwarting the father's common law right to control and custody of his children." What was true in Victorian times continues in courts across the country today, thanks, in part, to Caroline Norton.

Indeed, Caroline's winning argument was that mothers are inherently better suited for parenting young children and that keeping children in their mothers' care was in the best interest of the child. As such, the Custody of Infants Act prioritized the *best interest of the child* over the financial and legal rights of a father. Its passage was a pivotal if imperfect episode in the continuum of making custody laws both gender-neutral and child-centric (which I will later show is the same thing).

The British Custody of Infants law eventually percolated into U.S. law in the form of the "tender years doctrine," which held that young children were better off in the custody of their mothers because they needed maternal care. This well-intentioned principle would become a fundamental part of divorce law that still hovers over American courts—and our culture. Culturally and legally, custody laws that are guided by the tender years doctrine only codify our blind assumptions that children fare best under maternal care—a notion that helped to institutionalize feminine power but has come to shackle women to home and child.

The tender years doctrine began to give way in the 1970s, and by 1981, twenty-two states had passed laws abolishing tender years as the leading precedent for custody decisions and instead were taking a case-by-case, gender-neutral approach, known as "best interest of the child." Today, "best interest of the child" is the language dominating family law. In theory, *best interest* is gender-neutral, but given the lack of any guidelines in determining a custody schedule, families and their lawyers are left to duke it out to determine which parent is, in fact, the better caregiver. These arguments were deeply influenced by a 1973 book written by a law professor, a "child analyst," and a psychiatrist. According to scholar Mary Ann Mason, "In their book, *Beyond the Best Interest of the Child*, the authors created the concept of the 'psychological parent': the one individual, not necessarily the biological parent, with whom the child was most closely attached. In their opinion this person should have total and if necessary, exclusive custodial rights, including refusing visitation to noncustodial parents."

In essence, the tender years doctrine prioritizing mother care was replaced by a best-interest doctrine centered around attachment parenting—a supposedly gender-neutral practice of encouraging baby-parent bonding by way of feeding on demand and maximum physical contact that in effect prioritizes mother care and mother responsibility. After all, throughout these decades of debate, moms have been the ones spending the most time with babies. The tender years doctrine may no longer have been on the books, but it was still very much in our hearts, minds, and courts. The adoption of the best interests of the child was the advent of what New York divorce attorneys call "the Friday night special"—kids live with their mom and spend every other weekend and Wednesday dinners with their dad. The dad builds his career, the cliché goes, and pays the mom child support and maybe alimony. This keeps the dad connected, but the child benefits from the security of that primary attachment. But it didn't work out so great.

Early in the mass-divorce years of the 1970s and 1980s, about half of these dads checked out completely, and today about 25 percent of fathers are not meaningfully involved in their children's lives, with, of course, the mom picking up all that slack.

The Importance of Mothers Gets Taken to an Extreme

The debate over child custody is deeply influenced by the twentieth century's obsession with psychology and data-driven parenting. Increasingly, we turned to social science to answer what millennia of religion and tradition could not. This is where questions about parental influence meet gender politics, and what you may believe to be true about attachment parenting and the importance of your role in your kids' lives is probably all wrong.

Enter the father of attachment parenting, John Bowlby. Nearly a century ago, British psychologist John Bowlby pioneered the early field of child development and cemented cultural norms that blame mothers for their children's shortcomings. Bowlby's early research concluded that criminals and sociopaths were likely to have grown up without a mother, and the aftereffects of these findings still have a grip on modern parents' fears, no matter how dated and since disproven. After all, how many moms reading this (raising my hand) worried that failing to breastfeed or constantly snuggling our newborns would prevent our children from forming human connections, with results akin to warehoused Romanian orphans?

That's not the only assumption that Bowlby injected into the collective unconscious. In the early 1940s, Bowlby hypothesized that human infants bonded primarily with one parent—typically the mother (of course) up until the age of two (he later amended it to age five). As a result of this intensive bonding, he also theorized that periods of separation from the mother ("maternal deprivation") led to kids suffering emotional and psychological impairment. In 1940, Bowlby published his findings on his examinations of twenty-two children who had broken relationships with their mothers. His findings? "Fourteen had become affectionless thieves and three had become schizophrenic." In a follow-up experiment, Bowlby interviewed forty-four teenagers who had been caught stealing in their early lives and compared them to a group of forty-four teenagers who did not have criminal records. He concluded that fourteen of the thieves had been separated from their mothers for longer than six months before the age of five, compared to only two in the non-stealing group. Did he consider any other factors of these teens' lives—their relationship with their father, their economic conditions, their schooling, their diet? Nah. By his own admission, he ignored every other variable.

Even mothers who remained present weren't off the hook. In another experiment where Bowlby examined "neurotic children" who were raised by their mothers in a stable home (meaning, they were "looked after by their mothers and well cared for according to ordinary standards"), he observed a root cause of "the personality of the mother and her emotional attitude toward her child." It wasn't enough to merely be present; the mother had to be eternally beguiled by her child and not exhibit "impatience over naughtiness...odd words of bad temper...or a lack of the sympathy and understanding which the usual loving mother intuitively has."

Bowlby's ideas crossed the pond to heavily influence American thinking with his 1953 paperback, *Child Care and the Growth of Love*, which claimed that a mother's love and care was primarily responsible for her child's mental health and went so far as to herald the mother as a child's "psychic organizer," without whom the child's mind would be eternally discombobulated. Over the next ten years, that book was reprinted six times, was translated into fourteen languages, and sold more than four hundred thousand copies in Britain alone. News coverage around the world contained quotes such as "only the hands of a mother can shape destiny" (Italy), "a relationship of cause and effect between a mother's love and a child's behavior is almost mathematical" (France), and "social behavior depends on mother love" (South Africa). In the United States, Bowlby was invited to write for *Ladies' Home Journal*, with titles including "Mother Is the Whole World" and "Should Mothers Work?" (His answer? Need you ask?)

For Bowlby, it wasn't even a question of whether young children *could* have a primary attachment to their fathers, having said "it is fortunate for their survival that babies are so designed by Nature that they beguile and enslave mothers." (Enslave!) And that "little will be said of the father-child relation; his value as the economic and emotional support of the mother will be assumed." There was also a strong biological component to Bowlby's views—he explained attachment as an evolutionary necessity, for in order to keep their children safe from predators when living on the savannas, mothers needed to keep them close.

Bowlby's ideal twenty-first century mother, like her mother before her, was a woman enslaved by her power.

The Fetishization of the Stay-at-Home Mother

Thanks in large part to this history, there remains enormous social pressure on women in the workforce to forsake their economic power in lieu of family. Nearly two-thirds of American adults believe kids are better off when a parent stays home, and just shy of half of us still believe that that parent should be the mother if both parents' incomes are equal. I felt that pressure from my own mom. In my bougie neighborhood, I am often asked by new acquaintances if I work. (My answer: "Why wouldn't I work?") This pressure is so great that women who actually earn a living falsely label themselves "stay-at-home moms."

A few years ago, a project between my friend time-management expert Laura Vanderkam and *Redbook* magazine found that 62 percent of self-described stay-at-home moms contributed to their household income, including 25 percent who run businesses. I know a divorced blogger who earns $80,000 per year and calls herself a stay-at-home mom—a disconnect that is both common and destructive, since it perpetuates the perceived pressure for women to sacrifice our livelihoods for our children and husbands.

We fetishize stay-at-home moms despite the fact that research finds again and again that everyone is happier, healthier, and more financially secure when both parents work—including the kids. That obsession also keeps those gender gaps vibrant.

A Harvard Business School study of thirty thousand adults in twenty-four developed countries found that daughters of working mothers finished more years of education, earned higher salaries, and were more likely to be employed and in supervisory roles than their peers raised by moms who never worked. In the United States, daughters of working mothers earned 23 percent more than daughters of stay-at-home mothers, and sons spent seven and a half more hours a week on childcare and twenty-five more minutes on housework. "In other words, when mothers work outside the home, the pay gap narrows, and the labor gap inside the home narrows," the study's lead author, Harvard Business School professor Kathleen McGinn, told me. The study was replicated and results corroborated over a total of one hundred thousand adults in nineteen countries. In further good news for working-mom guilt: sons of mothers who had paying jobs earned just as much as their peers who had stay-at-home moms, tended to choose partners who were employed, and held more egalitarian attitudes. Best of all, both groups of adult children were not more or less happy than their peers.

But what about all those poor babies neglected by their ambitious mothers? And what about all those working single moms whose babies are abandoned to childcare?

We tie ourselves in knots over whether mothers should work, work too much, or otherwise spend a moment extra away from our children. Yet throughout history, including modern history, women have worked outside the home in large numbers.

First, a history lesson. Today, moms spend on average fourteen hours per week with their children—40 percent *more* hours than mothers did in 1965, according to Pew. For three- to eleven-year-olds, mothers spend an average of eleven to thirty hours each week either fully engaged in activities with their kids or nearby and accessible when needed. In 1975, moms spent just seven hours per week with their kids. And today, working mothers spend the same number of hours with their children as stay-at-home moms did in the 1970s.

Yet we uphold those post–World War II years as a family ideal we sacrifice to achieve. That period was marked by a worldwide need for nurturing and comfort from the traumas of war—not to mention rebuilding the economy. TV shows and magazine ads from the 1950s and 1960s lead us to believe that most women—at least middle-class white women—were home with their fancy new appliances, tending to a wounded nation. In reality, they were flooding into the workforce just like their men.

Despite the advent of the GI Bill, which guaranteed (mostly white) veterans attractive mortgage rates and free college most families relied on, women marched into jobs created by the postwar industrial boom (clerks, secretaries) and baby boom (teachers, nurses). In fact, women's participation in the U.S. labor force has steadily increased since World War II, more than doubling since 1940.

The truth is this debate over whether mothers should work is strictly one for the rich. Keep in mind that Betty Friedan penned her landmark *The Feminine Mystique* to document how miserable all the (rich, white) stay-at-home moms were during those postwar years, yet for most families since the dawn of humanity, resources have been simply too scant to devote any healthy adult to hugging babies all day. Most families need a woman's labor to survive.

Stephanie Coontz, emeritus faculty member at Evergreen State College and director of research and public education for the Council on Contemporary Families, challenges our collective nostalgia for bygone eras that were usually a lot more rotten than we remember. In an article for *Life* in 1997, Coontz wrote the following:

Families in which mothers spend as much time earning a living as they do raising children are nothing new. They were the norm throughout most of the last two millennia. In the 19th century, married women in the United States began a withdrawal from the workforce, but for most families this was made possible only by sending their children out to work instead. When child labor was abolished, married women began reentering the workforce in ever larger numbers.

For a few decades, the decline in child labor was greater than the growth of women's employment. The result was an aberration: the male breadwinner family. In the 1920s, for the first time a bare majority of American children grew up in families where the husband provided all the income, the wife stayed home full-time, and they and their siblings went to school instead of work. During the 1950s, almost two-thirds of children grew up in such families, an all-time high. Yet that same decade saw an acceleration of workforce participation by wives and mothers that soon made the dual-earner family the norm, a trend not likely to be reversed in the next century.

Nevertheless, old narratives—and prominent research—die hard. Bowlby produced papers until his death in 1990, and his work strongly influenced family law in the United States. His attachment theory then paved the way for attachment parenting, which hit American parents like a plague in the early 2000s when Dr. William Sears, a pediatrician, and his wife, Martha Sears, a nurse, published *The Attachment Parenting Book: A Commonsense Guide to Understanding and Nurturing Your Child*. This tome led a generation of parents to believe that co-sleeping, breastfeeding, wearing the baby, and answering their every cry were the only ways to raise secure, happy children. It was yet another brick in the wall of working mom guilt—one that has also hobbled our kids, which I elaborate on in the chapter about child development.

Despite our eons-long history of working mothers, the should-moms-work war rages on. While mainstream feminists are increasingly urging women to keep a foothold in the workforce, the default attitude about mothers and career for half a century has been *It's a choice. Do what you feel is best for your family.*

However, more often not, that choice isn't about what's best for the kids—it's about money. Surveys find that most women want to work. Today the question is about whether women can *afford* to work, with the cost of childcare for poorer women often higher than the money they'd earn.

Equal parenting addresses this issue. A 50/50 schedule means that neither parent has to choose between work and care while also making it clear that both parents are responsible for both earning money and caring for children. Less choice means less guilt.

All this to say, when it comes to parenting—both inside and outside a traditional marriage—many of us are aiming to replicate some feminine ideal that never existed, forces us into lesser- or nonpaying career paths, and probably doesn't serve our kids.

The Cost of Mommy Guilt

Mommy martyrdom is not just an ill-advised parenting tactic. It is the root of the pay gap between men and women.

Despite popular beliefs, lingering remnants of gender inequity are not the fault of bros like Mr. Hart in *9 to 5*, chomping on cigars, patting subordinate women's tushes, and commiserating in a C-suite about how to keep ladies in their place. A growing body of research paints an increasingly clear picture of the actual story of the very real gender income pay gap and its deep and gnarly roots of mom guilt.

Indeed, thanks to broad efforts by governments and business institutions as well as individual women and men who have advocated for change and those who have leaned in, we have made remarkable strides in equalizing education and opportunity for girls and young women. Ever since 1979, women have been the growing majority of college graduates, and they now make up a majority of many professional and master degree programs. By the year 2020, there were more than 3.2 million more women than men enrolled in degree-granting programs.

In fact, today, the higher education gender gap is wider than it was in 1972—15 percent versus 13 percent—but today it is reversed, with fewer men than women in college. Women enter the workforce in equal numbers, in equal positions, and with equal pay as men, and for younger women, this is reflected in an ever-shrinking pay gap.

The pay gap is the most-cited measurement of sexism, and both are very real. As of 2023, white women overall earn seventy-three cents to every white man's dollar while Latinas (fifty-four cents) and Black women (sixty-four cents) fare even worse. Asian women come the closest, at eighty cents. There are also gaps in overall wealth (fifty-five cents invested for every man's dollar), corporate board seats (28.9 percent female), and Congress (28 percent women as of this writing in 2023). Not to mention that women report being enraged at their male partners for not doing enough at home as well as feeling physically and mentally taxed, with mental health challenges for working women linked to pay inequity. I would be remiss not to remind us, in assessing our power, that since the 2022 reversal of *Roe v. Wade*, we have very few reproductive rights in most U.S. states.

Even the pay gap is showing signs of enormous progress. In 2022, the difference in pay for U.S. men and women aged twenty-five to thirty-four is just 8 percent in favor of men, though as these women age, like the women before them, they are likely to experience that figure grow as they sacrifice professional and earning power for parenthood.

Guilt may be a useless emotion, but it has consequences—mommy guilt does indeed slash our earnings now and in the long term. Working mothers experience parenting guilt at far higher rates than working fathers. A survey by the *Harvard Business Review* found an obvious difference in how men and women executives considered work-life conflicts. Fathers overwhelmingly chose work without regret while mothers were more likely to feel guilty—so much so that one female executive cited the fear of missing out on the joys of motherhood as a major reason women leave the workforce or decide not to seek promotions. While women sacrifice earning and career success, men sacrifice their parenthoods and family success for hours at the office.

In summary, although women and men start their careers out of the gate as equals, within a few years, the effects of mom guilt result in women in fewer leadership positions and with lower earnings.

This phenomenon is perfectly illustrated by Elizabeth, who earned equally to her husband when they met, was out of the workforce for about a decade, and now makes about a fifth of his income in a job that doesn't fully utilize her education or experience, largely because of her goal to parent full-time and long-term.

For single moms, the gender income disparity is especially stark but also more complicated. Using 2013 U.S. Census data, research concludes that single moms' income from work is just 65 percent of that of single custodial dads, though government programs are largely successfully addressing this issue for women but not men. The reality is that single parents overall are poorer and less educated and have fewer resources than married parents, and they are more likely to be a racial minority, with 64 percent of Black children, 49 percent of Native American children, and 42 percent of Latino children being born to single-parent families versus 24 percent of white and 16 percent of Asian children.

Single-parent poverty is a result of a complex tangle of racial inequities, generational poverty, and the simple fact that it is more expensive to maintain two homes than one (as would a "traditional" married couple). However, for single moms, garden-variety mommy guilt is compounded by additional factors:

+ The belief that children should be primarily with their mothers, which is institutionalized by the family court, welfare, and child support systems
+ Fear that the kids will be destroyed by living in a "broken home"—an attitude that keeps unmarried moms from leaning into earning opportunities and perpetuates the gender gap in lieu of more time at home, even when the risks and reality of poverty are higher than when women do so
+ The fact that single moms disproportionately parent alone (true to the stereotype), and the time and logistical burden of parenting prevents them from working and earning equally to their children's fathers

IN THE PURSUIT OF BEING A "GOOD"– MARTYRING–MOM, WOMEN

+ **Seek out lower-paying careers than men**, such as teaching (77 percent of the 5.5 million K-12 teachers in America are female), because of the flexibility they afford.

+ **Drop out of the workforce to accommodate caregiving**, meaning they then have less work experience, less seniority, and lower pay than men when they do return. In 2019, only 66.4 percent of mothers with children under the age of six participated in the workforce. Taking even one year off to care for kids comes with a steep price for women, who will earn, on average, 39 percent less a year when they return than women who never left.

+ **Play small at work** because of parenting pressure. A Pew survey found that 23 percent of moms versus 17 percent of dads said they turned down promotions for the sake of family time. I wonder about the parents who didn't even go for that promotion in the first place.

+ **Are more likely to work part-time**, and part-time jobs tend to mean lower hourly wages, fewer benefits, and fewer opportunities for promotion compared with full-time workers. A 2019 Pew survey found that 54 percent of mothers versus 44 percent of fathers said they've had to reduce their work hours to part-time to care for kids. Similarly, 54 percent of working moms and 43 percent of working dads say their parenting responsibilities mean they can't give 100 percent at work.

+ **Co-create parenting relationships** (both inside and outside relationships) in which the woman is the default and primary caretaker of children and home.

Is this just another version of *Lean In*, in which privileged white women yell at all women to buck up, plow through the hurdles, and be aggressive in their careers for the sake of equality?

A little yes, but also no.

Especially since the pandemic, there has been a groundswell of demand for more government family support: affordable, quality childcare, paid parental leave, flexible work schedules, and ample vacation time. These are benefits enjoyed by northern European countries that also model strong equal parenting practices. President Biden snuck in universal basic income with the child tax credit, which, along with other recent government programs, is credited with lifting single moms and their children out of poverty.

While some strides have been made in the United States and things are improving, it is a chicken-egg conundrum: without women in leadership, family-friendly policies are not advocated for. Without family-friendly policies, few women reach decision-making roles. One study looked at very affluent Americans, earning more than $845,000 annually (who technically qualify for the top 1 percent of earners). Of the male one-percenters, only 29 percent had a spouse who worked. When the top earner was female, 84 percent of their spouses also worked. This disparity can be explained by the fact that even though these high-earning men likely partnered with a similarly educated and professionally successful woman, his earnings so outsized hers that it was not a difficult decision for her to off-ramp her career to support his. These traditional roles are more common for the very rich than other couples, researchers wrote: "Related norms encourage women to use their household division of labor to signal social status: for high-income, high-wealth couples, a traditional division of labor may be seen as a luxury and a measure of these processes work together to lead super-rich couples to opt for a traditional male breadwinner–female homemaker/caregiver arrangement much more frequently than other couples."

They continued, "Married men, unlike married women, are more likely to have partners who perform the majority of unpaid labor in their household and are willing to compromise their own careers to favor their spouse's ambitions. This tendency is particularly pronounced once a couple has children." In other words, even though parents of this class can afford to hire help for housework and childcare, women still end up managing this realm of family life. Once again, that mom guilt comes at the cost of gender equality in the workplace, as these highly educated and likely once-professionally employed women stay home and their masters of the universe husbands keep dominating the galaxy.

The effects of this gender-typical circus among the one-percenters trickle all the way down the economic ladder. Another study found that men with wives who did not work outside the home were less likely to promote women or otherwise value female leadership. Without having to share parenting duties with a working spouse or an equal parenting schedule with an ex-spouse, these men were shielded from the struggles of balancing work and home, making them less likely to advocate for family-friendly work or government policies that would benefit all families.

Affluent couples that divorce tend to keep to these gender norms: the high-earning dad keeps at his big career while the now ex-wife continues with her hands-on parenting, afforded by alimony and child support—as illustrated by Elizabeth's support of Sean's career. In these cases, these women are far more incentivized to fight for that majority time since there is so much money at stake, and they may have lost much more career momentum than a middle-class mom who stayed home for a shorter time out of economic necessity. Even in this now-separated affluent family, it is still the woman who is on the call list for school, who manages the zillions of appointments, homework, and behavioral issues of childcare.

Feminist writer Jill Filipovic told Twitter, "More mothers at home makes for worse, more sexist men who see women as mommies. Men with stay-at-home wives are more sexist than men with working wives." It is poor women, including single moms, who are hurt the most by a lack of family-friendly jobs that pay a living wage and instead get stuck in low-earning jobs in a search for the flexibility that parenting requires.

There is no legal lever that might force wives to work or force husbands to take on more childcare or housekeeping (or require moms to lean back on the housekeeping and childcare). But we can legislate how families are structured and paid for when parents live separately and unmarried. A cultural and policy presumption of 50/50 would forcibly equalize these responsibilities, making men in power aware, firsthand, of the realities of caregiving. Not only does this equal schedule allow single moms to participate more in the workforce, it also frees men (or challenges them?) to broaden their focus and be influenced firsthand to advocate for policies that benefit all caregivers, now that they are 50 percent caregivers themselves.

Let's take a look at some of the cultural attitudes that are standing in the way.

Intuitively, it is easy to grasp the concept that an equal parenting schedule would net equal earning for men and women, but I could not find any data to substantiate this hypothesis. So a few years ago, I did my own research.

In my survey of 2,270 single moms, 86 percent said they are not reaching their full earning potential. Of those moms, 30 percent said the key to earning more is increased childcare, and 22 percent said more child responsibility sharing with their child's father would increase their income. A full 87 percent of single moms said that if their kids' father took on more parenting time, they could earn more money, and 30 percent said they'd be happier. Other highlights that shine on the money and co-parenting connection include the following:

+ Moms with a 50/50 parenting schedule were 54 percent more likely to earn at least $100,000 annually than moms whose kids are with them most of the time (with "visits" with the dad).

+ Moms with a 50/50 parenting schedule were more than three

times (325 percent) more likely to earn $100,000 than single moms with 100 percent time with their kids.

+ Moms with 50/50 parenting schedules were more than twice as likely to earn $65,000+ than those with majority time and nearly three times as likely to earn that sum than moms with 100 percent parenting time.

This was a survey from my blog readers (my blog is not focused on equal parenting but single motherhood overall, yet still not a terribly representative sample). What happens in real life when equal parenting is the law? In 2010, Spain passed an equal-parenting law that was adopted by five of the country's seventeen regions, which led to 40 percent of divorced families in those regions sharing parenting time equally. In 2022, researchers found that the Spanish law has resulted in numerous benefits, including a decrease in "contentious and wife-initiated divorces and increase in the employment of mothers relative to fathers." Researchers wondered if the reason could be that women now had more time to balance paid work and childcare or if the financial hit of divorce forced them into the workforce (which would be true no matter the parenting arrangement; two homes cost more than one). In any case, studies find that mothers who work are happier and provide more financial stability for the whole family, and that both boys and girls benefit from their influence.

While Elizabeth and Sean are a cautionary tale of how *not* to manage a marriage or divorce, let's take a look at Cassandra and Akim, an example of a good divorce—no matter how hard-won.

While married, like many moms, Cassandra felt like she shouldered far more than her fair share of the housework, childcare, and emotional labor—on top of working full-time as a program manager in the education industry. But no amount of therapy, fighting, or begging would change the relationship. After the divorce, Cassandra struggled financially on a single income, initially with child support. "I would create a budget based on what I earned plus the $300 per month he gave me. I hated that I constantly worried that I couldn't make it if that child support went away," she told me. "It was my goal to get off child support." It was also her goal to get to 50/50 time-sharing even though after the divorce, their three grade- and middle-school kids stayed primarily with her. "His schedule was Friday through Sunday every other weekend, with one night per week that alternated based on his work schedule," she said. "Plus, Akim lived with his mom in a small home, and there was barely enough room for everyone to stay comfortably."

Cassandra felt overwhelmed and became increasingly angry that despite separating from her husband, she still had to *do it all*. But she also saw how much her kids missed their dad and how depressed he was to be separated from them so much. A year into their separation, Akim was able to move closer and get his own place, and they switched to a 50/50 schedule and agreed to no more child support.

"That was two years ago, and we did go through some adjustments. I mean, at first he would pick up the kids late because he was still doing laundry! But then he realized that he *could* wash clothes while the kids were there. Things got better. Since then, I have been able to focus on my career without constantly worrying about when my kids need to be picked up from school or have their sports practices organized. That uninterrupted, kid-free time when I can just focus is priceless. I've been able to earn two promotions, my income has increased by $24,000, and this year I am on track to earn six figures for the first time. I never would have guessed this was possible, but 50/50 shared parenting was the best thing that happened to my relationship with my ex."

The Myth of the Maternal Instinct

Core to Caroline Norton's arguments in her pamphlet *Observations on the Natural Claim of a Mother to Her Children* is the idea that a mother's rights to her children are inherent to her sex. This argument would later be called *maternal instinct*, and it's the theory Bowlby furthered with his own research— the widespread belief that there is a biological hard-wiring that bonds women with their children in ways not possible for a man.

However, researchers have debunked the notion that the adult-child bond is gender-specific. "It's totally false that women have a maternal instinct. It is not true that babies form an attachment bond to their mothers that is stronger than to their fathers," said Linda Nielsen, PhD, a Wake Forest University professor who has conducted many studies on equal parenting and written books on father-daughter relationships. In reality, Nielsen said, "Babies cannot bond emotionally to anyone until they're seven to nine months old. The brain is not capable of it. Until you change that myth, people are going to say no to shared parenting for kids under the age of one because they fear it will cause an insecure attachment with the mommy."

In fact, scientists now know that men and women both have the capacity to bond with their babies—connecting to the baby's needs and being able to pick out their own baby from a crowd of baby cries. It is assumed that because women carry the babies inside their bodies, their ties to the child are stronger and that men can't possibly have an equivalent physiological and hormonal response to their own infant. Yet when their partners are pregnant, dads' estrogen and cortisol levels go up and their testosterone levels go down. "Those hormones which are affecting the mother are also affecting the father to get him and the baby bonding with each other. The same areas of the brain light up in the father's brain as in the mother's brain when they hear their baby cry," Nielsen told me. "It's a myth that women's hormones and brains are better wired to take care of children and babies."

In fact, it is the very act of caring for a baby that triggers the parenting, says Jodi Pawluski, PhD, behavioral neuroscientist at University of Rennes, France, and author of *Mommy Brain*. "We often think that parenting is a mother's job and that she is 'made to do it,' she 'just knows,' but in fact, parenting is all about learning, and it doesn't matter if you are a mother or father, birthing or non-birthing parent, you can also 'just know,'" Pawluski said, adding that this applies to adoptive parents and grandparents too. "Everyone, regardless of gender, has everything in their brain they need to parent. They just need time with their child to figure it all out. Parents aren't born, they are made."

But what about when a parent—any parent—does bond with a child and that child is taken away for hours or days at a time? What about when a mother deeply bonds with her baby, and then the baby is sent for weekends with a father with whom the newborn has not yet bonded? While family experts recommend introducing the child to the dad with shorter visits or more frequent check-ins with the mom, the science has found that equal parenting promotes stronger bonds with dads *without compromising the bond with moms*. In fact, it is not gender but the amount of time and intention that a parent puts into connecting with their child that strengthens bonding—yet another argument for a 50/50 schedule. If we fear that dads are not connecting with their kids, the answer is to have them spend more time—not less—together.

Ladies, this is good news. Science has freed you from your role as primary caregiver. Now we can all shimmy off those shackles and bask in equality, right?

Not so fast. In reality, many women *don't want* to share their dominance on the parenting front. Instead, we pride ourselves on knowing what's best for our kids and go to great lengths to control how and when our children's fathers parent. This tendency is so well established that scientists have named it: *maternal gatekeeping*. Maternal gatekeeping describes the phenomenon of women exerting control over their partners' parenting—and in the case of divorce, parenting time. It manifests as words and thoughts such as "You're not doing it right," "You don't know how to do it," or "You just don't care as much as I do."

There's a fine line between taking the lead in parenting and taking over to the point where the other parent has been diminished. Too many of us cross that line, and you can argue that either parent taking a lead by definition diminishes the other parent.

Linda Nielsen told me, "Mothers don't want to give up the self-esteem, the status, and the power that comes from being told, 'You're so special as a parent, you're superior as a parent.' Who wants to give that up? That's a good feeling." After all, those in power fight to maintain that power. But no one tells us we are powerful. We are told motherhood is victimhood. "What price are you paying in your relationship? What price are your children paying for you being mother superior? What price are you paying economically for that?"

That price is steep. A study by researchers at Brigham Young University found that women who were classified as "gatekeepers" did five hours more family care each week and had less equal divisions of household labor than women who were classified as "collaborators." And then we resent it. We resent our kids' dads. We resent our kids. We resent how much we become tied to the house and our kids' needs at the expense of our well-being, our interests, our careers.

Another divorced mother, Michelle, wonders if her marriage might have survived if she had gotten a grip on her constant criticism of her husband. "Max is not a bad guy—he really loves the kids and wanted to do the right thing. He still does," she said. But Michelle had a clear idea of how the kids should be raised: healthy, homemade food for all meals, a strict routine, a very tidy house. "I'd come home after a long day at work and the house would be a mess and he'd be warming up a frozen pizza for them and I'd lose my mind," she remembered. When he'd take on bedtime routines, she'd get frustrated if he deviated from her method and allowed the kids to run around naked after the bath or jump on the bed instead of getting straight into pajamas and preparing to read. "I had my reasons: I'd read all the literature about how important routine is and a calm nighttime ritual. But now when I look back, they were all having such a good time, and my bitching just made him not want to participate at all, which only made me madder."

Eventually the marriage broke down, and the couple did commit to a 50/50 postdivorce schedule, which ended up resolving a lot of parenting struggles they'd had when they were married. "At first I was overwhelmed trying to keep *my* way of things going at *his* house, and everyone was stressed out. One example: it was important to me to continue our ritual of showing the kids *A Christmas Story* every year on Christmas Eve—something that I'd done as a little girl with my parents. One Christmas when they were with their dad for the holiday, they came home and hadn't seen it. I blew a gasket. But our therapist helped me realize that I had to let go of so much control if we were going to be good co-parents. She also stuck it to me and said, 'Moms are not automatically better parents just because we're women.' That really got under my skin, but probably because deep down I assumed that I was the better parent because I gave birth to these kids, nursed them, and was so obsessed with them, frankly!

"Now I feel like he enjoys being a dad so much more than when we were married—and when I do want to discuss something, he's a lot more open to listening and participating. For example, I was recently worried about some behavior things with our son, and instead of just telling Max what to do to fix it, I called him and asked how things were at his house. He had some really good insights that I hadn't thought of. He suggested he call our son's teacher to get some more feedback and then report back to me, and together we figured out how to handle it. It was a little uncomfortable that what we agreed on wasn't 100 percent how I would have managed it, but I reminded myself that this was the sort of co-parenting that I'd always wanted. I just hadn't had the skills to do it when we were married."

It isn't just anecdotal that men who are belittled in their parenting take on a sideline, nor is it a uniquely American phenomenon. Studies in Taiwan and China have found a link between the presence of maternal gatekeeping and less father involvement—which only hurts kids, despite moms closing the gate in an effort to expose their kids to "better" parenting. When dads are shut down, kids suffer.

Maternal gatekeeping also exerts a big cost on dads. Men's innate parental instincts are just as strong as women's. Men too crave connection to their children. They want to love, hold, snuggle, and raise their children. When dads are held at arm's length—or worse, when they're legally denied meaningful time with their children—it robs them of an essential part of their humanity. In one early study, dads who received minority time custody after divorce became unengaged 50 percent of the time.

Consider Gary, a dad of three in his late thirties who found himself in a marriage that looked more or less like that of his minister father and stay-at-home mother. "I worked all the time building my engineering career, and she was a stay-at-home mom who had a lot of strong opinions about how to raise children," Gary said. She took the lead in insisting on attachment parenting, organic eating, and self-directed discipline. "I really wanted to be the involved dad and changed the diapers and put the kids to bed every night. But whether it was parenting or chores, I was criticized for never quite doing it right, and she would just come in and take it from me. I never had the opportunity to fail as a parent, and that is the only way you grow and learn. I just wound up with low self-esteem as a dad."

Ultimately, as women, we must accept that while we are at a disadvantage in the upper echelons of business and politics, we absolutely hold the power in the domestic sphere. Those with power have responsibility. If you and I have the support of family courts and our culture to control how our families are structured, how much time our kids spend with their dads, and how much autonomy our current or ex-partners have in parenting, it is on us to own that responsibility and use it judiciously— even if by most objective measures you are the "better parent."

Assuming both parents are not severely violent or actively

addicted, it doesn't matter who is the better parent. Kids are entitled to the parents they have. In the past three decades in the United States and beyond, we have defaulted to a rebuttable presumption of joint *legal* custody in which both parents have equal *rights* to decisions about education, health, and religion as well as access to records. We must take this a step further and equalize *time responsibility* for all parents, just as we assume equal rights and responsibility for married parents.

Divorce Corp., a documentary on the broken family court system, illustrates the fallacy of the "better parent" equation by illuminating how greedy lawyers and a corrupt court system egg on divorcing parents to duke it out in order to prove which one is the "better" parent and win majority custody. On a hypothetical ten-point scale, a very good dad who scores an eight would be denied meaningful parenting time if the mom in that family scored a nine. Likewise, a mom (perhaps struggling with addiction or mental health issues) who scored a three would win custody over a dad who scored a two. Both families would endure fights, family court appearances, money spent on lawyers, and lots of acrimony—all under the guise of "best interest of the child." Meanwhile, the latest child psychology research has found that the 50/50 schedule, which communicates to children that both parents are meaningfully committed to that child, is the one that serves the child best. In other words, the better parent is *both* parents. I'll cover this in much greater depth in chapter 3, but for now, the takeaway is this: in the vast majority of cases, a 50/50 schedule *is* in the best interest of the child.

Also, children are not entitled to *good* parents. They are entitled to safety, having their basic needs met, and, assuming it does not threaten their safety, access to their family of origin. After all, there are plenty of married parents who are twos and threes on the parenting scale who raise their kids without any question. Just as we no longer "reeducate" Native children in boarding schools or camps in the name of a subjectively "better" upbringing, it is no longer the role of the state to shuttle children around to marginally "better" homes.

So why do most moms continue to fight for majority time? Especially when the mom is not arguing over legitimate safety issues (in which case no parenting time or only supervised time may be in order)? The real reasons are usually about control and, most likely, money. If getting more child support is your underlying motivation for getting primary custody, here is a bit of unsolicited life coaching: just let him go. Go for a 50/50 schedule. Be proud that you are advocating for what is best for your kids. Model grace and care for one of the two people your kids love most. Embrace the unfettered time to work, chill, date, exercise, and live a life that is better than what you experienced in your miserable relationship.

If women can get over ourselves enough to open the parenting gate, dads have to figure out childcare for the portion of time that the kids are with them and how to work all day and still get dinner on the table and coordinate school drop-offs and pickups, activities, and playdates. Dads do their share, and moms get time off. And best of all, we don't feel guilty about it because we know that everyone is better off this way.

2

Beyond the Male Breadwinner

"Men want to be parents and need to be parents, but our systems and culture have not supported men. They actually create barriers. Men who check out have a story, and they need healing."

—Kevin Bremond, Alameda County Fathers Corps

When we talk about living in a sexist society, the conversation is nearly always about the sexism women experience: the pay gap, the leadership gap, rape culture. And we're right. Our world is sexist against women.

It's also sexist against men.

In the United States, men are falling not just behind women but also behind where they were just a decade ago in education, employment and earnings, mental health rates, and life expectancy. While women justifiably complain of finding motherhood overwhelming, men are denied meaningful engagement with their children, but the yin and yang of this story is rarely discussed, including for separated families.

Studies estimate that women initiate divorce about 70 percent of the time. Feminist scholars and everyday women alike estimate it is because *mothers are so worn out by doing it all and men just don't want to change.* In other words, women initiate divorce because men suck. However, others put forth another theory: men have more to lose in divorce than women and are therefore less inclined to file. After all, divorce and separation have meant that women get the kids, alimony, child support, and maybe even a house—all at the expense of their ex-husbands. Just 20 percent of single dads have primary custody, and a very small number of the rest have an equal parenting schedule. While men's suicide rate is four times that of women's, rates for divorced men are twice that of married men (while there is no difference in suicide rates between married and divorced women). In fact, divorced men die by suicide at a rate *eight times* that of divorced women, according to one 2003 study in which researchers called out sexist custody practices as a possible explanation. While divorce laws have changed for the better since that study, men's suicide rates still far exceed women's. Overall, a lack of contact or meaningful relationships between fathers and their children is closely tied to men's well-being and that of their children, both boys and girls.

We are evolved adults who are capable of holding two ideas

in our minds at the same time: women are subject to sexism, *and* men are subject to different sexism. Advocating for men should not detract from the experiences of women. We all need to take care of each other.

I hope this chapter will help foster a call to action for the men in your life and beyond, as many men in our communities and families are truly and deeply struggling—in part because they miss out on the fathering that children and mothers need too. In this chapter, I'll explain how these trends are especially grave for men who live separately from their kids, how even seemingly thoughtful programs can serve as a barrier to engaging fathers, and how they can be transformed to heal our families and communities.

Men Are Hurting

In this moment in history, while we celebrate strides in narrowing or even eradicating gaps in pay, leadership, and education between men and women, the pendulum is swinging devastatingly too far in the wrong direction. In addition to all the measures I introduced at the start of this chapter, men, particularly Black, Hispanic, and Native men, make up 93 percent of the prison population in the United States. Between 2019 and 2021, life expectancy for men declined by 3.1 years—nearly a full year more than it did for women. Young and middle-aged men are less likely to be employed now than at any other time in history. Men are also significantly more likely to use illicit drugs, commit a mass shooting, and become radicalized. Why?

Hurt people hurt people.

The story is also true for our boys, who are failing in schools that are not designed to serve them and who score lower than girls from the earliest grades through college, where women have outnumbered men for years yet for whom scholarships and special programs abound. I find myself pointing out these inequities in interactions in my daily life: replying to a local girls-only arts program seeking donations with a plea for more support for boys (complete with links to supporting statistics); giving the stink eye to a new acquaintance who, at a middle school event, casually told a table full of boy parents that he, his wife, and daughters think "middle school boys are the worst! I know how their minds work!"; or questioning a teacher about the appropriateness of a high school classroom poster that reads "Girls Are Perfect."

These are disheartening yet socially acceptable symptoms of our sexist dismissal of an entire half of our population. They are also closely tied to a lack of father involvement. It is impossible to absorb the avalanche of evidence that men and boys are in crisis and still hold on to the perpetual message that women are universal victims and men are the universal enemy. It's time to accept that our whole gendered system is universally broken.

I know what feminist liberals say. After all, I am one, and so are most of my family and friends. *But what about the gaps that still exist in pay and leadership? What about the constant and subtle discrimination and stress that women experience just from living in a patriarchal society?* While these are critical measurements of equality, they are also patriarchal measurements of power.

Another critical measurement that we rarely factor into the equation is power at home, over children and the domestic sphere. We never talk about the power of love. We rarely talk about the power of family. Women absolutely dominate in this realm, a fact that is very easily measurable: women are the dominant parent four-fifths of the time when parents live separately. We get the kids, and in theory, we get all the good things that come with parental love: influence, importance, purpose, connection, meaning. Parental love, I argue, is the lifeblood of a good existence for most of us, an element that science finds translates into good health, meaningful employment, community, and connection.

A quick tour through recent statistics on men's well-being is ugly. While I'm listing these effects one by one in tidy bullets, the truth is, they are all intertwined and have an effect on one another. Your mental health trends downward when your earnings do—especially if you've been told your whole life that your biggest contribution to society and to your family is as a breadwinner. The lower your education, the lower your income, the lower your likelihood of finding a romantic partner if your culture dictates your attractiveness is intrinsically linked to your career success. Yet for simplicity's sake, let's look at them one by one.

MENTAL HEALTH

While overall, women experience mental health issues at a higher rate than men, men are far less likely to seek and receive help. According to 2020 data compiled by the National Institute of Mental Health, 51 percent of women with any type of mental illness received mental health services, while only 37 percent of men did. Maybe not everyone needs therapy, but talking about your problems is important for gaining perspective and feeling supported, yet men are less likely than women to do even that. A survey of one thousand men found that 77 percent had experienced mental health challenges such as anxiety and depression, yet 40 percent had *never spoken to anyone* about those challenges. That may explain why, in 2020, the rate of suicide in men was nearly four times higher than in women in the United States and that men are almost twice as likely as women to binge drink. It is relevant to note that any record of mental health or substance abuse issues is often used as a weapon in custody disputes, further discouraging already disadvantaged dads from admitting these vulnerabilities.

EARNINGS

A report from the Becker Friedman Institute for Economics at the University of Chicago looked at six decades of data on lifetime earnings and found that despite how much our economy has grown in the last fifty years, median lifetime earnings for men peaked in 1967 and then declined by about $4,400 per year. Meanwhile, women's median lifetime earnings have been steadily rising. To be clear, women are still earning less than men over the course of their lifetimes as well as on an hourly basis. Between 1980 and 2018, women's median hourly earnings for nonmechanical jobs (requiring analytical, social, and managerial skills) grew by 45 percent to $22 per hour, while men's wages in the same category increased only 14 percent, from $23 in 1980 to $26 in 2018. For jobs that require mechanical skills, such as manufacturing, where you might expect men to outperform women in terms of wage hikes, women still enjoyed significantly more progress—women saw a 32 percent wage hike between 1980 and 2018 in these jobs, while men's wages rose only 5 percent. The pay gap is still real, and women still suffer from it, but as it closes, the suffering has been transferred to men in terms of unequal educational attainment and long-term employment opportunities—and the related toll on their mental and physical health.

EDUCATION

The education system is designed for kids who can sit still and pay attention—a learning style that is much more suited to girls than to boys. Boys tend to lag in literacy skills and are much more likely than girls to be disciplined or referred to special education. In 2022, just shy of 40 percent of men attending college earned a bachelor's degree in four years, compared to slightly more than 50 percent of women.

LONELINESS

Since 1990, the number of men who say they have at least six close friends has fallen by half to 27 percent, and the number who say they have no close friends at all has increased five times to 15 percent, while that number is 10 percent for women. Only one in five guys say they have received emotional support from a friend in the last week, compared with four in ten women.

HEALTH

Declining education rates for men are also tied to bigger declines in life expectancy for American men than for women. Life expectancy for men declined each year between 2014 and 2017. It started ticking upward again until 2020, when COVID-19 hit. Then, men's life expectancy fell by 2.2 years compared to 2019 levels, the biggest decline in the world. The group of men whose life expectancy has taken the biggest hit is white, lesser educated men, who are significantly more likely to die from suicide, drug overdoses, and alcoholic liver disease. Princeton economists Anne Case and Angus Deaton, who first drew attention to this disturbing trend in a seminal 2015 paper, have termed these deaths "deaths of despair."

It can be easy to dismiss men's stagnant wages as mere bruises to dudes' egos or justice served after millennia of misogyny. I ascribe to a brand of feminism that seeks equality for all of us—not punishment for those born into entitled social statuses. Tipping the financial and public power spheres to a net even should not come at the cost of the physical, mental, and spiritual well-being of half the population.

Boys are not finding a learning home at school or college, young men are not finding a place in the workforce, and men who father children are not welcomed into their children's lives. Because humans crave and thrive on community, some disillusioned men have created their own: Men Going Their Own Way (MGTOW, pronounced "mig-tau"). According to the Southern Poverty Law Center, which studies hate groups, MGTOW is "a community advocating for male separatism" made up of men who have "decided to withdraw themselves from the perceived toxicity of women" and who "deem women inferior and harmful, and think they get in the way of male achievement."

There are some relatable principles of the MGTOW movement: society is set up to favor women; men are valued only as financial providers; marriage is a losing proposition for men as divorce rates are high and the courts favor women postdivorce and force men to pay alimony and child support while also stripping them of the ability to see their children; and it's better for men to avoid relationships with women and "go their own way." Indeed, twice as many young men than young women are single, and a third more men than women are childless.

A MGTOW proponent summed up his views in an interview with the *Guardian*: "Men are supposed to pay for dates and bow down to women...anything less than worship is hate," and, "When it comes to marriage, the system is so stacked against men, it does not make sense." The reporter described the MGTOW view of divorce as "deeply one-sided, allowing women to rob innocent men of money, property and, in some cases, children." They also take issue with the fact that men are never taken seriously as victims of domestic abuse and violence.

Where the tenets of the group veer into hate is that all women are untrustworthy and lie about rape and abuse—and are therefore deserving of rape and abuse—and that the "feminazis" and "radfeminists" secretly run the world, conspiring to keep men down, and it's time for men to take the "red pill" (a reference to the movie *The Matrix* when the main character swallows a red pill that allows him to see the mass manipulation and enslavement of humanity) and stop playing into these shrews' manipulations.

It is easy to dismiss MGTOW as fringe misogyny, but I argue we have no choice but to pay keen attention to it as well as to the other corners of the manosphere, which include the men's rights movement, incels (short for involuntary celibate, or men who can't get a woman to sleep with them and so actively rail against women), and pickup artists (who use manipulation and coercion to sleep with women in a mocking of the recent emphasis on consent), as evidence that men are unsure about their value to society, feel powerless and unlovable, and are suffering. Plenty of scholars have linked these trends to the rise of mainstream extremist movements, such as the Tea Party, Q-Anon, anti-vaxxers, and January 6 insurrectionists. Some also lump in fathers' rights or men's rights groups, but that is not appropriate, as those groups are focused not on antisocial behavior but on actually engaging with government and changing laws. The shared-parenting movement has been closely aligned with a group called the Fathers' Rights Movement, which today is focused on offering mental and social support to dads with custody and child support issues as well as, of course, advocating for equal parenting time. Other efforts include Richard Reeves's newly formed American Institute for Boys and Men, and a group devoted to enacting a White House Council for Men and Boys, with the aim to research and fund policy to truly address gender gaps and serve in-need males, as well as various programs throughout state and local governments with similar aims.

It is easy to lump all these groups together into one and dismiss them as patently misogynistic, violent, and dangerous, and certainly some people in them are. They are also composed of people who are deeply suffering. Again, these issues are messy, complicated, human. They also need to be addressed. Righting the power imbalance in the family sphere can help provide men with that missing sense of purpose.

Dissecting Fatherlessness

I just googled "number of children without father in home" and the top results included these titles:

+ *View Heartbreaking Statistics*
+ *Number of Kids Living Only with Mothers*
+ *The Fatherless Generation*

What I was actually looking for was just this stat: twenty-two million children, or one in three.

Now, depending on who is citing these U.S. Census figures,

they may be spun in a few different ways: These twenty-two million children have no contact with their father; these fathers abandoned their children; the courts and malicious mothers have alienated twenty-two million children from their loving dads.

The actual truth is that we have no way of measuring how many kids live part-time with their dads *and* moms, because the Census Bureau only tracks these categories:

+ Children living with married parents
+ Children living with unmarried parents
+ Children living with a mother
+ Children living with a father
+ Children living with grandparents or other relatives
+ Whether children live with biological, adoptive, or stepparents

Just because those twenty-two million children live primarily with their mom does not mean that they are not *also* cared for by their dad. While it is true that back in the 1950s and 1960s, about half of divorced dads did slip out, moved away, and often started new families, many of today's so-called fatherless kids *do* have a relationship with their fathers. A study that used data from the Children of the National Longitudinal Survey of Youth database found that about a quarter of dads dropped out of their kids' lives when they lived separately, while three-quarters had either significant or moderate interaction with their kids. But the census only counts kids as living in one home, so even kids who live with their dads half the time are likely to be counted as living with their mothers only.

This is more than just symbolic evidence that our society doesn't value fatherhood. It often just comes down to who is in the home at the time the census worker stops by, and if kids happen not to be staying with their dad that day, then it is not counted that the father lives with the child. This may be chance or by choice, as moms need kids to be living with them in order to ensure welfare benefits. Either way, the result is that dads who do not live with their children full-time are largely erased from our data, and without data, it is hard to understand and serve families.

This flaw in the census process means that we also dismiss all incarcerated fathers and mothers. However, as I elaborate on in chapter 6, there is a wonderfully booming field of studying fathers of all kinds, which has been gathering speed for more than thirty years. One effort of this field is to understand how much time nonresidential dads spend with their children. Again, three-quarters of nonresidential dads do spend some or a lot of time with their kids. This time is deeply meaningful to the members of these families.

While it is exponentially harder for a child and parent to create a deep connection without significant and meaningful time spent together, rarely did children or fathers I interviewed who had a less than 50/50 schedule view themselves as part of a "fatherless" family. Even families in which the father is incarcerated often still hold tight to those connections through visits, emails, letters, and phone calls. About half of people in state prisons have minor children—58 percent of that population are mothers, while 46 percent are fathers. The majority report communicating by phone and mail, while a third have visited in person.

Priscilla's father went to jail for aggravated robbery when he was nineteen and she was a baby. She grew up visiting him in prison four hours away from her home several times a year with her aunt and grandma. "Seeing your parent being patted down in this strange environment, I was scared and excited at the same time," she remembered. "But when he came around the corner, I'd always know it was him, I'd run and jump into his arms. He'd pick me up and squeeze me. Even though I didn't know-know him, I knew he was my dad."

Priscilla says while it was sad and disappointing that he wasn't there to attend her talent shows and school events and she felt ashamed to tell other kids about her family, she did feel connected to and parented by her dad, even calling him "very hands-on." "He wanted me to succeed with everything in school and was big on learning other languages—he'd write me letters in Spanish and I had to write him back in Spanish. When I had a problem, I'd go to him for advice."

Today Priscilla is the mom of three teenage boys, the youngest of whose father is serving five years for violating parole related to domestic violence against Priscilla. Before his arrest the previous year, her son and his dad enjoyed a warm relationship with frequent visits, though there was no formal schedule and all three boys stayed primarily with Priscilla. However, after the beating that led to his initial arrest, Priscilla was wary about her son spending time with his father—and the boy was too. But he also missed his dad, which of course she deeply related to. "At first I was dead set 100 percent against the boys seeing him," she said of her now-incarcerated ex. Priscilla was angry and scared for her own safety as well as that of her sons. "But then I prayed and prayed and prayed on it, doubled back on my childhood, and remembered how it felt when I wanted or needed my own dad. I'm not the best mother, but I try. And I had promised myself that I would never keep my kids from their fathers." When we spoke, Priscilla had made plans for her son to visit his father, who was in a prison a six-hour drive away.

The Stereotype of the Doofus/ Disney/Playboy Dad

If millennia of conditioning have pigeonholed women into the role of mother at the expense of their earning power, men have suffered the inverse: they have been shoehorned into the role of default breadwinner at the expense of parenthood. For men in the 2020s, that is especially complex and devastating as we double-down on narratives that demonize men, from #MeToo to toxic masculinity to just dismissing them as idiots. One of the few safe places men have is the role of the doofus dad: the well-meaning but incapable father, the parent who can't be trusted, the lovable trainwreck of a man who is the mainstay of TV shows and movies and likely in your family and neighborhood too.

Homer on *The Simpsons*. Phil Dunphy on *Modern Family*. Dre Johnson on *Black-ish*. These well-known characters epitomize the dad who is dorky and incompetent yet tolerated because they make the money and they're nice guys. But the stereotype exists well beyond Hollywood.

Last year, I attended a beautiful wedding between two dear friends. Everyone present was happy for the gorgeous couple. The ceremony was lovely. The priest, funny and charming in his service, quipped, "People ask me how many children I have, and I tell them four. But I tell them my wife has five." Get it? He's the fifth child! Hahaha!

While many handsomely dressed wedding guests gave a knowing chuckle at the unspoken assumption that men are all a bunch of babies, this joke is a brand of sexism we can't afford to ignore. (Sorry to be a buzzkill. And they say feminists don't have a sense of humor.) This cultural norm that *men are children*, which has resulted in men believing that this belittling narrative is deserved, is not benign at all. It is at the root of deep sexism that is devastating an entire gender—including, likely, your son, your lover, and your kids' dad.

This has been dubbed by scholars and journalists as the "doofus dad" or, in the case of separated families, the "uncle dad," "Disney dad," or, its racist counterpart, the "deadbeat dad," and it is just as harmful to men as martyring is to women.

This doofus dad myth is insidious because it seems harmless, full of dumb but benign dad jokes, dorky clothes, and burnt dinners. We all know and love a guy like that. He's the everyman! Yet if you look just one level deeper past the endearing oaf, the doofus dad is an incompetent dope who women can manipulate and push around—so dopey that he can't be trusted with serious tasks like raising children, because he is essentially a child himself.

The doofus dad trope is also false. Despite stereotypes of apathetic fathers, studies show that men are just as committed to their kids as women are, with nearly equal percentages of moms and dads reporting that parenthood is central to their identity, and these numbers fluctuate very little among mothers and fathers who are married, cohabiting, or living apart from a spouse or partner. However, dads feel exponentially less confident and even more guilty about parenthood than moms. A Pew study found nearly *two-thirds* of dads said they spend too little time with their kids (even if they spend three times the number of hours with their kids than most dads did just one generation ago), compared with *one-third* of mothers who said the same —an even more extreme expression of the parenting guilt long expressed by moms despite our increasingly intense, helicopter parenting. Men also feel less confident and competent as parents. Just 39 percent of fathers said they were doing a "very good job" raising their children, compared with 51 percent of mothers.

Even perfectly competent, confident 50/50 dads face these toxic stereotypes. In the introduction of *Father Figure: How to Be a Feminist Dad*, Temple University professor Jordan Shapiro shared that while reviews of his first book on parenting in an age of technology were very positive, critics repeatedly dismissed him as an expert because he's a divorced dad. "As I traveled the United States promoting a parenting book, I discovered that many folks immediately jumped to the conclusion that I can't possibly know the best interest of my children because I'm divorced," wrote Shapiro, who has a 50/50 schedule with his sons' mom. "Apparently a lot of people think I live in some sort of velvet-upholstered Playboy bachelor pad, where lounge music blasts from audiophile speakers and children have no boundaries."

This blind assumption that dads gain financially in divorce, based on grossly flawed research, has had an incredible impact not only on how our systems financially tax the single dad (more in the money chapter) but also on how he sees himself. If he's supposed to be a fabulous, wealthy bachelor but actually just wants to be a regular-incomed guy and co-parent his kids yet is denied that opportunity by the courts and by his ex, who is he? Where does he fit in? What is his value?

Unsurprisingly, there is a direct correlation between how competent a dad feels in his parenting and how much time he spends with his kids. The more time a dad spends with his children, the more competent he feels—and probably is. To gain such confidence requires swimming upstream against all the toxic assumptions about his ability to be a dad, including lack of experience.

The argument that a dad who may not have spent a lot of

time—or any time—with his child should not be trusted with any meaningful parenting time in custody disputes is a common way that men are separated from their kids. Wayne heard that from the courts when he filed for parenting time after learning he had a four-year-old daughter by way of being served a $7,000 child support arrears notice. "Every lawyer in the state told me that the way the system is set up, no judge will give me partial custody because I am a stranger. This infuriated me," Wayne told me. "When a woman goes to the hospital to have a child, that child is going home with a complete stranger, and no one questions that. That is a 100 percent thumbs-up. But for a man, that is a 100 percent thumbs-down. I will always be a stranger until you give me a chance not to be a stranger."

Let's explore fatherhood's importance to men.

Men Take Pride in Fatherhood

In my talks with single moms, I hear again and again that 50/50 custody could never work for them because, they say, *He just won't show up. He just won't do his share.* But when I talk to the dads, a more nuanced story emerges.

I spoke individually with Darcy and Dave—divorced parents of a boy and a girl who were nineteen and twenty when I interviewed them. Darcy and Dave live in a small Midwestern city where primary custody—nearly always with the mother—was standard practice when they divorced in 2014.

When Darcy and Dave were married, Darcy stayed home

with the kids, and Dave worked full-time as a maintenance supervisor at a manufacturing plant. In addition to cost savings, "I just didn't want the kids to have all that negative influence of day care," Dave told me. Darcy was eager to describe Dave as a hands-on dad, getting up with the kids in the middle of the night on weekends, coaching their sports teams, taking his son fishing and his daughter out on daddy-daughter dances, and doing his half of household chores. He was well known and liked in the community as one of the high school basketball coaches, something he did on the side as a volunteer. The problem? "I am definitely not going to sugarcoat it: I can be controlling about things," Darcy admitted to me when I spoke to her on the phone.

According to Dave, she was constantly checking his phone and his Facebook messages for proof that he was having an affair. After three years of this, Dave said, he had enough. Despite saying he "never had or would have had an affair—I loved Darcy, I wanted to be with her for the rest of my life," word got out in their small community that their marriage was ending because of his infidelity, likely news spread by Darcy. "Before the divorce, I would go to a school basketball game and not be able to leave because everyone wanted to talk to me. After the divorce, I'd go to one of the kids' band concerts, and no one would even sit within fifty feet," he said. It also meant that Darcy was awarded primary parenting time and, since he was the sole earner at the time, steep child support payments from Dave. Dave had the kids every other weekend. But he often wouldn't show up for his weekends, Darcy said, stopped attending the kids' sporting events, and largely checked out of their lives. The way Darcy saw it, he didn't care about having a relationship with his children.

Yet when you talk to Dave about it, you learn that shortly after the divorce, he had open heart surgery, lost his maintenance job, and was unemployed for six months. In those early months and years postdivorce, both Darcy and Dave admit there was a lot of animosity between them and little communication. Dave failed to keep up with child support, which angered Darcy.

But that wasn't her only issue with Dave.

"I didn't always respect his way of doing things—like eating out at restaurants all the time. He felt as long as they were fed, it was OK, and I wanted him to keep food at home," Darcy told me. "There were definitely times I could have been less controlling. I'd just get so angry and lash out. It never did any good."

From the outside, you could say that Dave was a super intentional father during the marriage, but then they got divorced, and he checked out instead of bucking up (manning up?) and fighting for his kids. But then you hear how he felt ostracized by his whole town, was sick, lost his career, and struggled financially—eventually even moving in with his mom—and the picture gets more complex.

When I asked Dave why he didn't fight for equal time with his kids, he said that he wanted to see his kids every day, but he also didn't want to disrupt their lives. "I didn't want them to live one week with her and one week with me. It felt like that would be such a mix-up for their lives. I wanted it as simple as possible— even to the point of skipping Wednesday dinner visits because they had after-school activities and homework. I just wanted what was best for them."

I pressed him. Couldn't he have done more, been more involved with their sports, or otherwise stayed connected? Maybe I was voicing my own frustrations from early in my divorce or even my lifelong hurt that my own dad wasn't around. I'd often wondered why he hadn't fought more for me. Didn't he love me enough?

Dave struggled to find an answer. When he was married, he might work long hours, he said, but then come home to his kids, his family. After the divorce, most of the time, he came home to an empty, dark house. Darcy took over planning extracurricular activities, RSVPing to birthday parties, and scheduling out-of-town trips on Dave's weekends, "which angered me to no end." He said he was kept in the dark about school events, though Darcy pointed out that she learned about them from the school website, which he could access just as well as she could. The picture becomes one in which Darcy kept the kids, scheduled their life—a very nice one, Dave will point out—but he was painted out of it, with no clear way to engage or connect.

I could hear in his voice that Dave really loved his kids and even his ex-wife in the way that people who have a long history together do. Today, they are friends and see each other around town. He was very open when she asked him if he'd be willing to speak with me, knowing exactly what the topic was. Dave is a good guy, and he wanted to do the right thing, but what is the right thing when you are sick, broke, and shunned by your community and feel like a lousy dad because you believe you should be financially supporting the whole family but now are supporting no one, not even yourself? What do you do when you don't have money for a lawyer to fight the situation and haven't seen how you could win anyway?

"In divorce, being a man means being at a disadvantage, as the courts, the lawyers, and the whole system tend to sympathize with the woman and don't really hear the man's side of the story," Dave said. He described a man's position in divorce court as on the receiving end of the "raw end of the deal." His child support order was $340 every two weeks, and his after-tax pay was only $780. "But Darcy could afford to take the kids on cruises and to Florida."

Even Darcy doesn't see Dave as just another lousy dad. Now that they're well past the breakup and their kids are grown, Darcy still has nagging thoughts about how things went down. During the marriage, she set high expectations that he be a good, hands-on father, but that went away when they broke up. "I always feel guilty, wondering if I could have done things differently and helped him have a closer relationship with the kids." In many ways, Darcy acknowledges the power she had in the family, including over Dave's fatherhood both inside and outside the marriage.

I'll cover what science finds is the best postdivorce parenting schedule in terms of child development in the next chapter as well as how the shuttling back and forth between two homes, while logistically challenging, is ultimately the best schedule for them. It is also a win for parents, including dads. But one of the big reasons men slide out of their kids' lives—entirely or partially—is because their identities as men are so closely tied to their abilities to financially care for their families, explains Kevin Bremond, who heads the Fathers Corps, an initiative in Alameda County, California, that helps local public agencies better support and engage with dads. "Poor men especially feel that if they don't provide, they don't deserve to be around their kid," Bremond told me.

Men of all incomes feel pressure to be the primary payer of bills, and Americans readily put that pressure on them. A Pew survey found that three-quarters of adults say it is very important for a man to be able to support a family financially to be a good husband or partner, while just one-third say the same for women. In chapter 4, I'll detail research that finds that poor dads are eager to provide financial support, especially physical goods that the kids can see them giving, such as food, clothes, and toys, underscoring the connection men make between their worth as fathers and money. Interestingly, Black dads are less likely than other races to hold tight to this gendered notion and are more likely to co-parent with their kids' moms and value time with their children. Perhaps because Black men have a long history of both poverty and being removed from their children, they have also overcome sexist stereotypes that might otherwise stand between them and their kids.

Soon after their split, Darcy went back to work where she

succeeded as an administrator at a health company, bought a home, and eventually remarried.

Dave, meanwhile, is existing paycheck to paycheck and living with—and caring for—his ailing mother. While he and his son have maintained a relationship, his relationship with his daughter is tentative at best. "I think she believes I wasn't there as much because I didn't want to be, but a lot of the time, I had to work. That is part of being an adult," he said. "Her whole world got turned upside down in the divorce, but mine did too."

Dave's story nearly perfectly illustrates the findings of one small study of three hundred divorcing families, the results of which were published in the *Journal of Marriage and Family*:

> The findings focus on the difficult circumstances of divorced fathers, rather than on their defective characters. It is found that fathers continue visiting and paying at high levels when they perceive that they retain some degree of paternal authority. The loss of this sense of paternal authority appears to occur, in part, because fathers perceive that the legal system and their divorce settlements were unfair to them. It is also found that the custodial mother, who sometimes sees little value in the father's involvement, limits the father's role within the post-divorce family.

Whether it happens postdivorce or if the parents were having a casual relationship when the woman got pregnant, the loss of parenting time can and does devastate men. After all, parenthood is a fundamental human experience, regardless of gender. "Men want to be parents and need to be parents, but our systems and culture have not supported men in being fathers. They actually create barriers," Bremond said. "Men who check out have a story, and they need healing."

Malin Bergström is a Swedish child psychologist and expert in the benefits of shared parenting for dads, moms, and children. Sweden is one of the few places on earth where shared parenting is very much the norm, thanks in part to a 1998 national law that made it a legal precedent. In a country where nearly all separated parents share time 50/50, there is cultural pressure for dads to have their kids half the time. "If a dad is not equally involved or somehow shut out of his kid's life, there is so much shame. They may feel humiliated or not respected. It's really difficult," Bergström said. But it's not just shame, and it's not relegated to Scandinavian social paradises. "Not being allowed to parent your children and not being in contact with your children goes against a fundamental drive in us as humans. It's a life purpose for many people to be good parents and have good contact with their children." (Or, as Bremond explained it, "No one wears a shirt that brags, 'I'm a Piece of Shit Dad.'")

No matter where they fall on the economic spectrum, what race they are, or even when the pregnancy is the result of a casual hookup, when men are denied equal access to their kids, they are cut off from a primal source of human meaning.

Systems That Erase Dads

I'll say it again: it is impossible to legislate parenting equality inside a marriage, but we can legislate equality between moms and dads when they live separately. Laws and courts can make 50/50 schedules the default (with reasonable exceptions), do away with child support to erase financial dependence, and support programs that actively engage both parents in a child's upbringing.

If you are skeptical that government can influence gender inequality, let's take a look at how U.S. government programs effectively segregated men and their children over the past century—especially in Black families.

Two-parent, married Black families were the norm in this country for a very long time. From 1890 to 1950, Black women had a higher marriage rate than white women, and in the 1960s, two out of three Black children were being raised in two-parent homes. Today, 44 percent of Black fathers do not live full-time with their children, the highest of all races, while the rate of unmarried births to Black mothers went from 24 percent in 1965 to 70 percent by 2018. For white women, the rate of unmarried births rose from 3 percent in 1965 to 28 percent by 2018.

What changed?

Much of this swing points to the 1965 Johnson administration publication *The Negro Family: The Case for National Action*, also known as the Moynihan Report, which detailed the rise of poor and unmarried Black mothers in the context of economic challenges for the whole family—especially Black men.

The report and its author were maligned as racist by many civil rights activists, though more recent perspectives give credence to its goal to address systemic racial inequality beyond the newly signed Civil Rights Act.

Unfortunately, the report and other moves aimed at alleviating poverty and crime in the Black community had unintended consequences that plague us to this day. The Johnson administration and those that followed did beef up social welfare programs but also effectively discouraged not only marriage but even cohabitation between poor parents: In order to qualify for welfare assistance, affordable housing, childcare, and medical benefits, laws often stipulated that no man be living in the house.

Infamous "man in the house" laws meant that welfare workers would spot-check homes to verify that a mother was accurately reporting her family status. As conservative Black journalist Jason Riley noted in the *Wall Street Journal*, "the government paid mothers to keep fathers out of the home—and paid them well."

Even now that those programs are written to be gender neutral, it still behooves poor families to keep the number of incomes on welfare applications to a minimum—and keep men off official government records. "The famous stories are those of the dad hiding in the closet when the Section 8 housing officer would come by. If they found out the family actually had two incomes, they'd lose that subsidy," said Kevin Bremond of the Alameda County Fathers Corps. "When families were struggling financially, it wasn't beneficial to have Dad around because his presence could disqualify them from receiving government assistance. They'd leave Dad off the paperwork for medical benefits, school, the birth certificate. It created a norm of hiding dads' involvement so people can get resources they need as a family."

Then, in the event of a breakup between the parents, there is a paper trail that makes it that much harder for these poor dads to prove that they have been involved with their kids all along—much less that they are indeed the father.

Poor Dads' Battle to Prove Paternity

When a newborn's parents are married, the father's paternity and rights to his child are presumed. Both parents are automatically inscribed on the child's birth certificate before the new little family leaves the hospital. So sweet. This is how it typically goes for white couples, who are more likely to be married than Black and Hispanic parents. Should the marriage end, the divorce proceedings automatically include both child support and a parenting plan. Throughout that child's life, the fact that his parents were married better ensures father involvement.

However, if the parents are not legally married, it is the mother's choice whether to put the father's name on the birth certificate at the time of birth, though the father also has to agree. Even so, he doesn't have to agree to pay child support if she seeks it, and that child support order will not likely mention parenting time or custody. Poor men have an uphill battle to be fathers compared to more affluent men.

Regardless of the mother's choice as to whether to name the father on the birth certificate, any unwed father who wants to establish his rights as a father must take legal steps to prove his paternity before he has any rights to his child. Depending on state law, that can be accomplished by simply declaring he is the father, taking a DNA paternity test, or going through a legal proceeding. Additionally, about two-thirds of states have "putative fatherhood registries" in which any man who believes he has a biological child can register this relationship in a confidential state roster. A man can register any time he has sex with a woman, and states urge men to register in multiple states: where the sex happened, where he lives, where she lives, and later when either one of them relocates. Then, in the event that a baby born to a mother who is named in a father registry is put up for adoption or sent to foster care, the system will contact the registered father, who will be asked whether he agrees to relinquish his parental rights and allow the adoption or foster placement to move forward. This is designed to protect men and their children against women who fraudulently claim they do not know the dad or forge the father's name in consent of the adoption.

On one hand, we can commend states for this resource that might keep dads connected to their kids. But its flaws are symptoms of our anti-father culture. Even if an adoption triggers the registry to notify the father, there is no guarantee that he will be allowed to adopt his own child. Once again, these dads must prove their competence as dads. It is not intrinsically assumed.

Take, for example, Chris Emanuel, then twenty-five, who was dating his coworker when she got pregnant. Although they discussed raising their daughter together, she ghosted Chris halfway through the pregnancy and then, once the baby was born, attempted to put her up for adoption without telling Chris. "It was like, I lost a part of me. I was lost. I was so lost," Emanuel told a reporter. "No one can love my daughter the way I can."

The only reason Chris was able to locate his daughter was that he received a notification from South Carolina's "responsible father registry." Even then, Chris had to sue for custody in a three-month legal battle that was reported on by news outlets around the country. It was a battle he eventually won. "Having my daughter for the first time where she's supposed to be. I felt her breath for the first time, seeing her eyes, seeing her touch, and I felt complete. I felt whole again. All I could do was break down on my knees, and I cried and I thanked God for bringing my daughter home because all I needed was for her to get in my arms."

While biological fathers can face insurmountable barriers to parent their own children, paternity fraud, in which women lead men to believe they are the father of their children when they are not, is a common concern cited by men's rights activists across the spectrum from thoughtful advocates to extremist groups. Maury Povich would have us believe otherwise, but "misattributed paternity" is relatively uncommon and decreasing. One international study assessing data over a forty-year period starting in the 1960s found mean rates of misattributed paternity to be less than 4 percent, while a 2021 study of two million people in Sweden found that 1 percent of the population in that country grew up believing someone other than their biological father was their dad. Increasing access to DNA testing services like Ancestry.com makes it harder for paternity fraud—or even benign confusion—to persist.

This messy issue comes into play in separated families, as in some states, child support can be ordered to any man who has assumed a father role, regardless of whether he is biologically that child's father, and men who do not want to become fathers are forced to pay child support. Meanwhile, men who do want to be meaningfully involved with their children are denied equal parenting time. Paternity fraud, however, is not a punishable crime, even when a man pays child support for a child the mother intentionally lied was his. At the same time, unpaid child support is a crime, punishable by jail time.

The Mental and Physical Benefits of Fatherhood

If you have kids, you've probably joked to a friend that parenting takes years off your life. Worry, exhaustion, and the fact that children can be very, very annoying can make any parent feel the youth draining from their blood. Yet another myth busted here: parents live longer than nonparents, suggesting that the purpose involved in wanting to do what it takes to see your kids flourish pays off. Joy and general well-being are also connected to health and longevity. Another surprise: the boost in the life span afforded to fathers is greater than it is for mothers—2 years for men versus 1.5 years for women.

Part of this effect can be attributed to the fact that three-quarters of men report taking better care of themselves once they become fathers, including drinking less, taking fewer risks, exercising more, and eating healthier.

Fathers also enjoy a rise in status after having a child: in a group of men with similar experiences and achievements, men with children are more likely to be offered a job. Perhaps it is because these dads are more ambitious or their parenthood signals commitment and wholesomeness to employers. Or maybe it is because fatherhood is *good* for men's psychological development in ways that carry over to the office. But dads are more successful at work. Research finds that men have better focus, patience, time management, and a sense of responsibility after becoming dads, and these traits are noticeable to others— dads are seen as more mature, compassionate, and kind by their coworkers. They also experience greater job satisfaction and are less likely to leave their positions.

Underscoring all these benefits is the simple truth that men find a deep sense of purpose in fatherhood. British researchers who analyzed twenty-two studies conducted around the world that assessed the mental health and well-being of new fathers who lived with their kids between 1990 and 2017 found that while men found the transition to fatherhood stressful and at times overwhelming, "Becoming a father gave men a new identity, which made them feel like they were fulfilling their role as men, with a recognition of changed priorities and responsibility and expanded vision."

The correlation between the time a man spends with his children and depression rates is direct. While some postnatal depression is uncommon in married fathers (6.6 percent experience it), the risk jumps to 20 percent in dads who are not involved with their kids. Meanwhile, the more daily contact a dad has with his child, the lower his risk of depression. Dads who don't live with their kids but are still involved have a nearly 12 percent prevalence of depression, while 8.7 percent of fathers who live with their child but aren't married experience postnatal depression.

Studies find time and again that while living with a child even 50 percent of the time—versus every other weekend or only occasionally—comes with an undeniable grind of daily care, those efforts offer plenty of opportunities for physical contact and bonding as well as giving kids and dads the lived experiences of what it means to care for a child and to be cared for. It also provides opportunity for the joys and the little spontaneous moments and connections that you can't plan for. Janella Street, PsyD, is a clinical and forensic psychologist specializing in co-parenting in the San Francisco area. Central to her work helping families structure co-parenting relationships, Street aims to make sure both parents have an equal share of the fun weekend time and what she calls "gritty parenting" during the week. "When a parent is connected to school and the homework and bedtime routine, they get to be the 'everyday parent' without having the kids every day," she told me. Both the dad and child benefit from this bonding, and it connects the father to the different aspects of the child's life—their teachers, friends, and after-school activities. It gives the dad that much more experience being a regular ole parent, finding his groove, figuring out how to get the kid to *take a damn bath*, and also facilitating a smoother bedtime routine that can make those times more about sweetness and snuggling and less of a battle.

Occasional or even minority-time dads miss out on all that. And their kids miss out too.

Disney Dads and Memory Wars

To compensate for those missed days and weeks, some dads who don't live with their kids make big gestures—gifts for no reason and trips to theme parks. It's easy to dismiss these "Disney dads," but their actions are often simply an eagerness to make the most of precious time with their kids. Plus, it's hard to get into a groove with your kids if you only have them a few days a month.

For a part-time dad, Disney parenting can be a symptom of many things: a lack of daily schedule to fall back on, an eagerness to make the most of precious hours with his kids, and a desire to burn memories of him into his kids' brains within their limited time together.

It can be easier to plan big outings and keep the schedule full instead of just waking up on Saturday morning and falling into a more regular routine because you don't have any routine at all. Especially when divorce or a change in living arrangements is new, dads can be unsure of how to establish a new rhythm with kids, and a trip to the zoo provides a welcome distraction, a semblance of structure since it is *doing something* when you have no idea what to do.

Also, I believe there is a very human competition among parents for real estate in a child's memory. If one parent has an abundance of time with the kids, it stands to reason that parent will also take up a proportionate sum of long-term mundane— but often more powerful—memories of rituals of daily life (smells of favorite meals, the comfort of being cared for when sick). The dad, then, is left desperately trying to hardwire a few splashy memories into his child's developing prefrontal cortices during his four weekend days per month.

However, as we unpack in the next chapter on myths around child development, it is both the mundane and the extraordinary that children remember long term, both of which scientists find are rooted in feeling connected and loved by a parent. If a Disney trip was a highlight, for example, it likely wasn't the rides or the princess-themed hotel that made the deepest impression but how that kid felt while spending time with the family. Ultimately, however, we cannot control which experiences burn into forever mental souvenirs, which are forever forgotten, and which may be twisted into some variation of what actually occurred. What science *can* tell us is that when an adult has fond memories from childhood of their relationship with their parent—whether it be a mother or a father—they enjoy fewer depressive symptoms throughout their lives. When a kid spends a lot of time with both his parents after a divorce or separation, he gains a sense of security from knowing that both his parents are committed to him, and that security fosters a number of positive outcomes.

The Myth that Men Don't Really Want to Be Parents

Of course, there are dads who completely check out of parenting. We've all heard stories of someone who bolted, likely as part of a story that contains the phrase *deadbeat dad*—a term politicians love to throw around, perpetuating sexist and racist stereotypes. Or maybe you've heard or used the term *sperm donor*, which reflects the notion that he dropped his seed then split without taking any responsibility. In a Facebook group I run for single moms, use of that term was so pervasive, so toxic and myopic, that we created a special community rule that specifically prohibited its use.

If you're a dad, of course it's painful to feel and hear the trope of "the useless dumbass" applied to your parenting. Checking out of the dynamic that continually tells you you're parenting wrong or aren't valuable as a father at least gives a man the chance to find some joy somewhere else, whether that means moving to another state, starting another family, or just not having to face the painful reality of only being allowed to see the kids every second weekend. Someone who abdicates his fatherly role can only believe that he has nothing to offer his kids—a message that's reinforced by messages all around.

In the early 1990s, a small study found that dads who received minority-time schedules after divorce struggled with grief and mourning, and half checked out (or maybe were forced out?) of their kids' lives. While these numbers have improved dramatically, especially for dads who had been married to their children's mother, a survey from a few years ago based on U.S. Census figures found that 37 percent of noncustodial, never-married dads had not seen their child within the past year.

Despite racist stereotypes about deadbeat, MIA dads, the majority of Black dads live full-time with their children—either alongside the kids' mom or as primary custody parents. Also, Black dads of all living situations—same house or separate houses—spend more hours, more days, and more meaningful time engaged with their children, playing, bathing, feeding, and changing them, than Hispanic and white fathers—parenting that pays off in paternal bonding long term. "The Myth of the Low-Income Black Fathers' Absence from the Lives of Adolescents," a 2023 Temple University study, found no significant differences between any races about how teenagers perceived the closeness of their relationships or interaction with their fathers.

Mike can relate to these stats that connect parenting time with bonding.

When Mike was living with the mother of his children, he felt pressure to take on the moneymaking, even though he had all intentions of being a more involved father than his own. "She seemed so confident in how things should be done, while I was often overwhelmed by being a new dad," he says of his then wife. "I didn't even realize what I was doing at the time, but I gradually became the smaller parent and just gave up. But I needed to feel like I was contributing, so I focused on my career. But clearly, that didn't work either, and we broke up. I felt like a total failure."

In family court, Mike sought 50/50 parenting time, but his ex argued that since she was clearly the primary caregiver during marriage, the kids should live with her, with visits to Mike. In the state of Minnesota where they live, the law states parents going through family court have a rebuttable right to a minimum of 25 percent parenting time, about four nights out of fourteen, so that's what he got—and, I will emphasize, that is what the *kids* got, and what the kids *lost*. Because the time sharing was so unequal, Mike was also ordered to pay a sum of child support and alimony that forced him to work long hours, which limited his ability to rebuild his social life, date, or otherwise connect with others. He sank into a depression. "Every time I saw my kids after two weeks, it was like they'd grown into new people, and I was not a meaningful part of their lives. It was almost more painful to see them those few days each month and be reminded of what we were all missing out on than during the time in between when I was missing them. I felt powerless to improve my relationship with them or change my life for the better."

After a few years, Mike had an opportunity to take a higher-paying job in a neighboring state, which is also where his new girlfriend lived. Moving there meant only seeing his kids once per month and some holidays. "The new job and new girlfriend promised some kind of meaningful life, some hope, which I had lost entirely being a part-time dad on the margins of their childhoods."

If you talk to a dad who walks away, typically he'll have his own story about how bitterly painful that decision was.

Men Are Born to Parent

You may think that men evolved to spread their seed and perpetuate the race. But if our female ancestors hadn't had men who stuck around to protect the family, hunt and cook the food, and teach children how to survive in the world, our species would never have proliferated as it has.

As doctor of evolutionary anthropology Anna Machin relays in her book, *The Life of Dad: The Making of a Modern Father*, "It is a little-known fact, but fathers saved the human race." Five hundred thousand years ago, Machin writes, our ancestor, *Homo heidelbergensis*, experienced a leap in brain size and corresponding high-maintenance and vulnerable infants. Evolution has continued to select for males who invest in their young, meaning "fathers are not mere adjuncts to mothers, occasional babysitters or bag-carriers. They are the consequence of half a million years of evolution and they remain a vital part of the human story."

Evolution has seen to it that men experience dramatic changes in their physiology in the presence of children. The long-term, day-to-day acts of fatherhood are ingrained in their biology, right down to their hormones—those powerful chemicals that we attribute so much of maternal instinct and bonding to. Turns out men have a hormonal reaction to babies too.

+ Oxytocin, also known as the love hormone that is released after orgasm or in response to loving touch and contributes to that feeling of being bonded to another person, rises in pregnancy and while caring for an infant, not just in mothers but in the men they live with during pregnancy.

+ Dopamine, which gives a pleasurable reward and works with oxytocin to increase neuroplasticity (the ability of your brain to form new connections between neurons), rises along with oxytocin in mothers and fathers, helping them enjoy that feeling of emotional closeness.

+ Testosterone goes down after a man becomes a father, which makes men more responsive to a baby's cry, more likely to be an involved co-parent, and more affectionate and understanding toward a baby than men with higher testosterone levels. It also tamps down the desire to look for stimulation outside the family unit. Lower testosterone also makes oxytocin more potent, making it even easier for dads to bond and actively care for their kids.

+ Beta-endorphin, the body's natural opiate, is released when dads play with their kids. As a form of opiate, beta-endorphin feels great, even a little addictive.

In addition to the hormonal symphony of fatherhood, dads

also experience brain changes, with an increase in neural activity associated with empathy and emotional processing and regulation. The actual size of certain areas in the brain also changes—specifically the striatum, hypothalamus, and amygdala. These regions of the brain are active in attachment, caretaking behaviors, and the ability to interpret and respond to another's cues.

Men Are Better Fathers after Divorce

While it is undeniably difficult for dads to be truly involved in their kids' lives when they don't have them a meaningful number of hours each week or month, there are many stories and studies that reflect that some dads are able to flourish in their parenthood after a separation. This blossoming is often the result of being freed from a toxic dynamic with his partner as well as being forced to take responsibility for the real, gritty parenting duties that a wife or live-in girlfriend protected him from. There is no substitute for one-on-one time with your kids.

Gary is the dad of three kids of elementary school age who checked out of parenting in response to his stay-at-home wife's confident commitment to certain parenting regimens—and criticism of Gary. "Whatever I did, I was never quite doing it right," he said. So she stopped asking—or even allowing—Gary to do much hands-on parenting. What may have seemed like a good choice for efficiency's sake—"If you want something done right, do it yourself"—had a cascade of negative effects for Gary.

"I never had the opportunity to fail, which is how you grow

and learn," Gary told me. "I always want to feel productive and useful no matter what I'm doing. It's demoralizing to not feel that way. I felt exhausted all the time, mentally and emotionally. And in a lot of ways, I didn't really know my kids because I wasn't taking care of them."

When the wheels came off the marriage and they divorced, Gary and his wife had equal parenting time since they live in Arizona, one of just six states where 50/50 is the norm. Gary was nervous about figuring out how to be fully responsible for the kids on the days when he had to work, but that feeling soon transformed. "I didn't have to walk around on eggshells anymore. I didn't have to worry about criticism. It was liberating," he said. "I realized that I am perfectly capable of making meals, handling discipline, and even managing when my daughter got her first period."

Even better, Gary's self-esteem and his connection with his kids improved. "I have my own relationship with my kids and my own failures. If I yell at them, it's for me to figure out how to repair. I've learned how to self-reflect and then talk to my kids about it. Now I feel like I'm a really good father, and I feel productive and useful in all aspects of my life."

Gary's story illustrates the findings of a growing body of research that looks at solo care by fathers (versus parenting near or simultaneously with the mother). The research is often brought up in the context of advocating for more paternal leave for dads as well as moms, but the findings are so relevant in examining the benefits of more and equal time for men and women after divorce. Dads who spend plenty of one-on-one time "solo caring" for children report more bonding, more enjoyment, and a greater sense of satisfaction than dads who are more of the mom's assistant. The researchers also found that these dads were able to define their unique parenting style with increased solo time. Other research substantiated the bonding powers of dads doing what co-parenting therapist Janelle Street calls "gritty parenting"— caretaking versus merely playing with their toddlers. A study of eighty families found that dads who tended to their child's needs (making food, changing diapers, etc.) during the workweek had a stronger father-child attachment than dads who only played with their kids on workdays (and left the gritty parenting to their partner). Playing is great, but nothing forges you as a parent and that bond with your kids like doing the work.

When you hear Gary's story about how he grew as both a parent and a person after divorce, it makes you feel the loss experienced by families like Darcy and Dave's. When I interviewed Darcy, it was clear that the chasm between her kids and their dad pains her. She vacillates between being contrite about what a control freak she can be, feeling genuine care and concern for her kids and their dad, and indulging in a good dose of postdivorce bitterness about how things played out. Divorce is brutal, and both parents are likely to go through a rough period as they adjust to an entirely new reality, although one may have a tougher time than the other. Darcy did what divorce culture told her to do: get the kids and hold her ex accountable financially.

For Dave, it is tough to say what he should have done. He was sick, broke, and depressed and had scant access to any mental health or social support in his community—factors that were made worse by his ex-wife's anger and judgment. But if he'd been granted equal custody of his kids, he would have had to figure something out, and Darcy would have had a harder time trash-talking him because she'd have to partner with him on coordinating the children's care. We must extend grace to a struggling co-parent, let go of the pain of ending the romantic relationship, and never forget that the goal is what is actually best for the children.

I'd like to see more co-parenting and family counseling baked into divorce processes and family courts. When you see how conclusive the research is that shows how much kids benefit from 50/50 parenting and how much they are hurt when they don't have access to both parents, gripes about how their dad did you wrong or how he doesn't keep their clothes clean don't justify keeping your children from equal time with their father. That research is exactly what we'll unpack in the next chapter.

3

Shared Parenting *Is* in the Best Interest of the Child

"I'm absolutely convinced, as much as any scientist can ever be convinced, that we can improve the public health of this country by having states and family courts let the public know that they're going to be open to equally shared parenting."

—William Fabricius, PhD, University of Arizona professor of child psychology

Despite all the research we've unpacked thus far on how unequal parenting harms men and women, we are still stuck in a common but outdated and unfounded formula to answer the question about what is best for kids: the child hunkers down with one "primary parent" (Mom). Meanwhile, the other parent (Dad) is a satellite, rotating into view every few days before zooming off again, providing more financial support and less emotional or logistical aid. The thinking is that this arrangement is best for a child, because kids only have room in their hearts and minds for one deep, primary connection.

But this is not what is best for kids or what mitigates the negative outcomes of divorce. Despite all the controversy and misinterpretations about how to best raise kids, research and common sense tend to align in this understanding: kids raised by two biological parents in a single home fare better than kids raised by a single parent or a home with a bio parent and a stepparent. Poverty, education, early pregnancy, drug use, incarceration, and dozens of other outcomes have been attributed to children living without both parents in one home.

The one living arrangement that has been shown to produce a *very* close second to having both parents living together in a single home is equally shared time with each parent in separate homes—a 50/50 schedule.

To move our culture and laws toward this easy answer, we must first understand why we are so stuck in the current, unequal sharing of time. The standard parenting schedule is not rooted in evil. It doesn't persist because women are controlling and men are negligent. It's the result of two societal forces:

1. Deep-seated gender norms that even the most progressive of us struggle to shake off.
2. A dated and disproven interpretation of attachment parenting research.

The unequal parenting schedule is just one symptom of these forces, which have twisted parenting into a competitive, all-encompassing marathon of constant parental hovering and frontal-lobe nurturing, creating dependent, anxious young adults. But unlike education reform, passing universal healthcare, or any other political quagmire that could dramatically improve child outcomes, an equal, 50/50 parenting presumption is the one policy change that could dramatically help tens of millions of children, their families, and their communities *without any additional funding*. Equal parenting can save lives *for free*.

As much as I love to champion single moms and advocate for them to have plenty of time to pursue their careers, their well-being, and their joy, and as much as I want dads to have the ability to bond with and care for their kids (without having their kids' moms judging their every move) and enjoy the purpose and meaning that parenting can provide, the fact is, shared parenting is a child-welfare issue.

As you'll come to see in this chapter, kids who experience an approximately equal physical custody arrangement after a divorce have better outcomes in academic achievement, emotional health, behavioral problems, and physical health, and they have better relationships with their parents, stepparents, and grandparents. This is true even in situations where there is abundant conflict between the parents and when there is a drastic difference in income between the parents' homes.

A growing and influential body of social science dating back to the 1950s—which I'll elaborate on in this chapter—concludes that not only do children benefit from close relationships with both parents and that they are harmed when their dads are marginalized in their lives, but also that a 50/50 parenting arrangement is the living situation in which children whose parents are not cohabiting fare the best. That 50/50 number is critical. In fact, studies draw a direct correlation between incremental increased sums of parenting time with the father and better child outcomes. The closer the schedule is to 50/50, the better the kids fare in social, emotional, academic, and physical health outcomes—not just immediately but for the rest of their lives.

Dads and Moms Are Different but Equally Important to Children

If the evidence is so clear that children benefit from equal time with both parents, thrive when they have meaningful time and relationships with their fathers, and truly hurt when those relationships are underdeveloped or suddenly severed, why have we historically been so comfortable with downgrading dads in our children's lives?

While the world is changing for the better dramatically and quickly, dads are still considered disposable parents.

As researcher Linda Nielsen, a professor of adolescent and educational psychology at Wake Forest University, puts it, "We're brainwashed to think that fathers are not as good a parent to daughters as mothers are, or that fathers can't nurture the way mothers can, or that daughters raised by fathers only are going to be worse off than daughters raised by mothers only, or that boys need their fathers more than girls do." All kids need their dads—even when he's not a paragon of parenting.

How do dads benefit kids exactly?

For starters, dads are a vital piece of teaching our kids risk-taking, grit, and resilience. If you watch the way that dads and moms interact with their kids on the playground, for example, moms are often the ones reminding the kid to stay safe and not fall off the jungle gym, while the dads are encouraging kids to go for it. And if the kid falls off, the dad will encourage them to get right back on.

"The research on child development has always shown that there is a difference in the way that mothers and fathers parent," Nielsen said. "The mother always wants to get all the obstacles out of the way—*I don't want my baby to have any stress.* Even in college, the mother prepares the road for the child. The father prepares the child for the road."

Preparing the road is neither good nor bad, just as preparing the child is neither good nor bad. Kids thrive with access to both parenting influences, but our current parenting culture, which defaults to coddling and helicoptering, tends to overcelebrate female parenting, while the grit and resilience that we consistently bemoan our children lacking happen to be a strong suit of dads—the very parents who have been pushed aside.

A 2016 study out of Oxford University in the United Kingdom found that fathers who were attentive and responsive to their eleven-month-old babies had a significant impact on their child's cognitive development and language skills through age three, regardless of the father's socioeconomic background. (Meaning that the children of fathers who were more sensitive to their needs scored significantly higher on standardized tests that measured cognitive development at eighteen months and language skills at three years than children whose fathers were less responsive to their children's cues.) For moms, their sensitive parenting only had a significant impact on their child's mental development when you removed socioeconomic status from the equation. In other words, dads as a whole were more impactful on their kids across the board, while mom's impact was conditional on her economic stability. Frankly, the researchers were surprised by their findings, calling them "somewhat unexpected." But they cited other research that found that fathers' supportiveness when their children were infants was positively associated with greater emotional regulation in their kids by the time they were two—an association that was not found with mothers' supportiveness, suggesting that dads help their kids self-regulate. The Oxford study also found that father involvement could compensate for moms who weren't sensitive to their babies' needs and cues. It makes sense: when one parent is struggling in some way, such as with postpartum depression, mental or physical health challenges, or addiction, it is critical to have more loving adults in proximity to fill in the gap. More love is more love. More love is more security.

Granted, this study was conducted on only ninety-seven families. A larger study of 860 families found that a dad's attachment to his twelve-year-old child had a significant impact on the child's mental health. Kids who were securely attached to the dad had reduced symptoms of depression and feelings of loneliness, whereas kids whose attachment to their father was insecure were much more likely to feel lonely and have a fear of being alone. Then think about how these benefits can be lost when moms get primary custody and kids don't get equal access to their dads. Plus, remember that dads with minority parenting schedules are most likely to check out altogether.

In fact, the father-child bond is a hallmark of humanity, according to *The Life of Dad* author Anna Machin, who wrote, "All mammalian babies form attachment relationships with their mothers, but humans are one of the very few mammals where a baby forms this intense reciprocal relationship with dad." No wonder kids miss their dads when they don't have equal access to them—they evolved to bond with them.

A Definitive Definition of Best Interest

Good news: over the past few decades, egregiously sexist language has been abolished from nearly all state family law when it comes to providing judges guidance in determining parenting schedules when moms and dads live separately. In its place, save for just six states, Kentucky, Arizona, West Virginia, Arkansas, Missouri, and Florida, where a 50/50 presumption is the law, the language is typically some variation of that of Virginia, where I live:

§ 20-124.3. BEST INTERESTS OF THE CHILD, VISITATION.

In determining best interests of a child for purposes of determining custody or visitation arrangements, including any pendente lite orders pursuant to § 20–103, the court shall consider the following:

1. The age and physical and mental condition of the child, giving due consideration to the child's changing developmental needs;

2. The age and physical and mental condition of each parent;

3. The relationship existing between each parent and each child, giving due consideration to the positive involvement with the child's life, the ability to accurately assess and meet the emotional, intellectual, and physical needs of the child;

4. The needs of the child, giving due consideration to other important relationships of the child, including but not limited to siblings, peers, and extended family members;

5. The role that each parent has played and will play in the future, in the upbringing and care of the child;

6. The propensity of each parent to actively support the child's contact and relationship with the other parent, including whether a parent has unreasonably denied the other parent access to or visitation with the child;

7. The relative willingness and demonstrated ability of each parent to maintain a close and continuing relationship with the child, and the ability of each parent to cooperate in and resolve disputes regarding matters affecting the child;

8. The reasonable preference of the child, if the court deems the child to be of reasonable intelligence, understanding, age, and experience to express such a preference;

9. Any history of (i) family abuse as that term is defined in § 16.1–228, (ii) sexual abuse, (iii) child abuse, or (iv) an act of violence, force, or threat as defined in § 19.2–152.7:1 that occurred no earlier than 10 years prior to the date a petition is filed. If the court finds such a history or act, the court may disregard the factors in subdivision 6; and

10. Such other factors as the court deems necessary and proper to the determination.

The judge shall communicate to the parties the basis of the decision either orally or in writing. Except in cases of consent orders for custody and visitation, this communication shall set forth the judge's findings regarding the relevant factors set forth in this section. At the request of either party, the court may order that the exchange of a child shall take place at an appropriate meeting place.

What Virginia's law outlines is an all-out battle for determining which parent is "better," in the name of the *best interest of the child*. This process is arbitrary and expensive, with wealthy parents routinely spending tens of thousands of dollars to hire attorneys, therapists, guardians ad litem, custodial evaluators, and more to decide which parent is better. Poor parents either avoid family court altogether or represent themselves, which is rarely effective. Despite all these efforts, to paraphrase one family therapist who testified in family court in my city, "There is often one parent who is a 'better parent' or who has a closer connection with the child, but the parenting schedule should still be split 50/50."

I have learned firsthand as well as through hearing countless stories of other moms and dads how unequal custody agreements hurt children. Maya started out her single parenting journey with two toddlers who lived with her, while her ex-boyfriend visited occasionally and unpredictably. She worked full-time as an assistant at a medical office, took the kids to day care, and couldn't count on her kids' dad for any sharing of care. "I saw some of the parents on the playground who really shared in taking care of their kids—even if they weren't together as a couple—and how their kids really always had two parents they could count on," she told me. "After a while, things calmed down with my ex and me, and we got on a better schedule. He'd have them every second weekend, and then it was more like three days each week." She could see how her kids looked forward to spending time with their dad and seemed happy to come to her house after, too.

The more time they spent with their dad meant her son and daughter got closer with their grandma and cousins on their dad's side of the family, and even though his parenting wasn't 100 percent how she'd like—her daughter's hair was often tangled when she came from her dad's, and he fed them too much candy—the kids were doing great, in part, she assumed, because Maya wasn't so stressed out thanks to the breaks she was getting, and their dad seemed like he had grown up a lot as well. On one hand, Maya was still doing nearly all the emotional labor—the scheduling, the schlepping, taking time off work when a kid was sick, and lobbying for her son to receive accommodations from his school due to his learning delays. On the other, she did like having the upper hand that her 60 percent time-share gave her when tensions arose with her ex. "I do your share of parenting!" was a refrain she leveraged when he wiggled out of his time with the kids, but as they got older and could read a calendar and count days, her attitude shifted.

The 60/40 worked for a while, but as Maya's kids got older, they had persistent questions about *why* they spent the majority of time with her. *Why* did they spend four nights each week with her and three with their dad? Maya could see how this inequity burrowed into her kids' sense of consciousness, self, fairness, and security. After all, they loved their dad and had a good time at his house, and the world seemed to think it was a perfectly good thing for them to spend time with their own biological father, so why did they only go to their dad's house for three days per week, they'd ask her. Why wasn't it half the time?

I connect with Maya's story, as it is very similar to my own. How we answer our children's questions about how much time they have with each parent is profound. No matter how you word it, the way kids interpret your answers to their questions about the reason for an unequal schedule is either "It isn't safe for you to be with your dad any more hours," or "Your dad doesn't want to see you any more hours."

It is unlikely either of these statements is true. But that is what the child likely hears, feels, or internalizes, says leading shared parenting researcher, child psychologist, and Arizona State University associate professor William Fabricius. "There are two sources of emotional insecurity for children in divorcing families: ongoing parent conflict, and emotional security with each parent—the mom and the dad," Fabricius said. "It comes down to the child having a sense that they matter to each parent. What we find time and again is the amount of parenting time a child spends with a parent after a divorce is highly related to how secure that child feels and reassured that they matter to that parent."

If you are reading this and listing scenarios where 50/50 is just impossible or impractical, it always comes back to this: the spirit of the time-sharing agreement always needs to be rooted in 50/50. There are a million deviations and caveats, but (barring extreme circumstances) it should always come back to a goal and a spirit of equal time, communicated clearly to the child and both parents:

+ "You are spending more time at Daddy's house this month because Mommy has a special work project and has to travel. Then we will get back to our regular 50/50 schedule next month."
+ "Your mom has a lot of health issues, so for a while, you'll stay more with me and see her every few days, until she feels better."
+ "Your mom and you do Scouts together every Tuesday, but it is easier for me to take off work when you need to go to the doctor. Eventually, there will be other things that come up, and over the long term, it all evens out. Life happens! But the big point is that we both work together and equally love you."

I have met many families in which the mom says she is confident in her kids' dad to parent for 20, 30, or 40 percent of the week but insists that any more is simply outside his capacity as a father. This makes no sense. If he is safe to parent 10 percent of the time, then he is safe to parent 100 percent of the time. Any argument to the contrary is rooted in financial greed (as time-sharing can be linked to child support payments), identity issues linked to ideas of a mother's parental superiority, a blatant play for control, or simply some very human mess around trying to maintain a sense of order during a time of family upheaval.

There are also those who say that conflict between the parents makes handoffs that much more stressful if parenting time increases. Again, back to Fabricius's work: fighting parents do cause anxiety and upset in kids, but the simple knowledge that one parent is officially the lesser parent also makes the child insecure.

Another common argument against 50/50 schedules is that kids get stressed out when they go to the other parent's house. That may be true. The back-and-forth can be exhausting, and they may not have bonded as deeply with one parent—yet. They may also be feeling guilty for having a good time with someone their *other* parent dislikes so much. These are all real stressors for a kid, but they are mitigated by the benefits of securing the parent-child relationship with both mom and dad through a 50/50 schedule.

That doesn't mean that having an equally shared parenting arrangement with your kids' other parent doesn't have its difficulties. I know intellectually that the research suggests I'm not going to have a lesser relationship with my kids because they have 50 percent time with their dad and I'm writing a whole book on the subject! But on an emotional level, I still struggle with that fear. As I write this, I just got a text from my kids' dad, asking if it was OK if he organizes our son's thirteenth birthday laser-tag party. Now, I have managed every other birthday party for our fifteen years of co-parenting and, kids, if you're reading this, here is the harsh truth: I don't enjoy it. Until they are teenagers, I generally do not enjoy the company of other people's children, and I don't enjoy kid things like bouncy houses or princesses or arcades. I am not, as you know, terribly sentimental about holidays and birthdays, and, son, you know how I feel about guns, even those that only shoot colored lights.

So if their dad was eager to wrangle this task and its expense, why did it take me a few painful minutes to finger-type the obvious affirmative? Because I am a human woman living in North America in the twenty-first century, and I experienced a sharp twinge of fear that this one laser-tag party would ding my maternal role in the heart of my kid. Cry me a river, right?

These issues are complicated, especially for kids. Jesse, a ten-year-old whose parents are divorced and have a 50/50 parenting arrangement, told me that on Fridays, when he switches homes, he gets stressed out. "It's annoying that I have to pack up my stuff—every single week," the fifth grader told me. He gets emotional sometimes, especially when he realizes something he needs for a science project or his hockey equipment is at the other parent's house—a twenty-minute drive away. "Other kids don't have to deal with that," he said. But again, the science tells us that the very real challenges of equal parenting schedules are dwarfed by the benefits. That equal schedule signals to Jesse that his dad and his mom love him, that his dad and mom are important as parents and as people, and that helps him feel important as a boy and future man—because if one parent is deemed unsafe or uncaring or a doofus parent, that gets internalized by the kids as *half of me is bad*.

On the flip side, a large and growing body of research finds, devastatingly, that children without equally involved fathers are more prone to numerous negative outcomes. In particular, researchers at Princeton, Cornell, and University of California, Berkeley, reviewed forty-seven studies on children raised without father involvement, carefully controlling for factors that might influence outcomes. The kids included in these studies were more likely to display externalizing behaviors in childhood, such as aggression, bullying, and poor emotional control, risky behaviors in adolescence, such as smoking, drinking, and having unprotected sex, and were significantly less likely to graduate from high school. Their mental health also took a hit well into adulthood. Why would we fight to preserve unequal parenting again?

Do Kids Care about Parenting Schedules?

In preparation for this chapter, I talked to adult children whose parents had divorced when they were kids, like my friend Kate, who is in her fifties and whose parents split when she was in third grade. When they were married, both Kate's parents had professional jobs. Kate went to day care and then to a neighbor's house after preschool and then was a stereotypical Gen X latchkey kid in elementary school, getting herself off to school in the mornings and letting herself in afterward.

Although both her parents had careers, thanks to stereotypical gender roles that played out inside her parents' marriage, Kate felt closer to her mom than she did to her dad. Her mom was the patient, nurturing one who managed Kate's schedule and homework and got to know her friends, while her dad was the disciplinarian who spent most of his time at home reading the newspaper. "After my parents divorced and it was my weekend with Dad, we didn't really know how to be together at first. I remember a lot of meals at McDonald's, awkwardly trying to make conversation over a Happy Meal." Still, they eventually found things to do together that they both enjoyed, like camping, going to the beach, road trips to see family, and doing scavenger hunts. And there were perks. "We'd make meat loaf, and I'd get to mix everything up with my bare hands, for example, something I never did with Mom. And I think because Dad was a little lost on what to do with me, I had more friends sleep over at his house. My best friend and I jumped on his bed so many times that he had to put his mattress up on cinder blocks because we broke the legs off." In many ways, Kate's dad is evidence of how men thrive as parents after a breakup and are able to find their parenting groove thanks to forced one-on-one time with their kids. His more laissez-faire parenting style is also consistent with how men tend to parent and how Kate benefited from that very style.

All was going well until fifth grade when Kate's mom married a man from Oklahoma, halfway across the country from their Rhode Island home, and started planning a move to the Midwest. Kate's dad tried to get a court order to prevent the move, but it was denied. (Kate, age ten, had to appear on the stand and answer the judge's question, "Whom would you rather live with?" She chose Mom.)

After the move, Kate and her dad talked on the phone each week, and Kate would fly back to Rhode Island for visits during the summers and school breaks. Once, during one of those visits, Michael Jackson's "She's Out of My Life" came on the radio, and her dad started crying, saying it brought back memories of when she and her mom moved away.

"It was confusing. One day, I had this nice and growing relationship with my dad. It felt totally normal. The next day, I just moved across the country like that didn't matter. It felt unfair and sad. Now I look back and see it as a tragedy—for me and for my dad. We got off that path to closeness that we were on, and although we have a loving relationship now, we can sometimes struggle to connect." Once Kate got out of college and was ready to have an adult relationship with her dad, it felt like maybe they had missed their window. Phone calls would be awkward, and she struggled to share about her current life, but bringing up old times, even the good ones, took them both to a painful chapter.

"I look back and see my need for a father figure play out in controlling boyfriends and just feeling unmoored as a young adult. I see my adult friends now who are getting divorced and working with their exes to stay at least in close proximity and civil to each other, even when their exes treated them horribly, and wish that I—and every other kid who ended up living far away from one of their parents—had that same option."

Kate's experience isn't unique. Twenty years ago, 29 percent of noncustodial parents had moved more than an hour away from their kids by the time the child was in college—figures that have since shrunk thanks in part to the legal system's emphasis on creating custody arrangements that keep kids connected to both parents. Many states even have laws on the books that dictate how many miles away one parent can move and still have joint custody—Michigan's limit is one hundred miles, while Florida's is fifty. Although these long-distance moves do still happen, a 2021 law journal article for parents who are considering moving their children away from their other parent summed it up this way: "The relocating parent should anticipate having a very difficult burden of proof in court." That's as it should be, because when that move happens before the kid is twelve, it has been linked to anxiety and depression, behavior problems, and impaired relationships with both parents as well as any relationship with a stepparent.

Even if kids don't live far away from their dads, there is still a loss of access to Dad in the standard custody arrangements— one that kids often wish they could fix. When Fabricius conducted a survey of more than eight hundred college students whose parents divorced when they were kids, he found that a majority wished they had been able to spend more time with their fathers. "When we interviewed them, kids told us that they wished they'd had equal schedules," Fabricius said.

The True Trauma in Divorce

Since the late 1990s, researchers have been paying more attention to the effect of traumatic experiences or what are technically known as adverse childhood events, or ACEs. Since the very beginning of this line of study, divorce and separation from a parent have been included on the list of possible ACEs. Other ACEs include experiencing violence, abuse, or neglect, living with someone with addiction, experiencing or witnessing violence in the home or community, economic instability, having an incarcerated parent, being bullied, and experiencing racism. As a whole, ACEs have negative impacts on child development—affects that last into adulthood—and the more ACEs a child has, the more likely they are to experience depression, anxiety, PTSD, cancer, diabetes, or alcohol and drug abuse and to have lower levels of education and income as adults.

Fabricius says that early childhood stress, such as witnessing parental conflict, "sets up patterns in the child's brain and stress response system that heightens them to worry about other kinds of stress. And if it's extreme enough in early childhood, it can set up a stress response system that is in a chronic state of releasing stress hormones. That causes long-term stress-related physical health problems like cardiovascular disease and a lowered immune system. It also interferes with social functioning and can result in over-heightened anger responses." ACEs are even believed to become embedded in a person's genetic code: according to one study, people who had ACEs as kids were found to have experienced changes that caused their genes that regulate receptors for oxytocin—the hormone that helps us feel bonded to others—to be turned off. These changes in genetic expression can then be passed down to future generations. (If you need yet another reason to stop fighting over custody and embrace shared parenting, think about how resolving your current conflict could make things better for your grandkids, *genetically*.)

And yet controversy abounds over whether all divorces and separations qualify as ACEs. On the one hand, yes, having your nuclear family break up and your living situation change, witnessing your parents going through a stressful event, maybe being subject to some crappy parenting because your mom and dad are stressed, or seeing them argue with each other can absolutely make kids feel insecure. Kids tend to blame themselves and wonder if the fact that their parents stopped loving each other means that they can also stop loving their kids. Plus, divorce or breakup may mean a move, a new school, a decline in financial stability—all things that also impact kids' sense of security and stress levels. A 2019 review of fifty-four studies that took place between 1990 and 2018 and included over a half a million participants found a significant association between having parents who divorced in childhood and numerous negative mental health outcomes in adulthood, including depression, anxiety, suicidal ideation, suicide attempts, and alcohol and drug use. The researchers did note that the association declined between 1990 and 2018, implying that maybe we're getting better at not making divorce such a disaster for kids, including a significant increase in father involvement after a breakup. But still, the breakup inevitably did cause long-term upset.

As researchers, therapists, and courts try to figure out how to configure families so that children fare best, there are plenty of kids of divorce who have gone on to become well-adjusted, healthy, and successful adults. Which makes sense, as successfully facing any hardship can build resilience. From that, we learn that it's not the divorce itself but the circumstances that can accompany it—like losing access to one parent, poverty, witnessing your parents fighting, or having a stressed-out mom who can't tend to her kid's needs—that make the dissolution of the nuclear family a true ACE.

And guess what alleviates all those factors? Equal parenting. When kids have involved dads and close relationships with their fathers, it addresses so many of those ACE-related negative outcomes: they do better in school and graduate at rates similar to kids with married parents. Younger kids develop better communication and socializing skills. Kids of all ages become more likely to make a positive adjustment to their new reality when their dads are involved, and the change in living status becomes more manageable. When both moms and dads have time off to get their heads and lives together while the kids are with the other parent, they can be better parents when they are with their kids. And when kids know they will have equal time with both parents, they are not scared that one of them will abandon them. But don't take my word for it. Let's look at the evidence.

What Science Says about Equal Parenting

There is an extensive body of research on the benefits of shared parenting—one that has been evaluated from a bird's-eye perspective by Linda Nielsen, Wake Forest University professor of psychology. In 2018, Nielsen published a meta review of sixty studies from the past twenty-five years that compared children whose parents have joint physical custody to children with one parent who had solo primary custody (meaning they lived primarily with one parent with only periodic visits with the other).

Most of the research studies included in Nielsen's analysis define shared parenting as both parents having the kids for at least 35 percent of the time. Why? Researchers (who are often also advocates) want to be accurate and realistic, and 50/50 arrangements were pretty rare until the last ten or so years, which made it hard to find 50/50 families to study.

To the naysayers who argue that the sample size or quality of shared parenting research does not fall in favor of equality: these findings were more than substantiated by researchers at the University of Lausanne in Switzerland. In a 2023 meta-analysis of thirty-nine studies published between 2010 and 2022, with a sample size of 1.5 million, researchers found that while children raised in nuclear families fared better than those in separated families, 75 percent of the time separated-family kids did just as well as those who grew up in homes with married biological mothers and fathers, but also much better than those raised by just one parent. The Lausanne study factored in income and the presence of stepparents. "Maintaining connection with both parents outweighs any potential drawbacks of moving between households and supports many countries' policies around preference [shared-custody parenting] over [lone-custody parenting]," researchers concluded.

As for Nielsen, her work found that kids who share time with both parents have better outcomes related to each of these areas:

+ Academic achievement
+ Drug, alcohol, and cigarette use
+ Mental and physical health
+ Early sexual activity and teen pregnancy
+ Employment and earnings later in life
+ Likelihood of family stability in their own adulthoods
+ Relationships with parents, stepparents, and grandparents

These benefits existed regardless of parental income level and conflict, although Nielsen is careful to point out, "This is not to say that children do not benefit in any way from living in higher income families or from having parents with low conflict, cooperative co-parenting relationships. What these studies do mean is that the better outcomes for joint-custody children should not be attributed to higher family incomes or to low conflict between their parents."

Other studies have also found the following:

+ Shared parenting arrangements don't take away from kids' closeness to their mothers.
+ Shared parenting when kids are young tends to mean that fathers remain involved with their kids as they grow into adults, while fathers with less parenting time tend to be less involved in their

kids' lives over time, and this leads to negative outcomes for those kids.

The common-sense benefits of shared parenting are also compelling. When children have equal time with both parents, they also benefit from what researchers call "social capital": increased circles of family and friends and neighbors and a greater sense of security in having two homes of extended care and love. Two involved parents and their tribes provide for more financial security: two incomes, two parents and their families to weather economic ups and downs and provide childcare, transportation, homework help, hugs, advice, and any of the countless elements of emotional and logistical labor that kids require.

While the analysis of these sixty studies proves why meaningful father involvement is so important in separated families, it is the research on that seemingly evasive 50/50 number that we need to focus on and use as our North Star.

Fabricius has found that stress in children related to their parents' divorce, even in a high-conflict co-parenting relationship, decreases the closer the schedule gets to 50/50. "If a child from a divorced family has equal parenting time, they can have relationships with both their parents that are as good as those in intact families," Fabricius said. On the other hand, "If one parent is absent from the child's life until every other weekend, for example, the child is at risk of thinking that *that parent doesn't really want to spend more time with me* and…*maybe I don't matter that much to that parent.*" Even if there's conflict, kids don't have all those extra hours and hours away from Dad to worry that he is going to slip out. "We know from lots of research that these doubts set up chronic stress reactions that can damage long-term mental and physical health." For this reason, Fabricius calls parenting time a public health crisis.

In my family, my kids benefit from not just equal time with their dad but also a loving stepmom and stepdad.

When both of our households relocated from New York City to Virginia two years ago, we decided on Richmond. The only tie any of us have here is my kids' stepmom's family, through which my kids enjoy relationships with their young stepcousins. One lovely by-product of this is that my kids have both gotten very good at being with little kids, which they otherwise would not have had the opportunity to do. Recently, our neighbors came for dinner with their three-year-old daughter, and my son, age twelve, took it upon himself to entertain her with badminton and Connect 4 with an ease I did not realize he possessed (single mom FOMO). "I know I'm good at taking care of little kids from being with my stepcousins," he said with an annoyed tween shrug when I complimented him later. "That doesn't mean I *like* it."

Another co-parenting benefit: both my son and daughter grow up seeing that it is normal and expected that both moms and dads, men and women, care for children. Equal co-parents model, by osmosis, a better, more progressive future. What kids see modeled by the adults in their lives matters. As evidence, a 2018 study by researchers at Johns Hopkins University found that when Black children have at least one Black teacher by the time they're in third grade, they are 13 percent more likely to graduate from high school and 19 percent more likely to enroll in college than their Black peers who didn't have a Black teacher. Similarly, storybooks featuring positive LGBTQIA+ characters have a positive influence on gay children's self-image.

Equally shared parenting also benefits children by allowing them to grow up with gender-neutral roles as their mothers take on breadwinning and "traditionally" male household tasks like lawn care and to learn that men are equally competent caretakers capable of household tasks like meal planning and family scheduling. How parents embody gender plays a big role in how kids think about gender. For example, witnessing their moms doing more "guy-type" chores has been shown to result in kids who were less likely to stick to predictable gendered choices in activities, friends, and what they wanted to be when they grew up. And when dads do more household labor in general—naturally including things that moms have primarily done, like cooking and cleaning—daughters in particular are more likely to grow up to work outside the home and to choose careers from a broader pool than the traditionally female teaching and caretaking. More gender equality has also been shown to improve life satisfaction for adolescents.

If we really want to change the future of child-rearing and make life better for kids, women, and men, we can do it by raising kids for whom basic equal parenting participation is simply the way things are done.

Shared Parenting for Babies and Toddlers

It might be hard to wrap your brain around equally shared parenting when kids are babies or toddlers. Maybe the child is nursing, or you're co-sleeping, or they just seem so vulnerable that you can't bear to let them out of your sight. All of the above applied to me, and I get it. Here too, the research shows that kids three and younger benefit from equal time with their dads.

Fabricius has found that more parenting time—including overnights—when kids are three years old and younger predicts a stronger, more secure father-child relationship without harming the mother-child connection. This was true even when the overnights occurred when the child was still an infant and regardless of whether the parents had low amounts of conflict or high amounts. Most importantly, the results held true even when the court had to impose the overnights with dad despite the mother's objections. Those brutal newborn nights of little sleep are how you learn about your child and how you learn how to take care of a child even when every fiber of your being longs for rest. And for the kid, "that's how the child forms an attachment to that parent and starts to recognize this parent as a consistent caregiver," Fabricius said.

Shared Parenting Helps Kids Even in High-Conflict Situations

What about when parents have a volatile relationship? One side of the debate in the shared parenting world is that seeing your parents fight—even a fight where there is no physical aggression—is enough of an ACE to warrant that kid having limited time with the parent who shoved first. On the other side of the argument are those of us who argue that losing access to a parent can easily be an even bigger ACE. I'll detail this more in chapter 5 on abuse, but for now, let's answer the basic question: Is it better to have the kids live primarily with one parent so that there are fewer occasions for the parents to argue?

This thorny question has a simple answer: no. Not for the kids. In fact, having equal access to both parents becomes even more important when the parents don't see eye to eye and even when they fight a lot. As Fabricius explained, "When a child is watching their parents in a high-stress state of conflict, the child is worried that if the parents can't at least stay somewhat together and in communication, the child will be left alone. That's the fear. And it's a very deep-seated anxiety." Specifically, Fabricius found that this insecurity and stress in kids with high-conflict parents was at its highest when the time the child spent with the father was between zero and about 30 percent, because "that leaves enough time that the child isn't seeing dad for the child to worry that dad's just going to give up on the situation." That stress peaks at about 35 percent and then goes down at equal time. "If dad is providing an equal home it provides the security in the child's mind that neither parent's going away," Fabricius explained.

As we saw in the previous chapter on men and fatherhood, men without equal parenting schedules do tend to feel disconnected and disempowered and slip out of their children's lives. In other words, kids in unequal parenting families are afraid of losing their dads, and that fear is justified.

Fabricius also looked specifically at families in which there was domestic violence around the time of the divorce and teased out the independent effect of domestic violence, not just parent conflict, as they can exist independently from each other. The pattern was the same—when the violence was perpetrated by the father, the child's stress increased when the time spent with dad was up to about 30 percent and decreased the closer father parenting time moved to 50 percent. However, when it was the mother who was the perpetrator of domestic violence, the child's long-term stress stayed high across all levels of parenting time. "We think that probably means that the child was worried that she might take the child away or do something to push dad out of the child's life," Fabricius said. Again, justified fears, as I unpack in my chapter on domestic violence as it relates to parenting schedules.

Linda Nielsen also did a deeper dive into studies that looked specifically at joint custody in cases where there was conflict between the parents. Despite the common assumption that conflict between parents was more damaging than minimizing time with a parent (father), that was not the case. The highlights of her research include the following:

+ Keeping the bonds with both parents strong—as a result of spending a good amount of time with each parent—helps offset the negative impacts of high levels of parental conflict and poor co-parenting. "Although joint custody does not eliminate the negative impact of frequently being caught in the middle of high, ongoing conflict between divorced parents, it does appear to reduce children's stress, anxiety, and depression," Nielsen summed up.

+ Kids whose parents have a high level of conflict that is ongoing—including physical conflict—have better outcomes when there is joint custody than when there is solo, primary custody. "Being involved in high, ongoing conflict is no more damaging to children in joint custody than in solo custody," Nielsen wrote. So it's not the proximity to the angry parent that's harmful but the distance.

+ Most parents with joint physical custody in high-conflict situations did not originally agree to the arrangement. They only accepted the terms under pressure or order from courts, mediation, or legal negotiations. Even so, kids with joint custody had better outcomes than kids with solo custody.

+ No study has found that kids whose parents have a high level of conflict experience worse outcomes than those with parents who reach a parenting agreement without legal conflict.

Fabricius concurs. "We have not found a case where we found negative consequences of shared parenting time. In fact, shared parenting time seems to provide the child with security in the face of parent conflict. So the more parent conflict there is, the more reason for shared parenting time."

Can Shared Parenting Save Lives?

In 2013, Swedish researcher Malin Bergström and her team conducted a population study of two hundred thousand kids in Sweden ages twelve to fifteen years old and found that the health and well-being of children who enjoyed equal parenting schedules was nearly as good as that of those who had parents who were together as a couple and better than those living only with a single mother. "Since then, we have seen more or less the same pattern in all our studies: children with shared parenting have slightly worse health than those with parents who have stayed together, but better health than those living mostly with one parent," Bergström told me.

When I asked her why she thought that was, Bergström shared a view aligned with Fabricius: "Losing [or greatly reducing] contact with one parent creates loss and a sense of not being important. It is losing love from one of the two most important people in your life, which is of course difficult for children." But it's more than that, she went on. "Keeping both your parents gives you access to more resources—that could be financial resources, coaching, experiences, or network."

Still, the fact that kids in shared parenting arrangements are physically and mentally healthier than kids who live with one parent, including later as adults, is great—for Sweden, where shared parenting is a cultural norm and the population is regularly rated near the top of the global happiness scale from year to year. What about in the United States?

Fabricius secured funding from the National Institutes of

Health to collect data over a ten-year period, when children were between the ages of twelve and twenty-two. They checked in with the families to evaluate how much parenting time the child had with the father five times during that ten-year span. "Our field of psychology has devised a statistical method that gives the strongest evidence for causality that we can in a situation where you can't run a controlled experiment," he explained. "We applied those techniques to our longitudinal data and results were beautifully clear that at each age, an increase or a decrease in parenting time was followed one to two years later by an increase or decrease in the strength and the emotional security of the father-child relationship." And as other studies have made clear, father-child bonding is key to children's physical, mental, and emotional health. But Fabricius's study goes beyond those correlations to answer the question *Is it the parenting time itself that creates the positive benefits of shared parenting, or do they come as a result of good dads being granted more time with their kids?*

This finding has more implications than emotional benefits. It also has public health ramifications. The United States has been collecting mountains of public health data dating back to the 1950s on the contributing factors to chronic diseases, including family relationships, by soliciting answers to the questions *How well do you get along with your dad?* and *How well do your parents get along with each other?* The results show that the quality of your relationship with each of your parents and the level of parent conflict have long-term effects on physical and mental health. If either of your parental relationships suffers or if your parents have a high level of conflict, it can contribute to cancer, cardiovascular disease, and early mortality. Since shared parenting improves parental relationships and helps kids deal with the stress of parents who have conflict, Fabricius has gone on record as saying, "I'm absolutely convinced, as much as any scientist can ever be convinced, that we can improve the public health of this country by having states and family courts let the public know that they're going to be open to shared parenting." Mic drop!

The Prevailing Parenting Style That's Standing in the Way

If unequal parenting is a cultural norm that we must challenge and change to serve kids, it is not the only one. Parenting styles have ebbed, flowed, regressed, and progressed throughout time, and a shift to more father-mother equality is just one. So is another: helicopter parenting, and I argue that these two are intrinsically linked.

Everywhere I look, I see parents who insist their middle-schoolers would miss them too much to go to sleepaway camp for one week, who take on the apartment hunting and packing and relocating for their college graduates, and who happily drive their sixteen- and seventeen- and eighteen-year-old students around town because the kids aren't in the mood to get their licenses. I often found it hard to hang out with other parents if our kids were in the vicinity. Adult conversations are constantly interrupted by the demands of a snack, permission to download an app, or sharing about how they just performed on a video game—unannounced interruptions that are immediately met with that parent's full attention, even for children as old as middle school. While I tell my kids to leave the parents to chat, to go play alone, to entertain themselves, their friends expect their whims to be met immediately and fully—and they are. Parents in my circles are there not just to serve their kids but to be responsive to their every need *in real time.*

We've come to equate hovering and overdoing with good parenting. Simultaneously, we contend with the collective cry of moms: "I need a break! I'm overwhelmed! I'm stressed!" as well as now two generations of young people plagued with the inability to manage their own schoolwork, careers, anxiety, or relationships—a trend experts are increasingly attaching to the fact that their loving parents hovered and doted far beyond any historic or anthropological precedence. This culture of overprotecting and hyper-parenting children only fuels the flames of a dysfunctional postmarriage family culture. After all, what is arguing over small slices of time in family court if not an extension of mommy warring over the micro benefits of co-sleeping or crying it out?

Underpinning it all is the blind assumption that children are fragile, that more mothering is better, and that the parent-child bond is both tenuous and essential.

I have fought my way through the whole arc myself.

When my daughter was born in 2008, I joined my other

enthusiastic new-parent friends and devoured the then-current parenting bible, *The Attachment Parenting Book* by Dr. William Sears and his wife, Martha Sears, RN. Originally released in 2001 amid a popular culture where every week, a new celebrity mom was on the cover of *People* magazine gushing about how motherhood was the most important job she'd ever had, the Searses' book advocated spending as much time with the kids as possible—carrying them in a sling, breastfeeding them, and sleeping in the same bed with them. It even espoused going into financial debt in order to spend nearly twenty-four seven with the baby. That last part rubbed me, a financial journalist, the wrong way, but otherwise, I felt a euphoric love for my baby that made me want to spend as much time in her orbit as possible (as opposed to *her* spending time in *my* adult orbit!), so the pitch resonated. Besides, every other new mom I knew lived by it. We were tired, overwhelmed, and devastatingly unsure how to best raise these teeny, perfect creatures. The Searses' combined medical experience—and the fact that they had eight kids!—made their "kinder, gentler" approach a clear antidote to our parents' and grandparents' devotion to crying it out and the occasional spanking.

However, attachment parenting did us all dirty in a few ways. First, the notion that more time with your child is better discouraged a lot of moms from pursuing work outside the home and encouraged us to spend endless, exhausting, and stressful hours with our children. While attachment parenting didn't originate the pay gap—we can thank patriarchy for that—it has certainly perpetuated it. All those endless hours with our kids and the pressure to make every second so damn meaningful only add to maternal stress and anxiety, heightened by now having less money and being more financially dependent on our partners.

Family psychologist Eleana Armao, whom I met at a shared parenting conference in Athens, Greece, joins the chorus of shared parenting critics who point out how the Searses' literature underscores typical gender roles by assuming an inherent mother-child bond and assigning only a supportive parenting role to men. Armao's study on parents practicing attachment parenting revealed an imbalanced parenting dynamic, where mothers were excessively involved while fathers were insufficiently involved, leading to mothers bearing a disproportionate burden of caregiving and decision-making, ultimately affecting their mental well-being negatively. "The perception of the mother as the most significant and irreplaceable caregiver can create pressure for mothers and deprive fathers of opportunities to form fulfilling relationships with their children and experience meaningful parenthood," Armao said, adding that this dichotomy stands in the way of equal parenting for separated families.

Also, overwrought attachment parenting has hobbled our kids.

"We've known the consequences of coddling, overparenting, and protecting kids for years. When you hover, you're interfering with your child developing self-reliance," Nielsen told me. "What you get is the snowflake generation of kids in college who have to be protected from every stress and strain. We have to have safe places and we have to have trigger warnings. That all comes from overcoddling, helicoptering, and overprotecting." Friends who teach university share common stories: students routinely fail to meet deadlines or take responsibility for their poor grades and missed assignments, expecting the constant, kind accommodation of their upbringing to continue through adulthood.

Lenore Skenazy, journalist and author of *Free-Range Kids* and cofounder of Let Grow, a nonprofit focused on giving children back some measure of independence, is a longtime friend who has challenged us all to let our children have some free time and independence away from doting adults. Where did all this smothering culture come from? "We are enamored with the idea that [fill in the blank] will ruin your child forever," she told me. It's the net result of living in a culture that is mired in fearmongering media and data-driven parenting, leading to a belief that "one thing can knock you off the rails for life," Skenazy said. Plus, we subscribe to the notion that it is our job as parents to make our children happy—both now and for the rest of their lives. After all, how many of us have funded the self-help book industry and devoted countless hours to couch time to unpack how our own parents failed to give us the tools to make *ourselves* happy?

Yet throughout history, our species has perpetuated itself, despite great biological odds and in the face of thousands of years of plague, endless war, famine, and, until very, very recently, a dearth of parenting books or family therapy. In ancient Greece, 25 percent of babies didn't survive infancy, and half of kids died before puberty. Child mortality didn't take a steep nosedive until the middle of the twentieth century. Historically, those children who survived long enough to become adults and parents didn't fare much better: In the Middle Ages, the bubonic plague killed one-third of the European population, and religious wars killed tens of thousands. Kids *never* had stable upbringings, and still society advanced. Cities, trade, art, and universities flourished, as did children.

It is the human condition to forget history, to experience fear with greater acuity than with appreciation for the relative safety and abundance of living in the Western Hemisphere in the twenty-first century. And so we hover, interject, clear the road, and help kids negotiate their every upset. On top of that, we're obsessed with quality time with our kids. But this is a uniquely American view.

"In other cultures, a parent on a floor to roll the ball or play horsey is as strange as getting down on the floor to lap milk from a dish, and a mother is chastised if she's too attentive," Skenazy told me. Around the world, mostly it's not even a parent raising a child but an older sibling. In her book *Parenting Without Borders*, journalist Christine Gross-Loh wrote, "Around the world, it's common for older children to take care of younger children...playing with them, carrying them, disciplining them. Mother is more of an overseer than a laborer when it comes to childcare." One paper found that Kenyan grad students at Harvard think it's totally weird that American kids would even want to play with their parents and not seek out a sibling instead. In Mexico, toddlers were most often supervised by siblings and other children—not parents.

Whether you go down a rabbit hole of watching TikToks featuring school-age Korean kids using an adorable array of household gadgets to cook and clean while home alone after school, get sucked in by the Japanese reality show *Old Enough* that shows kids—some still in diapers—walking twenty minutes and crossing busy highways by themselves to pick up some curry at the store, or read an article about how Swedish preschools don't have fences around their yards, it's easy to find examples of happy, healthy kids spending time away from their parents or even much adult supervision. After all, how many of your best childhood memories include grown-ups?

Independent play, free time, problem-solving, and just being away from adults are basic childhood needs. Studies link autonomy to long-term motivation, engagement, a more positive attitude toward school, confidence, and better executive function. Neuropsychologist William Stixrud and educator Ned Johnson, in their book *The Self-Driven Child*, wrote, "Like exercise and sleep, autonomy appears to be good for virtually everything, presumably because it represents a deep human need."

Without that sense of agency, kids can have a harder time managing their emotions, navigating social interactions, and succeeding in grade school, and in college, they experience higher levels of depression and life satisfaction, research finds. Psychologist Holly Schiffrin concluded after studying helicoptered kids, "Parents who 'help' their children too much stress themselves out and leave their kids ill-prepared to be adults."

Considering how relatively safe, healthy, and thriving most people are in the Western world when compared with nearly all of history and how few hours our children actually need us, bickering with your ex about the holiday schedule or bedtime routine in the name of *best interest of the child* becomes futile at best, if not embarrassing. If rich white parents invest in international travel and economically diverse schools in the name of growing experiences, why do we frame living half-time with a loving parent as detrimental to a healthy childhood? If we're comfortable with sending our kids to summer-long camp at age seven with but one parenting visiting day—as has long been common among the affluent—how can we argue that our kids are going to be traumatized by a few more days per month with a nice dad? *Especially* when we now have solid science to support the fact that equal time mitigates so many other discomforts and even traumas?

"People wonder why kids are so anxious these days. It's really that they spend too much time with their parents," Skenazy said. "The brain is expecting a wide range of experiences to weave synapses together. Some of those experiences are great and fun and pleasurable, and some are hard and frustrating and painful, but they're all vital to becoming a fully fledged adult." Turns out that it's up to us to stop micromanaging every aspect of our kids' existence, and that includes allowing them to spend time with both of their parents.

In a study that I cite often in my work and interviews, University of Maryland researchers found that the sheer amount of time moms spend with school-aged kids (ages three to eleven) didn't lead to better outcomes in behavior, emotional health, or academics. What really matters is how warm and engaged the mother is—something it may be hard to be when you're constantly with your kids.

Lead researcher Melissa Milkie, who is now a sociology professor at the University of Toronto, said that the science finds that kids benefit from quality activities and care and support from larger communities of teachers, schools, extended families, affordable childcare, and fathers versus sheer numbers of hours with a mother. "It's the warmth and connection that is the important part," she said. "Mothers do not need to be providing 100 percent of care. That is impossible and exhausting." Even if our individualistic, sexist American culture pressures mothers to do just that.

It's time we strengthen our ability to hold two conflicting ideas up as truth: there are many hard and stressful parts of an equal parenting schedule, *and* kids benefit from equal time with both parents. You can be better off divorcing—or never marrying—your kid's parent, *and* your kids can be better off by having equal time with them. And finally, you and your child's other parent can experience a lot of conflict, *and* he is exactly the dad your kid needs now and into the future. It's not one or the other.

4

Money Always Matters

"Parents going through divorce often use money as a bargaining chip: 'I want my share,' or, 'I'll give up a day or two of parenting time in exchange for money.' As custody evaluators, we are not allowed to talk about money with families, but it is the elephant in the room."

—Janella Street, PsyD, custody evaluator
and co-parenting therapist

It is impossible to talk about co-parenting without talking about money. Money ranks as one of the top reasons couples break up, why they appear in family court, and why they experience co-parenting conflict.

Our systems and our attitudes work in tandem to reinforce the following paradigm: men have the economic power and therefore must be held accountable for financially supporting not only their children but the mothers of their children too. After all, women are unable to earn as much as men, the thinking goes, and are saddled with all the child labor.

Bad science on the subject doesn't help with this perception.

A seminal 1985 book by Dr. Lenore J. Weitzman reported that, in the wake of California's adoption of no-fault divorce, women's standard of living after divorce decreased by 73 percent, while men's rose by 42 percent. It was a jaw-dropper, a conclusion that influenced decades of judges, media, and lawyers, all of whom encouraged divorcing women to "take him for all he's worth." The statistic was even cited by the Supreme Court and still continues to inform casual conversations today. The only problem is that the data was erroneously wrong.

A 1996 analysis of Weitzman's initial data found the gap in divorced men's and women's standards of living to be much smaller. Yes, women's standard of living did fall—but only by 27 percent. And men's standard of living did rise, but only by 10 percent. But not every man saw an uptick in his fortune. In fact, nearly 10 percent of men saw their standard of living drop by 72 percent. Like many points in issues of gender equality, the story was messy and nuanced. Yet the dramatic initial numbers were burned in the zeitgeist, even after subsequent research painted a totally different story:

First, in 2012, the U.S Government Accountability Office reported that overall, men's standard of living *declined* by 23 percent postdivorce. Then, in 2020, a study published in the

Journal of Marriage and Family found separation, not divorce itself, had the most critical impact on each spouse's personal net worth—with men faring worse than women. In fact, 82 percent of men and 76 percent women experienced reduced personal wealth during the separation process, a loss that neither gender tended to recover postdivorce. This is common sense: women get the house, child support, and maybe alimony and qualify for more government benefits as head of the household, but both parents are poorer since two homes are more expensive to maintain than one, and a 401(k) split in half is a loss of 50 percent. Lots of people report that Marie Kondo-ing their ex out of their home makes way for new, more abundant energy, but basic math suggests it will be tougher financially, for the short term at least.

For affluent families, women often argue that they sacrificed during the relationship for the sake of their husbands' careers. For low-income families—who make up the majority of separated families—our systems are set up to force poor men to pay back the government for cash assistance paid to poor moms, a notion that politicians have sold as a "father responsibility" program. In reality, this welfare–child support system steals from the poor to give to the poor—all while deepening chasms between dads and their kids.

Legally and morally, both parents, regardless of gender, have a responsibility to financially support a child, and the state has an elaborate child support mechanism for holding both men and women financially accountable. However, there is no legal tool to hold a father responsible for the time and care children require, even though what children need most from their parents—both their parents equally—is time and care. When low-income parents are unable to meet their family's basic financial needs, government programs have proven to be the most effective way to support those families, not trying to squeeze more money out of poor dads.

Whitney and Jace are an example of a couple who came full circle in their child support and co-parenting journey.

Shortly after their daughter was born, the couple broke up, and Whitney hightailed it to file for child support, including Jace's share of expensive New York City childcare. She was struggling to find work in her field of online customer service, was really angry that he left while the baby was so young, and was deeply worried about just surviving. The child support payments were a big help to Whitney, but they came at the expense of Jace's ability to even keep his own apartment. "I was staying with a friend and then with my mom, sleeping on her couch," he told me. "I wanted to do the right thing and take care of my daughter, but I also had to take care of myself, which was hard."

As the months rolled on, the relationship mellowed, and despite Jace initially being flaky about showing up to see their daughter and Whitney sometimes turning him away when he did, the two sorted out a parenting schedule, which included their daughter, who was by this time one year old, spending weekends and some weeknights with her dad. During that time, Whitney landed a job and got a promotion, while Jace got laid off from his delivery job and started missing support payments. "I knew he wanted to pay, but he just didn't have the money," Whitney said. He'd point out when she bought a new-to-her dining set or got her nails done—luxuries he felt he was financing. They argued about the child support arrears, with Jace charging that he needed that money just as much as Whitney did. After all, they both had bills to pay, and they were both contributing to childcare costs. "I started to see his point, especially since he was having such a hard time that was not his fault, and I was earning more than ever," she told me. Meanwhile, their daughter adored her dad, Jace adored his daughter, and Whitney could see how important that relationship was to all of them.

Over the ensuing few years, Whitney and Jace appeared twice before a judge to formally deviate from the state of New York's child support calculator, once when Whitney asked the court to erase Jace's arrears, which had resulted in him losing his driver's license, and a second time to establish a payment from Jace to Whitney that was 50 percent of their daughter's out-of-pocket expenses—or "extras," which child support calculators separate from core household bills. "Our financial situations had changed so much over the time that we were broken up. Also, I changed my attitude about child support and started to see how it really got between us parenting," Whitney told me.

In both cases, they had to appear in court to attest to the agreement. Both times, female judges read flatly from a state-issued script that asked Whitney if she was making the decision to accept less than she was legally entitled to because either (a) she was under the influence of drugs or alcohol, or (b) she was being threatened physically or otherwise.

In other words, the state assumed the only reason a woman would deviate from its child support program is that she was high or had a literal or proverbial knife to her throat.

Even worse, because child support had previously been in play, there was no way for the sum owed to go to zero and both parents to get on with their lives. Instead, Jace was forced to pay the minimum twenty-five dollars monthly, which was automatically deducted from his bank account and appeared in Whitney's—an irritation that they worked out between them to reverse via Venmo but that stung each month no less. It was a symbolic gesture that a man's financial contribution to his child must be institutionalized and that a woman can never be financially free from a man—and that a poor family can never be free from the state's control. "We were both ready to move on and work it out peacefully between us, but the state of New York had other ideas," Whitney said. But she hasn't looked back. "Once I let all that money go, we started communicating better, and we rebuilt a lot more trust. It helped me realize that he really wants to be a good dad and is a good dad. We just had to get the money out of the way."

The Custody-Money Connection

For decades, family courts have separated custody hearings from child support hearings—as well they should. The spirit of that change is that unpaid child support should not stand in the way of a child's relationship with their parents. The two issues are separate.

The spirit of that is noble, but the reality is that money always matters, especially when it comes to child custody issues. Finances are central to most disputes between parents, whether they are married, divorced, separated, or never married. That conflict spills over to co-parenting in ways big and small.

A mom who takes on the vast majority of time with her kids—whether by her efforts or the dad's—is understandably bitter over an imbalance of financial responsibilities of parenting, plus the hit on her earning potential. She can easily take that anger out on her co-parent, perhaps by engaging in high-conflict texting (conflict has been shown to decrease a man's likelihood of willingness to parent), making unsupportive comments to the kids ("We can't afford that sweater because your dad didn't pay what he should"), engaging in outright arguments (which can lead to domestic violence arrests), or even withholding visitations.

A low-income dad saddled with unaffordable child support payments has a harder time being a dad: he is likely to struggle to afford housing that would facilitate overnight parenting time and more likely to string together a number of part-time jobs and gigs to make ends meet—often without a regular schedule, which makes any parenting time arrangement a challenge. No wonder it is common that these dads get critical or even combative when their kid's mom shows up in new clothes or a new car or takes a vacation.

Child support is more than a nuisance for millions of fathers. The impact of these payments for fathers is real. One study comparing the United States with the United Kingdom and Finland found that dads in the United States paid far more support as a percentage of their income, and those payments increased fathers' poverty rates by nearly 50 percent. Another program aimed at low-income fathers in the United States surveyed more than ten thousand dads and found that 58 percent paid more than half their income in child support, 40 percent had not seen their kids in more than a month, and 80 percent of them wished they could see their children more.

That same father will prioritize his support payments over paying rent or bills lest he face the loss of his driver's license or even jail time, which of course means zero parenting time for the kids, no child support, and no benefits of co-parenting for the mom. Again, these issues are racially stratified—while 24 percent of noncustodial dads are white, just 10 percent of men jailed for failure to pay child support are white; 41 percent of noncustodial dads are Black, but 78 percent of those jailed for nonpayment are Black. Local sheriff and police departments will publicize "deadbeat dad raids"—often on Father's Day—in which they round up those owing unpaid support in a public shaming effort as the dads are paraded in front of local news crews. A criminal record, destroyed credit history, and trauma experienced while incarcerated all mean fewer financial and emotional resources for those dads—and the whole family.

Despite the fact that debtors' prisons are unconstitutional

in the United States, we have a modern-day debtors' prison for parents too poor to pay child support.

OTHER FACTORS CONTRIBUTE TO CHILD SUPPORT'S MESSINESS AND UNAFFORDABILITY:

+ When a dad does not attend a child support hearing, 70 percent of the time, payments are set by default—typically at least the rate of a full-time worker earning minimum wage, regardless of whether he is employed at all. Sometimes, he is not served with a notice of court appearance and literally has no idea he has a child or is being taken to court for child support.

+ Low-income men, and men of color especially, who cannot afford an attorney, face high incarceration rates, and may have outstanding warrants are hardly inclined to willingly go to court for any reason. Arrears, plus interest, accumulate.

+ Things go sideways when there is a loss of employment and support payments are not immediately officially altered. The system is often not conducive to easily file for a change of child support order, so a dad living paycheck to paycheck sees his arrears grow while he awaits a court date, if he goes that route at all.

+ Biweekly child support payments often include "extras" like childcare, health insurance, and sports fees. Some of those are unavoidable expenses of child-rearing that can seem like extortion to dads who do not manage those accounts (yes, that is actually what childcare costs, and yes, day care benefits both parents equally). Sometimes things like expensive music lessons can be a point of contention between parents but are lumped into support payments pulled out of a dad's paycheck.

+ When parents are in conflict with each other over money and in conflict with the state over what they feel they are owed or forced to pay, everyone is incentivized to fudge their income, work in the gray economy, and, in some cases, intentionally underearn in order to either pay less or get more support and/or public assistance.

+ A dad who takes a less-demanding job to spend more time with his kids may still have his support payments based on his previous, higher salary—a judge *imputing* a salary based on what he previously earned.

In an equal co-parenting relationship, child support has no role. If both parents enjoy equal time to work and earn and equally take on parenting responsibilities, then each parent pays their own rent and bills, feeds and diapers the kids when they are in that parent's care, and splits up the kid-specific expenses—clothes, child and medical care, school and activity expenses—in an equitable way. Even though we don't enjoy a culture or laws that support such equality, I still advocate for an abolishment of child support—even as the financial pay gap between men and women persists. It is logically impossible to require equality of care without equality of financial responsibility. Equal rights, equal responsibility for everyone.

You might argue that such an equation is much more attainable when there are two professional parents who can afford to maintain their own homes—even if that home is smaller than the one they enjoyed when they lived together as a couple. Low-income mothers need all that child support just to get by, right?

Yes, low-income mothers—and fathers—do need more support, and that support should come from government programs. Thankfully, as I elaborate on later in this chapter, tax credits and programs that make housing, food, quality childcare, and medical care attainable for the poor have been very successful at lifting women and children out of poverty. Pandemic-era tax credits further reduced poverty and did so dramatically. Social support programs work. We need to extend these programs to support two parents when those parents live separately—not just moms. While child support payments alone *increase* fathers' poverty rates by almost 50 percent, they only *decrease* mothers' poverty rates by 25 percent. We must stop defending the broken U.S. child support system.

Unfortunately, in most U.S. separated families, child support is alive, well, unpaid, and unfair. Parents in the United States owe $11 billion in unpaid child support, most of which is owed by men earning less than $10,000 per year—mostly men who are incarcerated, disabled, or seasonal workers. A full 30 percent of parents with child support orders received no payments during the 2017 calendar year, and just 46 percent received the full amount—rates that have remained more or less steady since the program's inception in the 1960s. The court-ordered child support system is worse than broken—it incites conflict between co-parents, which breaks down fathers' relationships with their children and actually financially penalizes the whole family.

The History of Child Support

Why are these numbers such a disaster? At its root, the current child support program was built on good ideas that had catastrophic outcomes.

The focus of child support since its inception—even dating back to colonial times—has been to hold men financially accountable for their children and unburden the state from that responsibility. In our country's earliest days, so-called bastardy laws dictated that an unwed mother could be jailed or publicly whipped until she either named the baby's father or he came forward. Things are not much better today.

The modern U.S. child support program was established in 1975 as a way for the federal government to address what it saw as a problem of unmarried Black mothers relying too heavily on welfare while Black fathers did not financially support them. In reality, poor families were given rich financial incentive to actively remove men from their homes by making it so that the lower the household income, the higher the housing, medical, cash, and food subsidies they received.

Later, in the 1980s, Ronald Reagan decried the scourge of the "welfare queen" (a Black urban mother who lived a life of luxury by gaming myriad government programs and who turned out to be a figment of a speechwriter's imagination), and a CBS special featured an apathetic father of six as a "deadbeat dad." These smear campaigns recast in the public's mind these outlying characters as mainstream, taxpayer-swindling scourges.

It was President Bill Clinton who signed, as part of welfare reform, the Deadbeat Parents Punishment Act, which codified felony punishment and jail time for parents (dads) who fail to pay child support or "who moves to another state, or country, with the intention of evading child support payments." The media surrounding the program that conjured a freewheeling dad lounging on a Caribbean beach while his kids walked to school, shoeless, in the winter was a baseless, toxic narrative—albeit politically tantalizing.

It was Clinton's welfare reform that requires that, to this day, a mother applying for cash welfare assistance on behalf of her kids must name the father of her children, regardless of whether paternity has been legally established. That man is then held accountable for repaying the state for any government outlay for his kids. In other words, the mom gets welfare payments, and the state collects reimbursements for those payments from the dad who is considered too unreliable to pay his kid's mom regularly. Typically, she can't get both welfare and child support payments. One or the other.

In essence, a poor family cannot get government assistance unless the dad is making child support payments. Poor men are forced to pay the state to take care of their poor co-parents— women who are required to work to qualify for aid but still need financial help to make ends meet. Meanwhile, the federal government pays state agencies to enforce child support collections.

In fact, states will often goad mothers into providing much more than just the father's name. They ask for his address, his employer's address, his bank account numbers, the make and model of his car, and his driver's license number. They often even ask for the names and addresses of his friends and relatives, forcing moms to be accomplices in government and even police pursuit of their kids' dads with whom they may very well have co-parented amicably—only because she sought public assistance.

Not only is the root of these programs sexist and racist—and possibly corrupt since state agencies stand to profit by enforcing them—they also do not work. Of the $31.4 billion in child support collected in 2020, $1.7 billion never made it to the mothers' bank account; it was instead diverted to state and federal coffers as a repayment for welfare outlay. That's $1.7 billion paid by poor dads that never reached their kids.

Meanwhile, as I unpack in chapter 6, when states implement programs that promote father involvement and help make child support payments more manageable, parents fight less, and single dads are more involved with their kids and also more likely to financially support them. In other words, saddling poor men with child support hurts us all. When we treat single dads like human parents and not ATMs, we all win.

Kenya Rahmaan, a single mom of three, is one of the loudest voices advocating for child support reform. Today retired from the IRS, Rahmaan relocated from Ohio to Texas more than a decade ago in search of job opportunities after retiring from the U.S. Army. Once she applied for welfare benefits and was forced to name her kids' fathers, she was contacted by an Ohio state agency that asked if she would like to criminally pursue her daughter's dad for $30,000 in arrears. "I didn't think that was right for me to have that much power over another person," Rahmaan told me. But by then, it was too late—the arrears were established, and the case was out of her control. It took eight years of bureaucratic nightmare to get the debt discharged. During that time, Rahmaan educated herself about the history and workings of the child support–welfare system, and today, she advocates for policy and culture reform through her blog, YouTube channel, and self-published book, *The Child Support Hustle*. "A lot of people think I am talking about women hustling men for child support, but I am talking about the government hustling people—especially poor people—to make money."

Meanwhile, for middle-class and affluent families, child support orders are most likely to be paid directly and fully, right to the kids' mom. It helps that those orders are also more affordable. Poor men are ordered to pay 18 percent of their incomes, and more affluent men pay just 11 percent—in part because in most states, support calculators phase out or are capped at a higher income levels.

The Connection between Money and Father Involvement

Encouraging a spirit of willing financial cooperation is arguably most powerful in low-income communities in which the challenge is especially steep for men to pay their share while also maintaining a home and job schedule amenable to a regular co-parenting schedule.

A growing body of social science finds a direct correlation between dads' physical involvement with their kids and how much they pay in support. In fact, a few years ago at a committee hearing for an equal parenting presumption bill at the Georgia state legislature, a representative from that state's child support enforcement agency appeared, advocating for the bill. The connection between father involvement and child support compliance was so strong that he urged the Georgia representatives to get ahead of any federal mandates he expected to come down the pike—and pass the bill.

His understanding of the science was correct. Researchers at Cornell University looked at more than one thousand nonresidential fathers and found that child support arrears are associated with dads having less contact with children, being less engaged with them in daily activities, and providing less in-kind support. Meanwhile, the better the relationship the father had with the kids' mom, the lower the likelihood that he also had a child support order through the courts (versus voluntarily giving her money or buying in-kind goods like diapers and clothes). The correlation between positive co-parenting and money for his child was strong: the better the co-parenting relationship, the more he paid in court-ordered support and the more likely he was to pay *even more* in informal payments.

In-kind support is especially important to low-income families, and it makes sense: men want to support their children, and they also want their children to see, feel, and touch that support in ways that women may not crave. After all, food, clothes, and toys are symbols of traditional breadwinning masculinity that eludes so many men—especially Black men and perhaps most especially men who do not live with their children full-time or who may be contending with another man living in their kids' homes.

One Johns Hopkins study found that in-kind support makes up about one-quarter of total support, while children whose fathers lack stable employment as well as children of Black dads receive a greater proportion of their total support in kind. This study found that poor, noncustodial fathers spend an average of sixty dollars a month on in-kind contributions, while dads paying formal child support pay about thirty-eight dollars a month through the program.

Further, dads who were involved with their kids paid more: each additional hour of parenting time was associated with an increase of nearly one dollar per month in support. While there was no difference by race in how much dads paid, Black dads were more likely to pay by way of goods than dads of other races.

The researchers found that fathers see gifts as a chance to bond with their children. "They want their kids to look down at their feet and say, 'My dad cares about me because he bought me these shoes,'" said study coauthor Kathryn Edin, a Princeton University sociology professor and a leading chronicler of low-income separated families. "We need to respect what these guys are doing, linking love and provision in a way that's meaningful to the child. The child support system weakens the child/father bond by separating the act of love from the act of providing."

This quote makes me think of a young Black dad I met while waiting for my own appointment in Queens County Family Court. Nervous, he approached me and asked if I was a lawyer (I'm not, but maybe I dressed like one?), and could I give him some advice? This young man was representing himself in an effort to get a visitation schedule with his one-year-old daughter, whom he clearly adored, but whose mom was refusing to give him time with her. Having a job with a moving company after serving a couple of years in prison on drug charges, he proudly told me he bought his daughter everything she needed—diapers, food, and Gucci and Louis Vuitton jackets. I found myself both judging his financial decisions and feeling his deep love for his child that he expressed through gifts. He was living the cultural bias that connects his value as a dad with his ability to spoil his daughter with miniature luxury goods while also battling a culture that empowers his kid's mom to keep the baby from her dad.

I outlay a plan to reform child support in the solutions chapter of this book, but we need to largely get the state out of our families and allow loving parents to manage finances in ways they deem best, with some support as needed. Things can get messy and, at least in the short term, unrealistic. How many custodial mothers have initiated discussions/arguments/brawls over this issue at the thought of dads buying little kids expensive (if adorable) tiny Adidas while ignoring the cost of childcare, diapers, and healthcare? How many dads are oblivious about how much childcare or health insurance costs but feel confident they are contributing their share because they frequently buy for their kids and don't have much more to give?

However, if we agree to honor the research that father involvement trumps conflicts between co-parents, then there is room for embracing the very human fact that dads connect with their children through buying them things they may not want or need. Studies show us that the better we all get along, the more time those dads spend with their kids, the more financially involved those fathers are.

When Equal Time Creates Unequal Finances

One of the secret issues about child support and welfare is that no matter how truly equal a parenting schedule is, only one parent gets to claim the children as dependents. For affluent families, this matters primarily for tax purposes, and parents can agree (with or without a judge's help) to switch off years on whether the mom or the dad takes the kids as write-offs on their tax returns. Savvy parents can do the math with the help of a CPA to estimate how much each kid is worth on the respective parents' returns based on tax brackets and can settle the difference by way of a Venmo payment.

However, when money is tight for everyone and the cooperation between parents is low, who claims the kids on their tax returns or who has 51+ percent custody can be a devastating difference between one parent being able to afford a home where their kids can live comfortably and not.

Take, for example, a hypothetical Ohio mom and dad who were never married, live apart, and amicably co-parent their son, age eighteen months, and daughter, age four, take care of their own homes, and manage in an ad hoc but efficient way to keep the kids in diapers, shoes, and school supplies.

However, when the mom decides to apply for state welfare benefits, she is forced to file a child support court order in order to start receiving those benefits. The mom and dad each earn $25,000 per year, but since only one parent can be considered the custodial parent for government assistance purposes, the typical result is that the father is ordered to pay $381 in child support each month (support plus medical care), per the state's calculator. Ohio does not pass through child support to welfare recipients.

In addition to childcare subsidies and Medicaid (expenses that directly support the children and therefore both parents equally), the mother's home also reaps the following financial public benefits, because she can legitimately claim that she is a head of household with two dependents. Meanwhile the dad, who also has the kids at his home half of the time, can only claim that his is a household of one and therefore qualifies for far fewer benefits for himself and none as a parent.

Although the parents each earn $25,000 per year and each have the kids about half the time, their monthly finances are now dramatically different:

	MOM	DAD
Gross earnings from work	$2,083	$2,083
TANF (cash benefit)	$503	0
SNAP (food stamps)	$498	$166
Child support	$0, because what the dad pays goes to the state	-$381
Housing subsidy	$1,402	$758
Head of household tax credit	$56	0
Earned income credit	$401	0
Child tax credit	$333	0
Total monthly income	$5,276	$2,626

In this example, the mom's income is 50 percent higher than the dad's—even though they earn the same from their jobs and have equal time and logistical responsibility for the children.

The financial scales are tipped further in indirect ways. Eligibility for Pell and other education grants is based on income and household size, making it easier for moms than for dads to receive financial aid for college or training. Emergency and subsidized housing focus on families with children, meaning custodial mothers and their kids. There are very few men's homeless shelters and hardly any in which a dad and his children can stay. Overwhelmingly, services for low-income people, in both the public and private sector, are designed for mothers and their children.

These federal benefits have expanded over the past two

decades, with an enormous bump during the pandemic years that has been credited as a successful move for the Democrats to usher in universal basic income in the form of earned income tax credits and child tax credits. These no-strings-attached cash benefits have been credited with enormous success in lifting child poverty rates, which have now dropped by 22 percent over the past two decades. The *New York Times* published an extensive article on this phenomenon, noting that the average low-income family receives $18,000 in government benefits each year, benefits about which Brookings Institution researcher Robert Greenstein said, "The decline in child poverty is very, very impressive, and it is overwhelmingly due to the increased effectiveness of government programs." These programs are credited with reducing poverty for women and children by 59 percent between 1993 and 2019.

Meanwhile, in families not enrolled in welfare programs, an equal parenting schedule still financially penalizes the dad. As one father told me, "It becomes even more expensive for me to have 50/50 than a lesser schedule, since I pick up the regular expenses of parenting during those added days: food, entertainment, and all the things a kid needs day-to-day in addition to the child support that I have to pay no matter what."

The Future of Child Support

While these financial imbalances persist in devastating ways, the tide is turning. First, increasing numbers of states have sliding-scale child support calculators that account for the number of overnights a child has with each parent. While some attorneys bemoan this method as one that commoditizes kids and incentivizes more fighting, the spirit is one that helps to equalize the time-money equation that is the root of the work to promote equal parenting.

Second, judges—and the lawyers who advise clients in their jurisdictions—increasingly have little patience for a woman who does not work and expects to continue to stay home full-time with the kids while her affluent husband supports her through child support and alimony. Divorce attorney and mediator Susan Guthrie often recounts being in court with a stay-at-home mom client in an affluent New York suburb. "She was literally whining that her payments weren't enough," Guthrie recalled. "The female judge physically stood up at the bench and looked down at this woman and said, 'I get up every morning and go to work, and you can too.'"

Third, feminism. As more and more women are becoming breadwinners—as of this writing, a quarter of women in heterosexual marriages earn more than their husbands—they are certainly less inclined to broach the issue of child support or alimony, as *they* would be the payor. I am fond of saying, *Hell hath no fury like a woman paying alimony.*

This leads into my fourth point: alimony is increasingly rare, lifetime alimony nonexistent, and just 3 percent of alimony payments are made to men, despite the fact that 25 percent of wives earn more than their husbands. This latter discrepancy is explained in part by the pride of men, part female incredulousness in not wanting a man dependent on *her*, and part a simple sunsetting of a dated practice.

More evidence: millennials who marry are more and more likely to sign a prenup, often initiated by the bride, who is older and more professionally and financially established than any generation of wives before her and eager to protect what she has earned from what is now considered a financially high-risk endeavor: marriage.

Finally, moms are over child support. As I detail in the solutions chapter, the percentage of single parents applying for and pursuing child support through the state is down 36 percent over the past two decades. In surveys by the federal government, parents who are not involved with child support programs but could be say they do not want the state involved with their families and they appreciate that the other parent pays what they can. Nearly a quarter said they don't need to get involved in state-ordered child support because *the child stays with the other parent part of the time.* In other words, one-quarter of single parent families who qualify for child support but opt out are already doing the no-support-shared-parenting program on their own.

Anecdotally, in my decade of writing about and interacting with hundreds of thousands of unpartnered moms, I can share this: more and more women simply don't want to mess around with child support. They see it not as financial security but rather as a meager sum that causes conflict with their kids' dad, keeps them tied to a past lover, can put into jeopardy a man who they may care for, who is the father of their children, and who also just deserves respect that the system does not afford him.

The trend toward more financial independence for both men and women can also be explained by a healthy dose of rebellion against self-sabotaging women who came before them. These younger and more progressive moms inherently understand how child support hurts them, hurts feminism, hurts men, and hurts their children. When Juana, age thirty-two, broke up with her kids' dad, she took a note not just from all the 50/50 divorced families in her social circle but also from her own divorced mom's inability to stand on her own.

"It is thirty years since they divorced, and my mom is still angry at my dad for some money she feels he owes her! All that anger really got in the way of her moving on and building her own life, and all that fighting still affects me as an adult," said Juana. "I want women to know how fucking amazing it feels not to be dependent on a man. And I want my son and daughter to see their mom as independent of a man. We have all these opportunities to earn and achieve, but they are for nothing if we're in court fighting over child support or choosing to pay our bills with men's money we didn't earn."

In fact, like Kenya Rahmaan, it is often women who are the champions of child support and alimony reform. These are the current girlfriends or second wives of men paying exorbitant sums to their exes who fib about their incomes, chose to underearn, or otherwise keep their financial claws in men because they can. And I can tell you from years of experience dating in New York City, men who pay a lot of alimony to women who do not work or who underearn are not interested in dating similar women. They date professionally ambitious women, women who tend to be disgusted by women who squander their education and privilege by living off men in the name of being a primary parent.

5

A Deeper Look at Domestic Violence Postdivorce

"It's not a good thing when one parent batters another, but that should not be an absolute—it ignores that children lose more by losing that relationship than they gain by being never exposed to any violence any time in their lives."

—Leigh Goodmark, PhD, domestic violence expert

When someone I meet for the first time hears that I advocate for a 50/50 shared parenting assumption, one of the most typical responses is *What about domestic violence? What about child abuse?*

When we talk about dads having any more than minimal time with kids, many are pulled back to early divorced-dad protocols like in *Mrs. Doubtfire,* the 1993 Robin Williams / Sally Field classic in which the recently divorced dad must have his apartment periodically inspected by a persnickety social worker to ensure it is safe and sufficient to host his kids for Chinese takeout once in a while. While our systems have moved into a more humane treatment of families, dads still often find themselves on the defensive from the beginning of a separation, proving their basic competency and safety as a parent before they are allowed to spend alone time with their own kid—much less equal time.

Much more flagrantly, domestic violence is front and center when equal parenting laws are proposed, with domestic violence advocates usually the loudest voices in opposition.

This knee-jerk response to protect abuse victims at any expense is ingrained in our culture. But here is where mainstream attitudes and law diverge from facts, science, and common sense. This chapter sheds light on gross misconceptions about the prevalence of family violence and the assumption that only men can be abusive. Further, there is strong evidence that equal parenting schedules actually *reduce* both domestic violence and child abuse. I also show that equal parenting schedules are so beneficial for child well-being that they trump the upset and the trauma of conflict between parents, even when that conflict becomes physical.

I procrastinated on writing this chapter, and it is the very last one I completed of the whole book. It wasn't because of writer's block. It was because I was scared of getting it wrong. After all, I wanted to be a good feminist and a good person. I spent all my adult life up until the last few years believing at face value what domestic violence advocates say:

+ "Women are abused by men."
+ "Domestic violence is grossly underreported because women are too scared to seek help."
+ "If a man shoves you once, you leave immediately and forever, and he must be punished far more harshly than our sexist laws and culture dictate."
+ "We need more public funds, stricter laws, and increased programming and resources to stop the scourge of men abusing women."

Those are the messages that were ingrained in me by the media that I consume, the cautionary tales from the adults in my life when I was young, and the liberal bubble that I have often encapsulated myself in.

In essence, I fear being canceled as an abuse apologist.

And that same fear, I believe, is shared by many thoughtful journalists, activists, and scholars who know but don't publicly discuss the facts.

And the facts are these:

+ Domestic violence is far less prevalent than headlines report.
+ Women are abusers too, which means men are also domestic violence victims.
+ Male abusers do not typically succeed in using courts to victimize women.
+ Family violence is layered and complex, often triggered by a response to circumstances and perpetrated by both partners.

+ Family violence is not a definitive reason to permanently remove a child from a parent.

In other words, violence is not a zero-sum argument against a presumption of equal parenting time. In fact, all the 50/50 parenting activists I know thoughtfully include provisions for abuse in all proposed laws and practices promoting equal parenting. The argument is to start parenting schedules at 50/50 and, if needed, deviate. No one argues for equal parenting for all children, all the time, under all circumstances. As it stands now, best-interest language sets the discussion at 0/0 and incentivizes each parent to duke it out for maximum time. In fact, research finds this winner-take-all approach to custody actually incites physical conflict between parents, with some studies finding as much as half of first-time family violence occurring after parents separate and within the context of a custody dispute. According to Edward Kruk, associate professor of social work at the University of British Columbia and shared parenting advocate, "This is no surprise, given the high stakes involved; when primary parent-child relationships are threatened, the risk of violence rises dramatically. When neither parent is threatened by the loss of his or her children, conflict diminishes."

Despite an abundance of social science to the contrary, we take the risk of domestic violence as so common and so grave that we start the parenting time conversation at abuse, as if it were the rule and not the exception. If you ever read about shared-parenting legislation efforts in the news (sample headlines include "He Beat Her Repeatedly. Family Court Tried to Give Him Joint Custody of Their Children" and "'Shared Parenting' Places Ideology Over Children"), domestic violence advocates' insistence that a 50/50 parenting presumption promotes abuse against women rings loudly in the debate.

There are two major philosophical problems with this seemingly well-meaning, pro-victim automatic pushback to a presumption that kids spend time equally with each of their parents:

1. Women are categorized as presumed victims.
2. Men are presumed abusers.

Not only are these assumptions inaccurate, they are simply sexist.

I'll unpack these broad generalizations that we are still not only making in our own minds unconsciously but also using as a basis for our current custody laws.

The Cost of Presuming Men Are Abusers

While it is a no-brainer that most of us, feminists and chauvinists alike, are anti-abuse, the argument against a presumption of equality in the name of domestic violence is really an argument that men are presumed abusers and that fathers must prove their fitness before their humanity is recognized and they are granted fair time with their own kids.

When we discuss custody and violence, anti-50/50 activists

argue that male batterers leverage the inherent anti-woman bias of family court to control women and their children, and an equal parenting law would only give these men greater access to their kids and ex-partners.

First, a common-sense assessment of this argument:

Either we assume—as a society and as individuals—that single fathers are dangerous, or we assume that they are competent parents capable of safely taking care of their own children. After all, we don't assess married men's capacity for violence before permitting them to procreate or require new dads to pass muster before bringing their babies home from the hospital with their wives. If we did, it would be unethical, unfair, and, if you want to go there, *un-American*. The assumption that fathers are dangerous is supported by a subconscious—and false—belief that only men are violent and capable of physical and emotional abuse. These ideas promote a ham-fisted and vintage idea about family violence.

Family violence is rarely about men obsessively beating the crap out of women and children. It is often the result of a complex set of forces that I'll unpack later in this chapter, such as a history of witnessing or experiencing family violence, poverty, a history of trauma, and/or addiction. And men are by no means the only perpetrators.

For outlying cases where one parent is violently abusive, a zero-custody arrangement or supervised visits may be warranted, at least temporarily. But if a child is safe with a parent 10 percent of the time, they are safe with that mother or father 50 percent of the time or more.

Equal parenting time with both mom and dad is so strongly tied to child mental, emotional, social, and physical health that even when there is high conflict between parents, even when the child witnesses some violence, that child will have better outcomes than if they were to lose time with both parents.

Family Violence Is Trending Downward

The argument connecting intimate partner violence and custody goes like this:

If a presumption of 50/50 parenting time is the default, that puts the onus on the victim to prove her and/or her child's lack of safety to the courts—a lack of safety that has been heightened since a 50/50 visitation schedule would require her to interact with and her child to spend time with her co-parent frequently, for the abusive father to spend many unsupervised hours with the child. Further, these advocates charge that police and courts do not believe abuse victims and cannot be counted on to protect mothers and children when violence is reported.

These arguments often cite a handful of devastating and high-profile cases in which a young child was brutally murdered by the father while in his care, including Kyra Franchetti from 2016 and Kayden Mancuso from 2018—two tragic cases out of millions of kids who just want to hang out with their dads. These cases are reminiscent of the abduction of six-year-old Etan Patz, who disappeared while walking to school in the

SoHo neighborhood of New York City in the 1970s, which launched the missing child movement and became a grain of sand around which formed the pearl of five decades of helicopter parenting.

These horrific stories from years ago are brought up time and again because they are indeed rare horrors—so freakish an occurrence that the tantalizing story perpetuates itself. In cases where there are true signs of extreme violence and dangerously controlling behavior and a child is at real risk, it should go without saying these are instances where the child should not spend time alone with that parent, perhaps ever, assuming that there has been a conviction, in which case that parent would serve prison time. Otherwise, in cases where a parent is arguing for majority time based on unfounded examples of abuse, singular cases of upset between parents, or cases that can be mitigated by counseling programs, splitting hairs over 20 versus 30 versus 50 percent parenting time should not apply.

But this thinking flies in the face of current assumptions about family violence perpetuated by mainstream media and supported by the flow of federal domestic violence funding.

Case in point: throughout the 2020–2021 pandemic and beyond, there were countless headlines in mainstream and local media decrying the "shadow pandemic"—a supposed surge of domestic violence sweeping the country as women and their children were trapped in homes with their male abusers, with nowhere to turn to except maybe-open, jam-packed, virus-infected shelters.

From *Time*: "Domestic Violence Is a Pandemic Within the COVID-19 Pandemic"

From MSNBC: "Domestic Violence Cases Surge amid COVID-19 Crisis."

Yet the numbers tell a very different story.

The most frequently cited stat is that intimate partner violence *reporting* in the United States rose just over 8 percent for the two years of the heat of the lockdown—a stat that comes from a federal commission that analyzed crime reports in urban areas, helpline calls, and hospitalizations. However, in their reports, the researchers were careful to note that the reason for the rise in reports was not clear. The uptick, the researchers wrote, could be attributed to an increase in violence, but it could also just reflect more *reporting* of abuse thanks to the increased number of neighbors who were home and could hear fights and make hotline calls or a rise in the number of victims who sought help from the police—not necessarily an increase in the number of abuse incidences.

In fact, a separate report from the Department of Health and Human Services looked at how many people contacted 800-799-SAFE, the federal domestic violence hotline (thehotline.org), before and during the pandemic and found the numbers overall to be flat, with some variations in how people communicated with the platform (for example, there was a jump in texts versus calls) as well as an increase in contacts from Asian victims (possibly related to the surge of anti-Asian violence reported at the time, the researchers wrote) and third-party helpers—those now-at-home neighbors overhearing upset. Researchers interviewed helpline workers who consistently said that the many media reports on domestic violence coincided with a spike in calls. In other words, it is possible that more violence victims than usual were seeking help thanks to overhyped media on the issue, which in turn inspired victims to seek the help they needed. Lousy journalism may have resulted in good outcomes for abuse victims.

These inaccurate reports of "COVID domestic violence spikes" were the subject of an hour-long episode of *Freakonomics Radio*—the twenty-five-year-old award-winning franchise in which a journalist and University of Chicago economist peel away the layers of commonly held assumptions and prove them wrong or unwind their complexities. In this case, the hosts found that the assumption that the pandemic lockdown meant a surge in intimate partner violence is in fact incorrect. Eve Sheedy, former executive director of the Los Angeles County Domestic Violence Council, told show hosts, "People confuse rage with power and control. Those are not the same things. The narrative pushed an understanding of domestic violence that there were people, because they were locked in, who all of a sudden became abusive people." She went on to explain that lockdowns aren't the automatic breeding grounds for abuse you might assume they are. "When you're in a dangerous domestic-violence relationship, whether there is a lockdown or there is no lockdown, you are stuck in your home. The concept of a survivor having his or her movements limited because of domestic violence is not limited to a lockdown. That's their life."

It's not just popular culture that perpetuates gendered myths about intimate partner violence—it's also the domestic violence support organizations themselves. Denise Hines, PhD, associate professor in the Department of Social Work, College of Public Health at George Mason University, is author of the book *Family Violence in the United States* as well as dozens of published papers on topics about intimate partner violence in families with children, on college campuses, in the LGBTQIA+ community, in undocumented communities, involving female perpetrators of violence, and more. She is also an equal-parenting advocate.

In 2014, Hines published a report analyzing the fact sheets shared on the websites of the state chapters of the National Coalition Against Domestic Violence and other allied organizations. The analysis found that 338 of them included statistics that were false. Specifically, nearly 35 percent of the sites claimed "according to the FBI, a woman is beaten every 15 seconds," 26 percent said that domestic violence "is the leading cause of injury to women between the ages of 15 and 44 in the United States—greater than car accidents, muggings and rapes combined," and 21 percent lied that "95 percent of victims of domestic violence are women who were abused by their male partners."

Hines's report was published a decade ago. Does it still hold up? In 2023, I googled "a woman is beaten every fifteen seconds" and found that claim more than 330 million times, including on sites for the U.S. Department of Justice and *Good Housekeeping* magazine.

None of these claims are substantiated, yet they penetrate our collective ideas about gender, relationships, parenthood, and safety, convincing us that men are a violent risk to women and children.

In reality, according to reports published by the Department of Justice and analyzed by PolitiFact, violence against women by intimate partners fell by 60 percent between 1993 and 2012. While there are no parallel reports since then (which is astonishing in and of itself), I pulled DOJ stats and found that while they did bounce around a bit, between 1994 and 2020, rates of intimate partner violence fell by 83 percent. Some experts attribute these drops to the passage of the Violence Against Women Act in 1994, which devoted hundreds of millions of dollars annually to providing access to domestic violence hotlines and shelters, funding police responses to reports of domestic violence, and raising public awareness of the issue. Others point to a simultaneous sharp decline in violent crime overall and the increased economic power of women, since the more money a woman has, the more empowered she is to leave a dangerous situation if she has to—or wants to. I have not seen any studies but would like to understand whether the organic shift toward more equal parenting participation between moms and dads of all family types may have contributed to this decline.

These are stats that I pulled from multiple DOJ reports:

YEAR	RATE OF INTIMATE PARTNER VIOLENCE PER 1,000 PEOPLE AGED 12 AND OLDER	TOTAL INCIDENTS
1994	9.8	2,100,000
2001	3	691,710
2005	3.3	816,010
2010	3.6	907,000
2013	2.8	748,800
2014	2.4	634,610
2015	3.0	806,050
2016	2.2	597,200
2017	2.4	666,310
2018	3.1	847,230
2019	2.5	695,060
2020	1.7	484,830

Despite these falling rates and questions about whether there was indeed a bump in intimate partner violence during the pandemic, the U.S. Department of Justice doubled its awards to domestic violence organizations to $1 billion in 2022.

But what about the safety of children themselves in custody disputes? Doesn't family violence translate to child abuse? Wouldn't a presumption of equal parenting time give abusive men more opportunities to hurt their kids? Like domestic violence rates, child abuse rates are also dropping dramatically, and perpetrators are also nearly equally men and women.

According to the U.S. Department of Health and Human Services, child maltreatment rates fell by nearly a third from thirteen cases per one thousand children (including multiple incidents per victim) in 1990 to nine victims per one thousand children in 2017—a 31 percent drop. During that period, rates of substantiated physical abuse declined by 40 percent and sexual abuse rates by 62 percent. Despite assumptions that child abuse—just like assumptions about intimate partner violence—would have surged during the pandemic lockdowns, child abuse cases plummeted by 70 percent, with parents reporting feeling closer to their kids despite the unusual stresses unique to that time.

Dr. Robert Sege, a Tufts University School of Medicine professor of medicine and pediatrics, made the argument that more government support of parents means less abuse: "When parents' own problems and stresses have already pushed them to the edge, they cannot handle these normal problems and difficulties of raising children. We have known for a long time that supports for families—food benefits, utility assistance, all those things—decrease child abuse. We think that during the pandemic families were given enough support that they never got to that edge." Again, good government support keeps families safe.

This seems to also be true when it comes to equal parenting and child violence. The National Parents Organization (NPO), the leading U.S. nonprofit advocating for equal parenting laws, assessed parenting guidelines in each of Ohio's eighty-eight counties for how likely they were to provide children with equal parenting time arrangements, giving them letter grades A through F. NPO then compared these ratings against substantiated incidents of mental, physical, and sexual child abuse.

Child abuse rates in counties that had an A or A- grade were *half* those with a D.

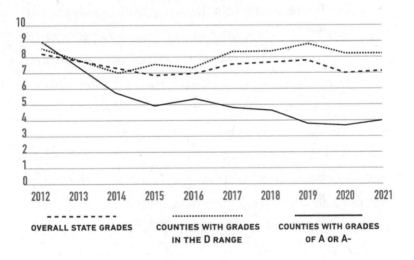

County Comparison Grades for Child Abuse or Neglect Over Time

OVERALL STATE GRADES

COUNTIES WITH GRADES IN THE D RANGE

COUNTIES WITH GRADES OF A OR A-

ACCORDING TO THE REPORT'S AUTHORS:

It could be that by reducing parental legal conflict over parenting time, courts are able to attend more closely to those cases that present significant risks of child maltreatment, stemming some of the harm to children. It could be, also, that lowering the conflict between the parents over parenting time reduces antagonism

that spills over to the children. And, of course, part of the explanation could be that, where two parents are equally engaged in
rearing their children, neither is as likely to feel overburdened
and stressed out by childcare responsibilities and both can serve
as a watchful eye over the children's well-being.

While efforts to curb violence should be celebrated for
their success and sustained going forward, practices need to be
updated, monitored, and scrutinized to ensure public and private
efforts are commensurate with the actual issue. We also need to
check our own assumptions about how serious a problem violence is and reconcile the unintended consequences that our over-
zealousness has caused. The media must take responsibility and
curb their misleading yet clicky headlines. Policymakers cannot
succumb to the extreme risk of outlying cases but should instead
look at the general well-being of the general population—in this
case, a bulk of children in this country who would benefit from
laws and culture that do not fear men around their children but
celebrate and promote dads as equal caretakers.

Women Are Perpetrators of Domestic Violence Too

A baseline assumption in the United States and around the globe
is men are more violent than women.

In fact, the rates of violence among men and women are
very similar.

The deeper you look at intimate partner violence statistics, the more complex and non-gender-specific violence becomes. A quick survey of popular culture is a jarring glimpse into just how acceptable it is for women to physically attack men.

I have been guilty of this brand of sexism. Once on my personal blog, Wealthysinglemommy.com, I embedded a GIF of Angela Bassett walking definitively away from a burning car—a known scene in which Bassett's character from *Waiting to Exhale*, in her grief and rage at her husband who left her for another woman, gathers all his meticulously organized luxury clothes and shoes, heaves them into his Mercedes, and lights the heap aflame in the driveway of their McMansion. This scene has been turned into a feminist meme: he did her wrong, and she made him pay. We justified her violence because her feelings were hurt—an absurd explanation that would immediately be flung out the window if the genders in that scenario were reversed. In fact, a friend filed a domestic violence charge against her boyfriend because he threw down and damaged her expensive oboe during an argument. Somehow, when the woman is wronged, it justifies all erratic behavior, no matter how violent. No such grace is extended to men.

Extend the spirit of that hypocrisy across media for the past century: women smacking a cheating or lying or mouthy lover while he simply takes it "like a man." The list of movies that have portrayed women slapping men includes such seminal flicks as *When Harry Met Sally*, *Groundhog Day*, *Pirates of the Caribbean 2: The Curse of the Black Pearl*, *Tomorrow Never Dies*, *Anchorman*,

Ratatouille, and *Frozen.* Even Miss Piggy has been known to slap and karate-chop Kermit when he did not return her obsessive sexual advances, refusing to take no for an answer.

I googled "woman slaps" and the AI auto suggested "woman slaps sleeping man" and "woman slaps snoring husband funny" as the top three search terms. Har, har, har—a spouse slapping a sound-asleep partner. Doris Day slapping a snoozing Rock Hudson, hee-hee!

You would think this would violate Google's own rules against violent acts, the one that prohibits "Beatings or brawls outside the context of professional or professionally supervised sporting events." But maybe our society—the one that Google itself has a complicated and powerful interdependent relationship with—finds woman-on-man violence a sport.

"Starting in the 1970s there was a huge public education campaign that was very effective at teaching us that men should never hit a woman," Denise Hines said. "Women are never taught that you never hit a man. Just the opposite: We learn that if he gets fresh with you, slap him."

And women do slap men. In a survey reported on by the *Telegraph,* one in seven American women admitted to hitting a male partner, compared to only one in twenty men admitting they had hit a female partner. In 2016, Natalia Milano wrote a Medium article titled "Why I Stopped Slapping My Boyfriend in the Face" and launched the #NoMoreSlapping campaign. She, like many young, impressionable girls, grew up watching their favorite actresses slap men and carried this behavior into her own life.

"I used to think that it was normal to slap my boyfriend on the face once in a while. As if slapping someone in the face was a legitimate form of arguing," Milano wrote. She wasn't alone in her thinking. "When I asked my female friends, I found out that many of them had, at least once, slapped their boyfriends or dates. Many of my guy friends have gotten slapped."

Of course, slapping is one thing; full-on assault is another. Here too, women are often perpetrators, and men are routinely victimized. The latest research concludes that there is only a small difference in the rate at which men and women experience physical violence at the hands of an intimate partner. A large and oft-cited study released by the Centers for Disease Control and Prevention in 2018 found the following:

+ 31 percent of men report some sort of physical violence, rape, or stalking by an intimate partner within their lifetime. For women, it was 30.6 percent.
+ 21 percent of women and 15 percent of men experienced severe physical violence by an intimate partner.
+ Overall, over 36.6 million women and 34.4 million men have experienced psychological aggression by an intimate partner in their lifetimes.

A further study found that in 2021, 1,690 women were murdered by an intimate partner, while that number for men was 1,078.

My friend Kevin is one of those men who was physically abused by a female partner. His longtime girlfriend on at least four incidents beat him when they'd argue, including punching him with a closed fist. Once, after an argument, he went to bed, only to be woken up by her slugging him in the face, giving him two black eyes. More frequently, she'd scream at him that he was an *asshole, a loser, a piece of shit* or follow him around the house yelling about his lack of loyalty or his interest in other women, often trapping him in a hallway or corner when he tried to get some space. Sometimes he'd yell back, and once he kicked her in the shin. He never called the police or even thought what was happening was illegal. Kevin is six feet tall, 220 pounds. The girlfriend is five foot six and 160 pounds. "I'm a guy. What am I supposed to do?" he thought.

His strategy was to hope it'd get better, until while staying at a hotel with some friends a few years later, the two once again argued after a boozy night out. She thought he was looking at girls at the bar. She punched him in the face, in the head. He locked her out of the room and told her to sleep in her friends' room down the hall. She insisted on coming back to the room to collect her things. "I sat down on the bed, and she started yelling at me right away," he told me. "I'm just sitting there, and she's screaming at me in the face, punched me right in forehead. She swung at me a second time, and I grabbed her by the wrists and told her, 'It's not OK for you to be hitting at me!' and tossed her on the bed." She punched him in the face, and he grabbed her bag and ripped it. "She started screaming and called the cops."

Kevin walked down to the lobby to await his fate, which he assumed meant jail time. "Who are they going to believe—a cute girl or me?" he said. After the police interviewed her, they returned downstairs and heard his side of the story. "I took off my hat and had a big bump on my forehead." A few minutes later, the girlfriend came down to the hotel lobby. "I saw her come out of the elevator, and she had a big ole smile on her face like she was proud of herself for getting me in trouble," he remembered. "She was lighting up a cigarette. Then they arrested her."

Despite Kevin's pleas to the contrary, she spent a night in jail. Later, because he did not attend the hearing, the charges were dropped. "I'd been to jail before for a DUI, and it sucked," he said. "I figured that it would be over since we'd break up."

However, the two were bound forever—they soon learned she was a couple weeks pregnant at the time. For the past six years, Kevin and his ex have been in conflict over custody and parenting time, with him fighting for a 50/50 schedule with his son and her arguing that he should have less time. Their parenting schedule has gradually settled into one that is about 60/40 in her favor.

These stories of male victims of intimate partner violence, thankfully, are getting some attention in popular media and by academics. But we have a long way to go to change the common notion that only men are violent. If you still are not convinced, look at child abuse.

The Children's Bureau of the U.S. Department of Health and Human Services found in its 2021 report that of 525,319 perpetrators of child abuse or neglect, more than one-half (53 percent) were women. If you are steadfast in the belief that men are more violent than women, it might be tempting to dismiss this stat. After all, women are the primary caregivers of children, so it follows that there would be more female perpetrators of child abuse simply by way of circumstance. However, many have written about and studied the reality that violence is a systemic, multigenerational cycle—if you grow up in a violent home, no matter your gender or the gender of your caretakers, you are more likely to be violent. Poverty, living in a dangerous neighborhood, substance abuse, and relationship and mental health struggles all predicate violence and are experienced by both men and women.

An argument for maximum time with parents is consistent with the goals of the state when it comes to child welfare. When kids are removed from their homes because of abuse or neglect, the state aims, when safe, to reunite them with their biological families and is successful at doing so the majority of the time. In 2019, 51 percent of kids in foster care were reunited with their families—an 8 percent increase compared with a decade earlier. There is also an increase in the number of children living with a relative after foster care—again, with the state prioritizing that biological family connection. A full 95 percent of infant adoptions have some form of openness that keeps that child and their biological family connected. This same understanding of the importance of keeping kids with their families of origin, despite claims of abuse, can and should be extended to moms and dads who are going through a custody dispute, which is stressful on multiple levels. In addition to presuming that kids do better with equal access to both parents, providing access to financial and mental health resources during tough times can help keep kids and parents safe and connected.

One of the most compelling illustrations that violence is gender neutral is the stats on gay women and intimate partner violence:

Lifetime Prevalence of Rape, Physical Violence, and/or Stalking by an Intimate Partner

WOMEN		MEN	
Lesbian	44%	Gay	26%
Bisexual	61%	Bisexual	37%
Heterosexual	35%	Heterosexual	29%

Research has found that nearly 44 percent of gay women have experienced intimate partner violence in their lifetimes, compared to 35 percent of straight women. Gay women are also more likely to experience severe violence at the hands of their partners—29 percent of gay women versus about 23 percent of straight women. If you find this surprising, you are not alone. Early domestic violence advocates had a tough time reconciling their belief that violence against women was a mere product of the patriarchy with the prevalence of woman-on-woman beatings they were contending with. In an excellent *New Yorker* history of the first U.S. domestic violence center, Transition House in Cambridge, Massachusetts, the founding members found it impossible to accept the realities of female violence in the 1970s:

At Transition House, everyone believed that battering was a result of male domination in a sexist culture, so the idea that women battered other women was incomprehensible, and therefore ignored... It was the idea of violent women that was impossible to understand... There was a lesbian couple working at the shelter who would get into terrible fights, but no one thought of it as domestic violence. "One of the women came in with bruises because her partner was throwing rocks at her on the beach at P-town, but we didn't think this was battering, because women don't do that to each other," Carole Sousa says. "We thought they were just having a fight and it got out of hand." Soon afterward, the shelter hired a lesbian who said that she had been in a violent relationship, but still nobody could believe it. "She would argue with us, but there was a lot of denial," Sousa says. "People's response, including mine, was, How could that be? It threw out the window everything we knew. It just didn't make sense."

That was fifty years ago. As I type this chapter, I am texting with a friend in her forties who is a highly educated feminist and progressive activist and is fascinated by and skeptical of everything I just wrote. She loves her dad and boyfriend and stepson and has many male friends, has not personally experienced intimate partner violence, and knows just a couple women in her circles who have. Yet she is dumbfounded by evidence that violence is not gendered. "It is just totally against everything that we are taught, which is that men are a bunch of assholes," she said.

No matter how compelling the argument that violence is gender-neutral, our prisons and family structures hardly reflect this reality.

In fact, studies that use national, population-based data instead tell a very different and much more gender-neutral story. Despite the fact that women are abusive in roughly equal numbers, the U.S. Department of Justice reports that about 77 percent of the arrests for domestic violence are men, with Black men being much more likely to be convicted than white men.

Domestic Violence Laws Might Hurt Women

About half of states have mandatory arrest laws on their books, meaning when police are called to a domestic dispute, they must arrest at least one (the "dominant" aggressor) or even both parties. In most cases, whoever calls the cops doesn't want their partner put in jail; they just want the abuse to stop. One member of the household going to jail means legal fees, loss of income, and loss of access to a parent for the whole family—costs that are harder to cover for low-income people. Plus, many people who have been beaten up still love their partner and don't want them in jail. People are complicated.

Leigh Goodmark is a law professor at the University of Maryland who wrote a book on gender, violence, and the law that I found equally compelling and challenging. In *Decriminalizing Domestic Violence: A Balanced Policy Approach to Intimate Partner Violence*, she argues that arrest mandates for any domestic conflict are deeply racist and sexist, disproportionately removing

Black men from their families and communities and perpetuating cycles of abuse and poverty. Goodmark on one hand casually dismisses "the men's rights movement that argues that women are as violent as men, and that the system is unfair to men on a regular basis—the standard fathers' rights stuff" —a statement that made my blood boil. Yet she also makes the very sensible argument for the abolishment of mandatory arrest laws and imprisonment that often lead to the arrest of the woman or both partners—even when the cops arrive only because a neighbor overheard arguing and even when the victim does not want the partner arrested.

"The idea that women are so coerced and so weak that they can't make decisions for themselves around violence that the state has to step in and do that for them undermines women's agency and self-determination," Goodmark told me in an interview. "I don't believe criminalization is an appropriate way to address domestic violence because it harms victims." Arresting men for intimate partner violence only heightens the effects of violence, as men in prison are likely to experience violence while incarcerated, lose contact with their children and communities, and then lose employment opportunities—all of which perpetuate cycles of trauma, poverty, violence, and family separation. There is also evidence that domestic violence arrests make that relationship even more dangerous for the victim.

Instead, Goodmark calls for restorative justice programs, community support, and, most of all, diverting domestic violence budgets to programs that provide economic development for women. I add that we also need more economic programs for men and co-parenting classes for everyone.

The Silver Bullet in Custody Cases

In family court, allegations of any form of violence are referred to as "the silver bullet"—for many years and still in many places, a mention of violence of any kind gives the woman the upper hand in any divorce or family court proceedings.

One woman I know casually told me that she hoped to strategically use a few incidents in years past in which her husband shoved her to gain a financial advantage in her divorce negotiations. She was keenly aware of the statute of limitations for filing an intimate partner report with the police, which she really didn't want to do, but she was prepared to press charges to get the majority time-sharing that she really wanted.

Ron, a New Jersey dad, told me that he'd enjoyed a quiet family life with his wife and four kids for ten years. When his marriage started to fall apart and arguments started, his wife suddenly started to cower and say, "I don't feel safe around you."

"Years before, a couple we know divorced. The wife is a divorce lawyer, and he got locked up overnight only because she told police she didn't feel safe. She used that against him in the divorce and got primary custody." At the time, Ron's wife was incredulous at hearing this legal maneuver. "I thought she was being empathetic, but it turned out she was taking notes."

That was six years ago. While the domestic violence charges, filings for restraining orders, and sexual molestation charges that Ron's wife filed against him have been dismissed by judges, those same judges have also given her primary custody.

This is not uncommon. Ashley-Nicole Russell, a North Carolina family attorney, told me she routinely hears from women asking about filing phony domestic violence claims to gain leverage in their divorces—advice they hear from friends, family, and in online forums. "I tell them, 'Actual domestic violence is a very important issue, and the system has many avenues to manage it. Using extortion to keep children from their father is detrimental to children now and in the long run.'"

The hard truth is that research estimates that in the United States and around the world, only about 10 percent of claims of child abuse are substantiated. The other 90 percent run the gamut from overly cautious neighbors who hear strange things to malicious ex-partners fabricating abuse claims. While historically, these charges were considered a useful silver bullet in winning custody, increasingly, judges are very good at carefully assessing cases in an effort to keep children safe and keep them connected to both their parents. There is also a movement to penalize false accusations in family court by way of proposed legislation and judges' incredulousness.

One important insight into how equal parenting can help heal family violence: our current parenting paradigm of mothers being the primary caretaker may be worsening the abuse suffered at the hands of their fathers. One study by student researchers at Grand

Valley State University found that while mothers are more likely to be physically violent with their children, fathers are more likely to be severely physically abusive—resulting in serious physical harm or death—in part due to lack of parenting experience. The author of the study concluded, "In general, fathers are more likely to favor authoritarian punishment and to use corporal punishment. Fathers' high rates of corporal punishment may be a result of lack of experience in resolving child conflict due to lower levels of parental involvement."

Give dads more support in parenting, and they will be better—and safer—parents. Give all parents the resources they need to thrive, and moms and dads alike will be better and safer parents.

Abuse and Custody

Despite being physically and verbally abused by his girlfriend and what Kevin (and the law) view as violence, Kevin believes his son, now age six, benefits from equal time with both parents. "His mom isn't violent toward him, and I think he deserves that time with her," he told me. Instead of a complicated parenting schedule, Kevin wishes they could do a week-on, week-off schedule, with the child switching homes after school on Fridays. "There'd be less contact between the parents," he points out. "The only other time you'd have to see them is at school events."

Kevin's assessment of his family is not naive but consistent with what domestic violence researchers understand about violence: it is complicated.

Denise Hines, who has studied family and intimate partner violence for fifteen years, said, "We're schooled to think that [family violence] is the men who are slapping women and men who are killing women, but that is incorrect. And cases where that progresses into severe violence are very rare." Instead, there is a lot of gray area. "Parents may be violent with each other but not necessarily bad with their kids. It may be a particular relationship or a particularly difficult time when the violence happens. And most of it is bidirectional. People who are saying 'No shared parenting because men are terrible people who hit their wives' are not seeing the complexity—they're only seeing the women who show up in shelters." There are fewer than five shelters for abused men in the United States as I write this.

Leigh Goodmark, the attorney and advocate for decriminalizing intimate partner violence, urges us to challenge the notion that all violence should be treated equally or is always a reason to remove a child from a parent. "There is a range of violence. We can't treat every stabbing the same as every slap," she said. "Lots of my clients told me, 'He's a terrible partner and an excellent father.' It's not a good thing when one parent batters another, but that should not be absolute—it ignores that children lose more by losing that relationship than they gain by being never exposed to violence any time in their lives."

Parental Alienation and Abuse

Campaigns for equal-parenting laws are often led by people who have lost contact with their children because the other parent turned the child away from the perfectly safe and loving mom or dad in an attempt to eradicate that parent from the child's life. This dynamic is called parental alienation, which almost exclusively takes place in divorced/separated families, where it occurs about 13 percent of the time. Parental alienation can include these actions:

+ A campaign of denigration against the targeted parent
+ The child's lack of guilty feelings for rejecting the target parent
+ When asked, the child giving irrational and frivolous reasons for the criticisms of the targeted parent
+ The child painting the parents in black and white—one parent can do no wrong, while everything the second parent does is horrible
+ The child's knee-jerk defensiveness of everything about the favored parent
+ The child parroting the favored parent's words, often using phrases of an adult to describe the rejected parent or citing scenarios that he or she heard the favored parent speak about but did not himself experience
+ Spread of the child's animosity toward the targeted parent's extended family or friends
+ The child insisting that his feelings are entirely his own, such as calling his father to say, "I don't want to come to your house anymore. Mom had nothing to do with this decision. I made it all on my own."

+ The alienating parent being quick to protect the child's "right" to choose whether he wants to visit the targeted parent

+ Children showing warmth and affection toward the targeted parent when alone with them but then speaking poorly of them to others, including the alienating parent

Parental alienation is different from estrangement, in which a child does not have a relationship with a parent because of a good reason, which is a normal response.

Children who are victims of alienation suffer not just the loss of the targeted parent but also a convoluted sense of truth, trust, and self. These kids grow up to experience heightened rates of anxiety, substance abuse, and relationship and career challenges. Parents who are the target of alienation are 47 percent more likely to have considered suicide within the past year and suffer from PTSD symptoms than those who aren't targeted.

Many alienated parents, devastated by lost contact with their children, hope that changing laws to equalize parenting time would help parents like them maintain relationships with their children.

My equal parenting advocacy work spends little time on parental alienation because I see them as separate issues. Equal parenting is a sociological issue of culture and law. Parental alienation is a psychological issue. However, it is common for alienators to use family court to allege abuse and otherwise fight for primary or sole custody. An equalization of parenting would hopefully make frivolous fights overall rarer and highlight the extreme cases that could benefit from court intervention—like parental alienation.

I chose to write about parental alienation in this chapter because social scientists and child psychologists categorize parental alienation as child abuse: parents who systematically remove their child from a loving parent, essentially erasing the kid from one half of their family and community and gaslighting them, are committing emotional child abuse against that child. Alienators are also guilty of committing emotional violence against the ex-partner.

Parental alienation is a deeply studied phenomenon, with more than two hundred well-documented and recent studies published in noteworthy science journals globally. The science is tight. The science is also a prime example of the wars in science and misinformation that can make it nearly impossible for even the most educated and thoughtful among us to separate facts from dogma.

Case in point: some high-profile domestic violence advocates and legal scholars routinely dismiss parental alienation as a phony gimmick used by abusive men to take children away from protective mothers. These same activists and scholars routinely argue against a 50/50 parenting presumption for the same reasons: it puts women and children at risk of violent men.

One of the most influential voices in dismissing parental alienation is Joan Meier. Professor of clinical law and director of the National Family Violence Law Center at the George Washington University Law School, Meier has for decades been a leading voice advocating for domestic violence victims, earning prestigious awards, appearing in the media, and being recognized as a leader in domestic violence advocacy. She often refers to parental alienation as "junk science" and "pseudoscience" and frequently consults on passing state and federal laws advocating for stricter treatment of domestic violence allegations.

In 2014, Meier won a National Institute of Justice grant of $500,000 with the aim "to debunk 'junk science' that mothers make false accusations of abuse to alienate fathers from their sons or daughters, a misconception that Meier said has put many children in danger," according to the George Washington University student newspaper, the *GW Hatchet*. Meier's study, "Child Custody Outcomes in Cases Involving Parental Alienation and Abuse Allegations," originally published in 2019 on a George Washington University website, unsurprisingly concluded that men are far more likely than women to commit domestic violence, and when these women seek custody, abusive men claim parental alienation and tend to win, placing those children in the custody of abusers.

In her paper, Meier details how her team reviewed all electronically published appellate court custody cases between parents in the United States between 2005 and 2014 that involved abuse or alienation claims. They concluded that mothers' claims of intimate partner violence and child abuse were rejected by the courts about two-thirds of the time, their claims of child abuse by fathers were negated 80 percent of the time, and courts frequently awarded custody to fathers whom the mothers had accused of either intimate partner violence (22 percent of the time) or a combination of intimate partner violence and child abuse (56 percent of the time). In other words, Meier asserts that truthful women were systematically not believed by the courts and children were being sent to live with their abusers at alarming rates.

Meier's research, with its large government grant, was quickly reported in national media and was immediately considered in state and federal family law reform. The study has been cited in national media including *Forbes*, Buzzfeed, and the *Washington Post* and is the foundation of new family law mandates included in the renewed Violence Against Women Act.

These findings rang alarm bells for those who study parental alienation and abuse in family courts, including Jennifer Harman, PhD, an associate professor of psychology at Colorado State University, a leader in the field. Jennifer and I have connected several times over the past few years on this issue, and I consider her a colleague in the shared parenting movement. Like me, she identifies as a feminist. She also identifies as a survivor of intimate partner violence, having lived through a physically abusive relationship with her children's father. Needless to say, Meier and her grant were very much on the radar of Harman and other parental alienation and shared-parenting academics.

"I did what you do in science, which is to replicate the research to see if it holds up," Harman told me. Together with legal scholar Demosthenes Lorandos, Harman set out to examine the same data set evaluated by the study—but with much trouble. Deviating from scientific methodology, Meier did not post her process on Open Science Framework—a tool academics use to document and store entire research projects, open to the public, in the spirit of transparency and good science. Even when Meier eventually published the results of the study in a peer-reviewed paper the following year, that paper did not include information on the sourcing of statistics. "We're not saying her paper is bad. We're just saying it does not have enough information to evaluate it," Harman said. "If there is no information, you can't gauge whether the work is good. My graduate students would never submit work like that. It would never pass peer review."

Without knowing exactly which court cases Meier studied, it was impossible for Harman and Lorandos to truly replicate and prove the validity of Meier's work, so Lorandos and Harman recreated the data source and published their findings.

The new study found exactly the opposite of Meier's. While Meier reported that men were much more likely to be accused of violence and claim parental alienation, Harman and Lorandos found that alienation claims were generally gender-neutral, and upon examining details of the cases, they concluded that family courts are generally good at identifying actual abuse and keeping victims safe, and cases where custody changed hands because of abuse was very rare. "It was good news: family courts are doing what they are supposed to do, protecting victims," Harman told me.

Their findings, published in *Psychology, Public Policy, and Law* in 2021, also highlighted flaws in the process of the study created by Meier, charging her with cherry-picking study subjects, intentionally slanting the findings, and refusing to share her processes publicly. Within months, Meier published a rebuttal defending her work and calling out flaws in Harman and Lorandos's research.

If this sounds like an academic and political catfight, it is. It is also an illustration of science wars that make it hard to understand what is true and what we should believe. After all, scientific papers are not written in plain English, and they are written by biased, fallible humans. News outlets often relay scientific findings, but polls find that most of us distrust most journalism—and for good reason. What "facts" can one trust? In this case, which researcher is most reliable?

In my quest to make an educated assessment of this scholarly showdown, here are some ways that I evaluated which of these researchers are more trustworthy:

1. The quality of the publications in which the science is published: There are tools such as the SCImago journal ranking, which assigns an "H-index rating" or an "impact factor" to measure the number, influence, and quality of the articles a journal publishes. In other words, a journal with a high H-index rating is considered more competitive to be accepted into, more influential, and more trustworthy. The journal *Nature*, for example, currently has the highest H-index rating on SCImago with a score of 1,276.

   Meier's 2019 paper was first published on a university website that does not have an H-index rating and later in the *Journal of Social Welfare and Family Law*. **H-index rating: 27.**

Harman and Lorandos's 2021 paper appeared in *Psychology, Public Policy, and Law*, published by the American Psychological Association. **H-index rating: 67.**

Meier's 2022 rebuttal was published in *Journal of Family Trauma, Child Custody, & Child Development*. **H-index rating: 21.**

Since then, Harman has published a number of related articles, including an argument for the validity of the scientific field of parental alienation in *Current Directions in Psychological Science*. The summary calls out that 40 percent of the 213 (and counting) papers on parental alienation have been published since 2016, indicating that this is an area of research that continues to warrant further study and is hardly "junk science." **H-index rating: 185.**

2. The rebuttal process: It would have been typical in academia for Meier to publish her rebuttal to Harmon and Lorandos's teardown of her study in the same scientific journal where it was published: *Psychology, Public Policy, and Law*. However, it was published in a different journal of lesser repute, which critics argue means her research standards did not meet muster of the higher-quality journal. Meier, in an email, told me her rebuttal was denied by *PPPL*, because, she believes, "it casts doubt on their own peer review and editorial process which failed to identify all of these problems."

Meier also dismisses relying on H-index ratings to assess research quality. "Impact factors are not proxies for the integrity or credibility of studies published in journals," she wrote in an email. "Particularly in this highly contested field, readers must be trusted to judge for themselves, and not simply look at impact factors or journal names to determine whether a particular article has integrity or credibility. Unfortunately, when articles contain statistical jargon, few people do the work that our team did, to discover the lack of accuracy in a published study."

Which is exactly the issue here: all the articles in this quandary are written in academic jargon.

The possibility of bad science has powerful, real-world implications, including how we treat fathers, children, and mothers in family court.

Further perpetuating scintillating but unsubstantiated headlines, Meier's old and new research has been cited as fact in dozens of other research settings. A 2021 paper published in the *American Journal of Family Therapy* (H-index rating: 66) found that some permutation of the unfounded statement "parental alienation theory assumes that the favored parent has caused parental alienation in the child simply because the child refuses to have a relationship with the rejected parent, without identifying or proving alienating behaviors by the preferred parent" has appeared in forty different journal articles, books, and presentations by critics of parental alienation between 1994 and 2020.

Beyond her media power, Meier has been sought out to provide expert testimony in family court cases and in front of legislatures seeking to pass laws that would make parental alienation inadmissible in court. Most noteworthy, Meier's work was key in drafting and passing Kayden's Law, named after Kayden

Mancuso, one of the famous cases I mentioned earlier in the chapter—a pretty blond girl who died at age seven in a murder-suicide by her father during his parenting time. Kayden's Law became federal law when it was included as an appropriations bill in the 2022 renewal of the Violence Against Women Act, meaning it never had a public review period and was never heard in committee or debated on the floor in Congress. The law focuses on dramatically limiting parenting time when a parent has any history of violence, including reduced custody time and supervised visits. The law errs on Meier's denial of parental alienation science, as it states, "Scientifically unsound theories that treat abuse allegations of mothers as likely false attempts to undermine fathers are frequently applied in family court to minimize or deny reports of abuse of parents and children." It then goes on to decree, "any order to remediate the resistance of a child to have contact with a violent or abusive parent primarily addresses the behavior of that parent or the contributions of that parent to the resistance of the child before ordering the other parent of the child to take steps to potentially improve the relationship of the child with the parent with whom the child resists contact." In other words, if one parent is accused of abuse, the court should default to the assumption that the accused parent is the primary problem. It's a presumption of guilt.

To become effective, states would have to pass and enact the law.

Harman told me, "The basis of the law is taken directly from Meier's 2019 study, which is not a legitimate scientific study, but they cite it directly in the law as being definitive."

Kayden's Law has been touted as a victory for women; Angelina Jolie was a spokesperson for the law and did an extensive media tour to promote it. However, the American Civil Liberties Union campaigned against it on the basis that it keeps *mothers* accused of child abuse from their children and financially penalizes poor people, especially women of color, who cannot afford a legal fight to keep their kids.

It is gravely disappointing that the ACLU does not address how much the law hurts dads too, not to mention ignores the perils of child neglect. Per Jennifer Harman, Kayden's Law "leaves out entirely neglect as a possible reason why you might take custody away. Which is weird because three-quarters of abuse allegations that are investigated by Child Protective Services and found to be true are neglect. And most of the perpetrators of neglect are women. So why is it that neglect is conveniently left out and the only focus of Kayden's Law is on child, physical, and sexual abuse?" These are behaviors our society mistakenly ascribes primarily to men, especially noncustodial fathers. Female victimhood sways hearts, minds, and votes.

While Harman and Lorandos's papers are gaining academic steam and the field of parental alienation continues to gain widespread acceptance as a very real thing, in April 2022, Meier was awarded an endowed professorship at the George Washington University Law School within the National Family Violence Law Center to the tune of $2.75 million "in recognition of her groundbreaking work to support victims of domestic violence."

This is a long story that helps explain how our assumptions

about family violence—and those who profit from the family violence industry—systematically stand in the way of equal parenting. How do we assess the arguments that equal parenting presumptions will result in spikes in family violence or discourage victims from going to court? Luckily, there is a simple answer to these questions. And it's found in Kentucky.

Abuse Rates When Equal Parenting Laws Are Passed

In 2016, the Kentucky legislature passed the country's first mandate of equally shared parenting time when parents separate or divorce. What's happened since that date has torpedoed arguments that a 50/50 presumption will increase family violence.

Since the law was enacted in 2017, Kentucky family court filings dropped by more than 16 percent despite the population increase within the state and the nationwide increase in divorce filings. Longtime Kentucky family court judge and Child Support Commission chair Lucinda Masterton told the state's *Courier Journal,* "Since the [shared parenting] statute, we've had a lot fewer disagreements about parenting time."

But what about domestic violence? Doesn't this new law discourage abuse victims from seeking sole custody if they fear an uphill battle under a 50/50 presumption?

That change is even more dramatic. Between 2017 and 2022, the number of domestic violence claims filed alongside family court filings fell by *half.* But this is not the whole story. Rates of family court filings involving claims of violence had already been on the decline—with rates down by more than 80 percent since 2011, the drop picked up steam in the years since the 2017 50/50 law passed. Those who observe these issues recognize these trends as good news: take the fight out of divorce and family law, and false claims go away.

Circuit Civil Domestic and Family Cases Filed 1/1/2020–12/30/2022 Statewide Cross-Referenced with Domestic Violence Cases

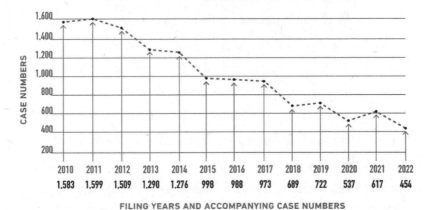

	2010	2011	2012	2013	2014	2015	2016	2017	2018	2019	2020	2021	2022
	1,583	1,599	1,509	1,290	1,276	998	988	973	689	722	537	617	454

FILING YEARS AND ACCOMPANYING CASE NUMBERS

Statistical Analysis Considerations
- Data provided from the CourtNet Database. Unit of count is circuit civil cases. A single circuit civil case may have more than one cross-referenced domestic violence case.

This seems to be what happened in Spain, where equal parenting presumptions were mandated in five regions starting in 2009, after which the rate at which parents shared time equally after divorce went up 400 percent. Researchers compared the rates of intimate partner violence in those regions and found that such violence declined 50 percent during that same period when compared with the other thirteen regions of Spain, which still operated under high-conflict, best-interest statutes.

One more report of evidence that equal parenting laws correlate with lower domestic violence: in Arizona in 2010, a mandate required judges to order "maximum parenting time" to both parents, which courts have since interpreted as 50/50 time, but also gave judges leeway to make exceptions—as do all passed and proposed equal parenting laws. Since then, researchers polled family court professionals (judges, lawyers, therapists, mediators) who overwhelmingly liked the law, said it was effective in mainstreaming 50/50 parenting schedules, and saw that it had a positive effect on children. These professionals reported that after the new policy was implemented, there was *not* more conflict between parents or increased litigation, though they did perceive a slight increase in allegations of domestic violence and child abuse—a half step above a neutral perception. There was no data on whether those allegations were substantiated. But again, these mostly pro-50/50 court professionals also saw overall less parental conflict after the law was in effect.

Those who study family law suggest that the uptick in Arizona domestic violence allegations could be attributable to false allegations in an effort to gain a legal upper hand in custody disputes where 50/50 is the presumption. There are also those who theorize that 50/50 presumptions clear courts of false claims and make room for courts to appropriately support actual abuse cases. The verdict is still out, though this 2018 paper on Arizona suggests that in the absence of more parent conflict, the increased abuse allegations are more likely of the false variety.

Old versus Young Feminists

In working on this book, I find myself dismayed by and even disgusted with feminist scholars who default to be outdated concepts about gender and family. I find myself really, deeply resenting the Joan Meiers and Claudia Goldins who perpetuate the "man bad, woman innocent" pat narrative that hurts us all.

But in an effort to embrace the complexities of these issues, it is important to put into context the continuum of feminism. Joan Meier, who graduated from Harvard University in 1980, came of age when there were far fewer rights for women, when family violence rates were substantially higher, when life for women overall was so much more challenging than when I was growing up (I was born in 1976), barely a generation later. Similarly, older judges and lawyers come from a time when women were financially dependent on men, and the culture and science of that time dictated that mothers were the only parents that mattered.

Meanwhile, younger men and women today have an even more egalitarian understanding of gender, said Denise Hines, who is about my age. "I typically do not have trouble teaching undergrads about other forms of domestic violence, such as male victims. It does not faze them," Hines said. "They are thinking in terms of equality as equality, but it is because they don't have to fight so hard to get basic rights. Older feminists had to work so hard to be looked at as equals, perhaps they overdo it."

6

The Future Is Now

"The notion that the child benefits from permanence in one home
has been dispelled."

—Justin Pfaff, Pennsylvania attorney

I have been working in the single parenting space for more
than a decade, and I have been astonished by how quickly the
understanding and practice of equal parenting are becoming the
norm. In fact, in writing this book, I could hardly keep up with
all the changes afoot.

Culturally, equality for parents who live apart is snowballing
in not just popularity but also normalcy. Even without 50/50
laws, concerted public service announcements, or activists like
myself getting traction, our culture, our society, is organically

just moving toward more father engagement, more women who assume the role of breadwinner or co-earner without much ado, a rise in parents starting time-sharing at 50/50, and many who eschew child support orders and nasty divorces and just do the right thing.

Social norms are powerfully influential. What the moms on the playground tell you to expect during your divorce influences how you proceed with your soon-to-be ex. When the weekly celebrity rags report equal parenting schedules of now dozens of A-list celebrities—including the likes of Bradley Cooper, Jason Sudeikis and Olivia Wilde, Adele, and some of the Kardashians—it seeps into the collective consciousness, and change happens. When your lawyer tells you to give up hope of arguing for majority time with your kids because any judge in your county makes it really hard to deviate from 50/50—no matter the law in your state—common sense takes hold. And when you commiserate over coffee with your colleagues about the struggles to carve out time for yourself as a parent and the lack of any national family leave or affordable childcare, a fight for anything more or less than 50 percent parenting time simply does not jibe with the zeitgeist.

When I started actively advocating for equal parenting laws in 2016 and 2017, the only shared parenting law on the books was in Arizona, where its custody law language is somewhat flexible, mandating that judges seek "maximum time" with each parent. Since then, five more states joined, each of them with a true equal parenting presumption, making a total of six with active bills in at least thirty other states. While enormously exciting, this snowballing of law passage is just one indication that equal parenting schedules will be the norm for future generations. In this chapter, we'll tour the meta forces that are guiding our culture toward truly equal parenting for all families, not just divorced ones.

I have no doubt that a norm of 50/50 schedules for families with kids in which the parents live separately is upon us. If you have any doubt about how to structure your family, sticking to the status quo "Friday night special" today means you will be a dinosaur and possibly harshly judged by your own children. The every-other-weekend parenting schedule is the drinking and smoking while pregnant of the 2020s.

Fifty-fifty parenting is not a far-off distant dream. Fifty-fifty parenting is now.

Young Parents' Idea of Family

Younger men, women, and families inherently understand the benefits of equal parenting. After all, parents of kids ages eighteen and younger are now the product of a society that has struggled through at least three generations of mainstream divorce. We have a pretty good idea of what we want and what we don't, and what we want is to avoid the fighting, missing our dads, and broke moms of our own childhoods. Even when people aim for a two-parent, heteronormative, married, and cohabiting home, it still looks very different than just one generation ago.

In 1977, just 11 percent of U.S. parents were unmarried, while today, that number is 25 percent. Today, the makeup of parenthood is shifting dramatically, further away from ole June and Ward (*Leave It to Beaver*) of the 1950s or the Connors (*Roseanne*) or Huxtables (*The Cosby Show*) of the 1990s that I grew up on or even the straight, two-parent TV families my kids see on shows like *Black-ish* and *Bob's Burgers*. Two-thirds of millennial moms will at some point have a child outside marriage, and a third of kids have parents who are unmarried but live together as a couple. There are no signs these trends are reversing—just the opposite. Today, gay marriage is codified in the Constitution, the rate of people in the United States living in multigenerational housing is on the rise, and while many young people aspire to marriage, they have largely decoupled the institution from parenthood. Even engagement rings are going out of style.

Sociologists find that while younger adults want to be parents, they are simply over the idea of traditional marriage. For them, parenthood is a life stage independent of marriage. Millennials are also jaded by their parents' bitter divorces and the emotional trauma they suffered at the hands of their parents' breakups. A few quotes from members of the Wealthy Single Mommy Facebook group sum up why more and more women are choosing to have children outside partnership:

+ "I never wanted to get married if I wasn't with the right person. But I always knew that I wanted a child. My parents had an incredibly acrimonious divorce when I was 12, so I had to go through a lot of therapy before I could commit to my fiancé."

+ "I saw my mom raise five kids on her own, so I knew it could be done."

+ "I didn't want to get married. The divorce rate is so high, and I have seen more unhappy and unfair marriages than great marriages."

+ "I got pregnant on accident and there was no way in hell I was marrying him."

+ "None of my pregnancies were 'planned.' Things happen and I'm certainly not marrying someone just because I'm having a child by them. Sex is one thing. Partnership is something entirely different."

+ "He asked me to get married many times. I didn't want to. My parents had an unhappy marriage and I felt like my mom felt stuck. I didn't want to be trapped. But I wanted a child. So I had one. Plus, previously marriage was a must because women needed the financial security of a man. I didn't and don't need that."

In short, married parenthood is now viewed as just one way to have kids, and the answer is *not* to bring marriage back. The past fifty years have seen countless government and religious movements try and fail. And for the growing majority of those who choose another way, equally shared parenting time is swiftly gaining traction. Compared with when I was a new mom in 2008, I see so many more dads of all races in all kinds of neighborhoods strolling around with babies strapped to their chests, involved with the PTA, and, sometimes gratuitously, in my opinion, being celebrated on social media: dads mastering elaborate hairstyles on their daughters, dads wittily grumbling about picky eaters and sharing touching posts about sweet things their kids say. You know, being a parent.

What about 50/50? That is on the rise too.

In my survey of 2,270 single moms, 13 percent had 50/50 time-sharing arrangements, and 98 percent of them were happy with that schedule. Of all moms polled, more than half either had or wished they had equal time-sharing arrangements, with the most common reason for not having them being a lack of interest from the dad. Meanwhile, celebrities in film, TV, sports, and beyond are increasingly promoting their positive co-parenting stories on social media, making lovely, loving, and nontraditional families not only normal but #parentinggoals.

Fifty-fifty parenting also aligns with other larger social trends at play. It is a matter of gender equality, family equality, love, and an inherent sense that kids and parents simply belong together. We can see this notion play out across our culture in myriad ways.

Again, nearly all adoptions in the United States are open adoptions, keeping kids at least somewhat connected to their biological families—and those families connected to their children—to the benefit of all involved, studies find. Collectively, we agree that children and parents should not be separated at national borders (67 percent of all Americans find the practice unacceptable). The huge surge in popularity of genetics testing networks like 23andme.com and Ancestry.com has connected millions of biological relatives who did not know of one another's existence and many times caused enormous pain at learning the real identity of one's parents after decades of deceit. (I am astonished by how many people I know personally who found unrealized siblings and learned that the dad they thought was theirs actually was not.) Customers of these sites take on enormous emotional risk in exchange for the promise of the ultimate reward of family connectedness.

The fight for LGBTQIA+ rights and marriage equality is a model and inspiration for changing our views on shared parenting. Although activists had been lobbying for years for such a change, many of us in the general public were stunned in 2015 when the Supreme Court made gay marriage legal in all fifty states. Although there wasn't a broad groundswell of advocacy, the ruling quickly polled high with the general public and was soon credited for higher earnings and employment for queer people. Today, 71 percent of the U.S. population supports gay marriage. The change in law was simply the tipping point in a changing culture, normalizing this common-sense message of love and family for mainstream America.

Also, as I covered in chapter 2, we have new attention on the plight of men and boys, which seems to be largely accepted by the left and right alike. Richard Reeves, a journalist and scholar at the liberal Brookings Institution whose excellent book *Of Boys and Men* (2022) is a manifesto for all of us to wake up and pay attention to the crisis of our males, told me, "I think for a generation of feminists, it was all about economics, but now there's a real sense that we're not getting it right. We don't want for women to live like men with wives at home. We actually want to live in ways that allow us to raise our kids. It's really struck me how many people who consider themselves very liberal, very feminist acknowledge that we need more men in our kids' lives." Despite his worries that the left would cancel him for his effort, the book has been widely accepted, well received, and named a Best Books of 2022 by the *New Yorker* and the *Economist* magazines.

Equally shared parenting sits at a similar precipice of becoming a new social and legal norm.

After all, between celebrities, friends, community members, and family, most of us know or have heard of someone who is sharing parenting duties equally or where it is clear to us that would be a logical path, just as most of us know and love at least one gay person.

Courts Are Changing, Regardless of Law

I have heard from countless parents who do not live in a state with equal parenting laws yet assumed that was the law where they lived. This is because 50/50 is the most common arrangement among parents they know, or perhaps they called a local attorney who told them to forget any notion of arguing for a majority of parenting time because the judges in that district don't want to hear about it unless there are critical concerns at play.

There is also an increasing number of attorneys who simply give their clients good counsel (versus those who fight for what their client wants, no matter how irrational or damaging to that family) and a growing crop of family therapists who do the same. Sometimes these professionals are versed in the research that supports equal parenting, and sometimes they understand on a gut level that kids spending equal time with mom and dad is equitable and healthy for everyone involved. We don't need to fight for equal parenting laws if culture has organically achieved our goal of a 50/50 presumption. After all, Denmark is one of a handful of countries in which equal parenting time is presumed when parents separate, even though there are no equal parenting laws on its books. Similarly, in Arizona, child psychologist William Fabricius educated law professionals and the court system for years about the benefits of equal parenting time. By the time activists proposed a 50/50 law, lawyers and judges had already made it a cultural reality.

It is hard to say how all these 50/50 parenting pockets come about, but here is an anecdote from Julie Johnson, a family law attorney in Louisville, Kentucky. When I interviewed her, she had been practicing family law for twenty-six years and had seen the trajectory of standard custody arrangements move from kids with mom (who often stayed home full-time and did not work) to a 50/50 default for years before the equal time presumption law passed in that state. "Even before our statute changed to a presumption of joint physical custody, a lot of our judges in urban areas over the past fifteen years had gotten to that point on their own," she said. While rural areas, with older and male judges, tended to be more conservative, urban moms were more likely to have careers and demand that the dad do more of his share of childcare, she said. Plus, the world was simply changing and becoming more progressive, even in the very red state of Kentucky. "In Louisville, in one year, we lost eight out of ten judges to retirement, and their more modern replacements favored joint physical custody," she said.

In 2017, even before the full law went into effect, news of the bill's passage had spread to the public and lawyers, and there was suddenly a culture of equal parenting throughout the state. A friend who was going through a divorce in Lexington at the time was overwhelmed and unsure of how to move forward with her parenting plan. "Every attorney I called told me, 'Judges are now ordering 50/50 schedules so you might as well just do that.'" She had an unusually complicated situation that involved international work visa challenges for both her and her husband that could have very easily justified one of the parents relocating overseas in order to legally earn a basic income. Yet they stuck it out, together, equally, and she is glad for it. "Now the kids have both their parents, and I have time to work and spend weekends with my boyfriend," she told me. The spirit of this initial agreement has carried this family forward through an international move and several job changes with both parents equally caring for their kids—all because a thoughtful lawyer relayed the new norm in that family's community.

Even in states that still have "best interest of the child" laws at play, things are changing quickly.

A few years ago, my boyfriend and I were having dinner with Justin Pfaff and his husband, whom I met while campaigning for Joe Biden in 2020 in Pike County, Pennsylvania, a rural community in the Poconos Mountains where they live and where my boyfriend owned a home. Over dessert, I found myself elaborating on the equal parenting movement. Justin, who practiced general law in that rural community, shrugged and said, "Yeah, judges and lawyers around here still mostly give the mom the majority of parenting time, but what you're saying makes total sense."

Pike County, like many rural areas, suffers from a shortage of lawyers and an abundance of low-income parents. The moms there would benefit from more time to work, Justin pointed out, and dads would benefit from lower child support payments— and the overtaxed legal system would benefit from fewer warring parents. Justin invited me to speak to the local bar association in a continuing education session about the benefits of 50/50 parenting. There were about a dozen of us in a room at the county courthouse, including lawyers and a custody magistrate who worked closely with the judges. My focus was on the benefits of equal time for kids, of course, but we also spent a lot of time discussing why shared parenting is good for women and gender equality and for stemming the male crisis. Also the very fact that equal parenting is quickly becoming the norm and that everyone in that room really needed to get on board, like it or not.

There were good questions, lots of interest, and none of the angry pushback one might expect if you spoke only to the front-line shared parenting activists who say money-grubbing lawyers hate 50/50 parenting.

A couple years later, I caught up with Justin, who confirmed that at least one judge in that county now strongly defers to a 50/50 parenting schedule when custody is in debate—a shift that has dramatically affected the counsel he and other local lawyers give clients. "We tell them that the judge works from a presumption of 50/50, so unless there is real abuse or a serious scheduling issue, they should work it out with the other parent. Usually, they do," Justin told me. "The notion that the child benefits from permanence in one home has been dispelled."

A by-product of this deference to equal parenting is that parents are forced to live close to each other, as illustrated by the unique nature of Pike County. The area is a two-hour drive from both New York City and Philadelphia, and many families relocated to the mountainous area during the pandemic or own a second home there. If the relationship between parents ends, some moms assume the freedom to relocate with the kids, which would only be possible if she has custody the majority of the time. Instead, when forced into a 50/50 schedule, everyone has to settle into living and co-parenting in the same town.

But what about cases where a parent is not safe? Justin said that the exceptions to a 50/50 default are real, especially when it comes to drug use. Drug use, mental health issues, child neglect convictions, and other factors are always circumstances that judges can and do consider when a parent is fighting for sole custody. But that does not mean that a single incident or even ongoing struggles call for a parent and child to lose their relationship. Increasingly, courts and social service agencies refer families to programs aimed to heal these situations. California, for example, has a formalized plan for parents convicted of domestic violence to regain increasing time with and rights to their kids, including batterer intervention and parenting classes. Thanks to welfare reform in the 1990s, hundreds of millions of federal dollars have been spent on fatherhood programs, which were reviewed in a meta study that found they were effective at helping men with parenting and anger management skills and especially co-parenting.

A barrier to equal parenting presumption is convincing judges to get on board. No judge, especially in states where judges are elected officials, wants a headline trending on Twitter that a child was harmed under a controversial custody ruling from their bench. But even domestic violence advocates are calling for equal parenting, including the workers at the shelter where Priscilla, whom I first introduced in chapter 2, whose father was in jail and whose partner then went to prison related to intimate partner violence against her, wound up. "[At the shelter] they told me that conflict between he and I should not be a reason to keep the kids from their dad," she said. It took her some time to think about that, but today she agrees.

Activism Successes

A few years ago, I doubled down on working on shared parenting advocacy as a priority. I spent a lot of hours networking, asking for phone meetings with people working on getting shared parenting laws passed and with academics researching the topic, and generally listening to the experiences of hundreds of moms, dads, and adult children contending with unfair and painful parenting situations. The more I learned, the harder it was to believe 50/50 was not widely accepted and enforced. After all, the research overwhelmingly supports a presumption of equal parenting time for separated parents, so of course laws should reflect that! And once there are laws on the books, then most parents and kids would enjoy all the benefits of 50/50 schedules—it would be the *law*, for crying out loud! Furthermore, the game of passing a law is ours to lose: NPO polls across genders, races, political beliefs, and geographic areas have found that more than 80 percent of those surveyed believe it is not only in a kid's best interest to spend maximum time with each parent but they'd vote for a political candidate who supports equal parenting. How could we *not* pass a law?!

What I found in these conversations was that for the more than forty years since divorce became mainstream, mostly white, mostly politically conservative men worked to do away with sexist family laws and replace them with laws promoting a presumption of equal parenting time and fairer child support calculators. If you ask these activists today how the issue looks, most will decry a persistently unjust system that robs children of their fathers and punishes men. They blame greedy lawyers, corrupt politicians and judges, malicious women, and an absurdly "woke" culture that ignores facts in lieu of a dogma of female victimhood. Feminism is a leading enemy.

While I am grateful for their work—although they've only managed to pass a handful of equal parenting laws, they've made significant strides—their angry rhetoric has tainted the movement. Very often when I talk about shared parenting, the very first response I get, even in casual conversations with strangers, is "Isn't that the work of the men's rights movement? Those guys who use the courts to abuse women?" Noses scrunch and mouths frown.

On one hand, I get the disgust. Shared parenting activists typically present as belligerent, which is understandable, given the trauma of losing your children, yet plays poorly in the public theater. They have also lacked the humility to acknowledge the skill and resources needed to get laws passed (lobbying and PR are bazillion-dollar-per-year industries populated by skilled experts, not DIY projects, guys!). They are also usually tone-deaf to the fact that for the past twenty-plus years, media, politics, and our culture have swayed far to the left in many ways, from #MeToo to the girl-boss phenomenon to the myriad ways the public and private spheres have clamored to—largely successfully—equalize the economics of gender. White guys screaming about their victimhood simply does not play well before a state legislative hearing, no matter how right they may be. And speaking of victimhood, most of us are adults and realize that when it comes to personal relationships, there are at least two sides to every story. A rambling narrative about how your ex did you wrong begs more questions about your role in the matter than it automatically damns the other party.

In short, I saw a whole lot of fumbling and not a whole lot of success. I also saw how the movement actually held shared parenting back. Until the past few years, the only image most people had of shared parenting was flamboyant public hearings and media events. As a PR strategy, it was a disaster. Such tactics only give megaphones to the powerful domestic violence activists and deep-pocketed bar associations who routinely oppose such laws with horror stories and dated and misquoted studies—and win.

By contrast, in all six states with good shared parenting laws, those victories were won by way of low-key, under-the-radar efforts by thoughtful activists who took the time to educate court employees and lawmakers and get their bills passed.

My friend Matt Hale, who is heralded as a hero in this space, is credited with passing Kentucky's law in 2017. Matt is not a career politician—he sells construction equipment for a living. And he is also not an estranged dad but someone who grew up without an involved father after his parents divorced and appreciated the benefits of 50/50 parenting his own kids when he divorced. When he speaks about family law, Matt is calm, fact-based, and strategic. In his campaigning, Matt held no media events, and the only person who joined him in testifying before the Kentucky legislature was his mom, who stood by and listened. The bill passed the state's house 81–2, simultaneously with the state senate. Shortly after the new law was enacted in 2018, a poll of Kentucky adults found that about 84 percent said a child would benefit from having equal time with both fit parents following a divorce, and 70 percent believe that family courts are more likely to give fathers less than equal parental rights. "I tell all the activists, lead with love," Matt told me.

In addition to Kentucky, Arkansas, West Virginia, Missouri, and Florida all passing strong shared parenting laws since 2017, there have also been many other successes:

+ Activists have been successful in removing from state law nearly all the blatantly sexist language preferring women as primary caregivers.
+ A presumption of joint, equal *legal* custody has been on the books, successfully, for decades.
+ Child support calculators are increasingly less punitive and fairer.
+ More public and private programs have arisen that focus on fatherhood as a priority, relieve child support arrears, and support dads being in their kids' lives.
+ Fifty-fifty parenting is cropping up around the nation, and the parenting landscape is only getting better every single day.

Yet despite all these positive trends, 50/50 parenting is still a relative rarity. As I mentioned, when I surveyed my audience of single moms who follow my blog and asked them about their parenting arrangements, only 13 percent of the nearly two thousand three hundred respondents said they had equal parenting schedules. Similarly, as part of a University of Miami graduate research project, Casey Sowers, former executive director of the Fathers' Rights Movement, surveyed more than five thousand separated families and found that about 15 percent said their kids split their time between households 50/50. We need these numbers to rise for the sake of kids, women, and men.

Is Child Support Going Away?

Thanks to federal guidelines issued to states in 2016, child support calculators and laws have come a long way in being fair and affordable, with the payer's ability to support themselves now in the forefront of calculation. When dads protest that they can't afford their payments or that arrears are hobbling them, the story is often far more complicated than a sexist law that saddles him with a paycheck garnishment that leaves him with $30 each week. Instead, calculators are mostly fair and take into account both parents' incomes, allowing the payor enough to live on and an option to adjust payments in the event of unemployment or job changes, thanks, in large part, to the 2016 federal Flexibility, Efficiency, and Modernization in Child Support Enforcement Programs Final Rule, which requires a basic standard of living be considered when child support is ordered.

Anecdotally, more and more moms tell me that it just isn't worth it to file for child support—not worth the tension it causes with their kids' dad, not worth the paperwork. It is true: state child support filings are on a dramatic decline, especially those that go through the public assistance programs. Between 1999 and 2021, the total number of families served by state child support agencies dropped by 36 percent (not adjusted for population growth) to eleven million families. Many are eligible but do not apply.

Why?

According to U.S. Census survey results, moms' attitudes about child support have shifted from an entitlement to frivolous or even toxic, and they now extend grace and common sense to their co-parents. They also want to keep these decisions in the family and keep the government out of their business.

THESE ARE THE TOP REASONS CITED BY PARENTS (MOSTLY WOMEN) NOT FILING CHILD SUPPORT THROUGH THE STATE:

"Did not feel the need to make it legal" (39 percent)

"Child's other parent provides what he can" (38 percent)

"Child's other parent cannot afford to pay" (28 percent)

"Child stays with other parent part of the time" (23 percent)

I choked up reading these stats. Despite a system that has a long history of driving parents apart and away from their children, despite a culture that has told women that their power lies in punishing men financially, a system that is incentivized to turn parents against each other and *fight, fight, fight,* large numbers of mostly low-income moms are telling us that they prioritize kindness, fairness, and decency toward their co-parent. I want to highlight this: *"Child stays with other parent part of the time" (23 percent).* Reader, nearly a quarter of separated moms who could be getting child support believe it plays no role in their family because they co-parent. We are getting there. We are getting there!

Governments are getting there too. Today, just 5 percent of state child support cases are those that involve government assistance reimbursement—down from 25 percent a few decades ago. Instead, some moms who once were on government assistance got off it, while more and more states have committed to "pass-through" policies, in which some or all child support paid goes directly to the other parent and is not redirected to the government.

Things are changing on the state level too. The language of new 2022 child support guidelines in Kentucky, for example, address this very argument of leveraging parenting time for more or less child support owed. Previously, deviations to child support in shared parenting cases were at the discretion of the court, which varied by county. The new order specifically addresses concerns that child support be ordered based on how much time each parent actually cares for the child (not just what is written in a parenting arrangement), as well as the paying parent's ability to support himself:

As signed by Democratic governor Andy Beshear:

→ The law created a "self-support reserve" that considers the needs of the paying parent to support themselves when imputing income in the child support calculation.

→ The Court must consider the number of "overnight stays" each parent exercises, then provide for a calculation based upon equal parenting time or unequal parenting time. The law now provides that merely providing a place to sleep for a child does not constitute an overnight stay. The Court can consider who is feeding, transporting, entertaining, helping with schoolwork, attending activities and athletic events, and paying for other expenses of the child when determining whether time is equal.

→ The Court can consider the likelihood of a parent to exercise their parenting time when determining whether to deviate from the child support guidelines. They can also consider the ability of the obligated parent to maintain basic necessities for the child in their home, geographical distance between the parties, and whether all of the children are actually exercising shared parenting.

In addition, a growing number of states have programs that pause support payments (and interest) when debtors are in jail. States and counties are investing in more programs that help dads manage or reduce arrears, find work, and better navigate the child support system. About half of states now pass through at least some of the dad's child support payments directly to the moms versus taking those funds to repay federal welfare payments. Studies find that dads are more likely to pay when they know those funds go directly to their kids—and not the feds.

Overall, the number of "zero orders" in which only medical expenses or no child support payments at all are issued has increased by two-thirds to 10 percent since 2010, which experts describe as a result of federal reform. Once more, this is evidence of powerful movement toward successful co-parenting and fair financial sharing.

Public assistance programs are successfully filling in the financial gaps when families need it, as poverty rates for women and children have plummeted in the past two decades.

The Legal Field Is Changing

While state bar associations have consistently opposed equal parenting bills for obvious financial reasons (less fighting = fewer billable hours), the legal profession is a burst bubble, with law schools producing far more debt-saddled graduates than the market has jobs for and salaries for new hires at all-time lows. Meanwhile, millennials are marrying less (and therefore there are fewer divorces per capita) and are more likely to resolve parenting disputes between themselves or through lower-cost methods like mediation, collaborative law, and just going to family court without an attorney.

There are market forces at play in the legal industry that are pushing family and divorce law toward kinder, gentler attorneys who aim for good long-term outcomes for their clients, not to mention better quality of life for themselves. These are pressures employers across all industries are contending with.

My friend Ashley-Nicole Russell, the family attorney in North Carolina and 50/50 parenting advocate, practices collaborative law, in which both parties enter into an agreement to settle the case and stay out of court. She promotes this model to other attorneys, laying out a business model that is just as lucrative as high-conflict litigation, as the hourly rate is the same for both methods. The work is also far more meaningful for the lawyer, she says, as collaborative cases are more likely to produce better results for the whole family: less fighting, less expense (Ashley-Nicole says a collaborative divorce costs $10,000 to $15,000 versus $50,000 to $150,000 for litigation), and a greater likelihood of a low-conflict, 50/50 parenting schedule. The tenor of the divorce sets the tone for the rest of the co-parenting relationship, which, despite what you may fantasize, actually never ends when you have kids.

Attorneys committed to low-conflict divorce resolution win too: they experience higher quality of life because, unlike in litigation, mediators and collaborative practitioners are not sucked into the toxicity of warring spouses, being at the mercy of last-minute subpoenas and late-night calls and emails, "putting out a million fires all the time," Ashley-Nicole said. "Everything is so aggressive in that world, your relationships with colleagues become more aggressive, and that spills over to your personal life." Meanwhile, divorces settled through a collaborative process go through a fixed number of prescheduled sessions with a finite, transparent processes that all parties can plan for, including the attorney. "I have incredible life balance," Ashley-Nicole said. "No one, including no court, has any control over my schedule—because we don't go to court."

Similarly, attorney Susan Guthrie, who now specializes in divorce mediation after being a litigator for decades, echoes that low-conflict legal models are not only better for the client but also better for building a successful business. "In the courtroom, everyone hates you: the other party, their opposing counsel, and usually your client is not going to be happy with you," Susan said. "The best way to build a business is through word-of-mouth referrals from happy clients."

These low-conflict models are gaining ground in divorce and family court. Collaborative law was certainly given a boost when in 2023, the International Academy of Collaborative Professionals was nominated for the Nobel Peace Prize. Increasingly, family and divorce courts rely on mediation to resolve conflict, which is true against many fields of law. It is estimated that 95 percent of family law cases are settled out of court—amicably or because one or both parents are emotionally and financially exhausted and give up, give in, and settle.

This is how culture changes: activist attorneys steer clients into successful 50/50 co-parenting relationships. Judges who read these settlements are aware of what is possible and are more likely to order equal parenting in their courts. This makes it easier for activists to get equal parenting laws on the books, all of which are important and effective stitches in moving the issue forward.

Everyday Activism

However, once again, the power of peer pressure and social norms do the heavy lifting of social change. Whether you are a blissfully married parent, the loved one of a parent going through a breakup or divorce, or a human who cares about humans, you can do your part to promote equal parenting.

I've learned that when you lay out the arguments in neutral, fair terms, skip your own sad story, and cite the research, 50/50 parenting is an easy sell. For example, my friend Hanna has heard me talk about my shared parenting work for years and had adopted my stance through osmosis. Recently, she told me about counseling a friend who was going through divorce:

> "Everyone around her—her mom and sister, her friends, her lawyer—all urged her to really take this guy down, get as much money as she could, and get the kids most of the time. He'd cheated, and everyone wanted to support her. And that meant to make him pay. I told her, 'Look, I know he's a shitty husband, but you always say what a good dad he is. Why don't you just do 50/50? I know you can't see it now, but you're going to want to date, and you need to get back to work now.' She ultimately agreed to a 50/50 schedule. That was a couple years ago. She recently told me, 'I'd never considered 50/50, and everyone but you encouraged me to do the opposite. Now, I can't imagine parenting any other way.'"

The opportunities for equal parenting activism are endless.

I recently consulted with a tech startup that serves parents of newborns. I pointed out that all the marketing featured moms, no dads. The next week, the images were updated to include fathers. That is activism. Speaking thoughtfully on the topic to people who are really appalled by the idea of a presumed 50/50 schedule is planting the seeds of change—no matter how brutal their reaction. Just being that 50/50 family is activism: you are modeling for those you know what is possible, modeling for acquaintances who may be navigating a breakup or are open to reconsidering their current parenting schedule what is possible. You are most certainly putting your child's best interest at the center of your decisions, modeling equality, and giving your sons and daughters the gift of two parents—which will reverberate for generations.

7

Solutions

So what is the answer? How exactly do we move everyone forward so that 50/50 schedules become the norm?

Here I outline five plans of attack:

1. Invest in fatherhood programs.
2. Create healthy co-parenting public service campaigns.
3. Pass—and support—equal parenting presumption laws in all fifty states.
4. Continue to reform child support.
5. Give men reproductive rights too.

Invest in Fatherhood Programs

Looking for the Shangri-la of equal parenting? Big surprise: it's in Scandinavia. While northern European countries lead in laws and practices to normalize moms and dads splitting parenting responsibilities equally when they live separately, Sweden is held up as a golden example because of its strong laws—the country passed its equal parenting law in 1998—and culture of gender equality. Of course, it also offers ancillary benefits like extensive paid family leave for mothers *and* fathers and affordable and subsidized childcare that make it infinitely easier for parents to work and care for their children without one parent sacrificing for the sake of the other's career. As Malin Bergström, the Swedish researcher, told me,

> "Shared parenting doesn't start after a divorce. This is something that parents have to build together from the very first blue line on their pregnancy test. In Sweden, fathers are expected to have participated in a parenting class before birth and to be there during delivery—they can even stay in the hospital. The family stays together always. And when they get home, a nurse will come to have a home visit and has to meet with both parents. And then there is a program that provides meetings with a nurse to address the mother's issues, the father's issues, and the co-parenting issues. Both parents are encouraged to always come together to the rest of the visits."

It sounds like utopia, but even in Sweden, equal parenting required a thoughtful, concerted effort. "Just to get this working has been a challenge," Bergström said. "It sounds so natural, but having these female nurses address both parents equally, it's been a lot of work, actually."

Sweden has an extraordinary advantage in its universal, single-payer healthcare system, which extends a unified path for the whole family from before conception through death for every member of society. Because of this system, it's much easier to implement programs that invite fathers into prenatal ob-gyn visits, birthing centers, pediatricians' offices, and home health visits and bake into each of these interactions messages about the importance of dads.

While the United States may never adopt any sort of unified healthcare system, we can find some glimmer of hope and replicable models in California. Alameda County's Fatherhood Initiative is an umbrella effort that incorporates fatherhood into every touch point throughout the system that serves the 1.8 million residents of the San Francisco Bay Area county. For example, the county's family health department is called Maternal, Paternal, Child, and Adolescent Health, making it the only such department in the country that includes any reference to fathers in its name. Further, the department ensures fathers' health and men's role in family life are central to every aspect of the services offered. This is not just lipstick on a pig—dads are baked into every part of the department's programming and far beyond.

For example, Alameda County's health department website and education materials include images of men and fathers, advertise support groups and parenting classes for fathers and mothers, and ensure dedicated seating for dads in pediatrician and obstetrician offices. It also trains its staff on how to best engage with fathers in its offices. "Think about it—how many schools or libraries are welcoming to dads?" said Kevin Bremond, who runs the county's Fathers Corps program. "Is there an extra chair in the pediatrician's office where the father might sit? Is the nurse or doctor welcoming to the dad and asking him if he has concerns about his baby's health, or the health of his partner, or his own health? Are you training your staff to acknowledge a personal bias they may have against men?"

Fathers Corps also looks to right gender inequities by granting $50,000 to local agencies with the stipulation that they incorporate father-friendly principles into their services—including that fathers be included in all family service programs in the county, these programs are inclusive and supportive of fathers involvement, fathers are recruited as employees of these agencies, and staff are trained to better serve and support fathers. This has resulted in the probation department's prioritization of father reunification programs and county libraries that are equipped with changing tables in all bathrooms and book sections about fatherhood. The local child support enforcement office, which Bremond said is staffed by 95 percent women (while 95 percent of payers are men), has set up a parents' advisory board that he called "groundbreaking."

In the United States, the closest we have to a national system that could mimic the from-conception programs in Sweden is the Maternal, Infant, and Early Childhood Home Visiting (MIECHV) Program. This voluntary program serves a third of U.S. counties in all fifty states, with a focus on helping low-income families connect with services that provide support and education about parenting, such as the importance of reading, safe sleeping, and nutrition, and maternal mental health. About $400 million is allocated to the program annually, providing home visits to 140,000 families—only about 10 percent of those eligible. The program is generally considered effective, well received, and a cost-efficient way of delivering services, and in its current form, it could benefit from further expansion. The MIECHV program has been credited with improving its clients' financial self-sufficiency, juvenile delinquencies, emotional and behavioral health, abuse and neglect rates, and academic performance—just as father involvement has.

Today, while some of the local agencies making the MIECHV home visits do intentionally address fathers, there is no national effort to include or support dads. That could be expanded to borrow from Alameda County's requirements to train staff to actively engage with dads in an inclusive, thoughtful, and unbiased way, educate the staff and clients on the importance of father involvement throughout a child's life, and support healthy and equal co-parenting.

We can also learn a lot from the $700 million the federal Administration for Children and Families spent on fatherhood programs between 2006 to 2018. A meta-analysis of thirteen studies of the effectiveness of these programs, titled "Do Responsible Fatherhood Programs Work? A Comprehensive Meta-Analytic Study," offers a thoughtful road map about what is and is not effective in supporting moms and dads in better fathering and better co-parenting. Findings indicate that fatherhood programs are effective when dads participate in extensive, ongoing training that involves an in-person parenting curriculum taught by a facilitator, as opposed to peer-to-peer support or online training. Domestic violence education as well as co-parenting training for both the mom and dad also improve father involvement, the study found. Most of all, this review found that fatherhood programs do work, in part because they help men understand that dads are so important.

Create Heathy Co-Parenting Public Service Campaigns

While kids still benefit from equal co-parenting even when their parents have a high-conflict relationship, that conflict is linked to lack of father involvement. Instead of blaming the dad for checking out, which was at the root of President Obama's floundering National Conversation on Responsible Fatherhood and Strong Communities, or blaming women for gatekeeping their children, as men's rights groups tend to focus on, those in the trenches of working with struggling families whom I interviewed repeatedly suggested a potential solution: more public messaging about healthy co-parenting.

Alameda County's Kevin Bremond is one: "I get moms who tell me her kids' dad shouldn't see the kids because he smokes weed, but I tell her, 'Hold on. You smoked weed together every day while you were together, and now you say he shouldn't have the kids because he smokes weed?' We need a culture shift." That same mom who may seem unreasonable or the dad who seems negligent likely did not have healthy co-parenting models themselves. "He watched his dad fight with mom and then wasn't around, and she watched her mom fight with her dad and then he wasn't around," Bremond said.

There are countless successful, culture-shifting public service campaigns that local municipalities could work on and that could be invested in through the Ad Council, the federal agency behind campaigns that promoted initiatives for war bonds, polio vaccines, and car seats for children; combatted drunk driving; and introduced the slogan "This is your brain on drugs." In the absence of and/or in conjunction with government campaigns, nonprofit organizations and private businesses can and should fund thoughtful, data-driven marketing efforts to educate the public about the importance of equal father involvement and positive co-parenting. Celebrity culture and popular media are already doing the heavy lifting on this effort, with *Grey's Anatomy* and *Parenthood* organically depicting separated parents amicably raising kids, not to mention Kim Kardashian hitting the talk-show circuit to share about the importance of Kanye's involvement with their three children, despite his mental health struggles and the famous exes' public spats.

Another model we can borrow from is the Geena Davis Institute on Gender in Media, which produces research on gender representation on- and off-screen in the media. The research, training tools, and corporate consulting her foundation provides Hollywood are a model for change that equal parenting activists can emulate.

There is also opportunity within faith communities to support equal parenting and as part of initiatives that promote fatherhood. I'd like to see organized outreach to religious leaders about child development in separated families and the importance of 50/50 schedules as well as to those working in faith-based community programs.

Pass—and Support—Equal Parenting Presumption Laws in All Fifty States

As I write this, bills proposing a rebuttable presumption of equal parenting time are active in about thirty states, which is consistent with the landscape over the past half century. The main difference is that in the past five years, six states have passed laws that make a 50/50 schedule a rebuttable presumption, meaning that if you take your case to family court, parenting time is split equally unless you can prove that a deviation is warranted. The activists working on this, typically in conjunction with the NPO, tend to be very good at including thoughtful bill language that protects children in outlying cases: abuse, neglect, when the parents live too far apart, mental and physical health concerns of parents and children, and whether domestic violence is at play. Here are a couple of playbooks to borrow from:

In Kentucky, activist Matt Hale approached policy as a child welfare issue and pushed the bill forward, working in conjunction with NPO and a social scientist at a Kentucky university, and skipped the media events and other fanfare. The bill was passed nearly unanimously in 2017 to immediate voter popularity.

In Arizona, starting in the early 2000s, Arizona State University child psychologist and professor William Fabricius began to give talks to family court employees on basic child development and shared parenting research with local judges, attorneys, custody evaluators, and other family court employees using his insights to organically change the judiciary's minds about parenting schedules. Early on in this journey, "I started my talk by saying that developmental psychologists had known since the early 1980s that infants become attached to their fathers as much as they do their mothers," Fabricius recounted. Those family court employees, who were responsible for establishing and maintaining custody arrangements, could not believe what he was saying. "They stopped me in my tracks and could not get past that point." By the time a new custody law was drafted in 2010, the custody culture in Arizona had already changed—judges were largely ordering equal parenting time, and as such, attorneys recommended their clients agree, out of court, to the same. The bill, requiring a presumption of "maximum parenting time," sailed through legislature and into law, and like in Kentucky, it has since been favorably received and credited with less parenting conflict, less family violence, and better child outcomes. In both states, the law was in fact implemented, and equal parenting time is reportedly the norm.

Language in both laws, as well as those more recently passed in Arkansas, Florida, Missouri, and West Virginia, allows judges leeway to deviate from 50/50 based on their interpretation of "best interest of the child" while also defaulting to the science that finds that frequent, regular, and equal parenting *is* in the best interest of the child.

You may note that four of the six states with equal parenting laws are true-red Republican states and Arizona and Florida are purple, swing states. This is a branding issue with which the movement has long contended, even though equal parenting is truly a nearly universally embraced social movement that polls positively in groups across the political spectrum, across the country, genders, and race, with voters universally saying they would favor a candidate who promoted equal parenting.

The issue appeals across the political divide.

To conservatives, 50/50 parenting promotes more father involvement and elevates the importance of men in family and community, means less government involvement by keeping courts out of your family, and is a men's rights issue.

To liberals, it addresses gender inequality in child-rearing and further helps to correct the pay gap, is a progressive practice that upends old restrictive gender roles, and especially supports the poor and people of color.

To everyone, equal parenting creates enormous benefits for the whole of society—no additional funding or resources required. None!

It's what the science says is best for kids. We all care about kids, right?

In addition to just passing good laws and calling it a day, I call for further family court reform to really clear the courts of all but the most contentious or difficult cases and move toward more mediation immediately—including for cases involving violence, mental health, and addiction issues. For cases where equal parenting schedules are not appropriate, in general today, courts do a decent job of keeping the kids connected to both parents through limited or supervised visits. However, to change any parenting schedule typically requires the expense, stress, and time for one parent to file in court again, make their case again, and once again beg for more parenting time.

I also argue for any court-ordered parenting plan that is not 50/50 to have in it a road map for getting back to equal time. Today, plans can be devised by the court-ordered mediator, but we need a standardized course of action to minimize conflict. Such a plan would give all parties steps and milestones required to make that relationship equal. Depending on the family, this may involve a rehab program, breathalyzer tests, clearance from a mental health professional, anger management and parenting classes. Not only does this support the struggling parent during their difficult time. It also signals to everyone at the table that 50/50 parenting is the goal and that we extend one another grace and forgiveness for our humanity with the long view that the parenting road is bumpy and hard, and no one is cast aside for their worst moments.

As I have mentioned, while equal parenting laws have been the focus of the shared parenting movement, we do not need laws on the books if we invest in creating a culture of parenting equality. In Phoenix, equal parenting was the norm before the law was passed, just as in pockets around the country where many parents assume 50/50 statutes govern their states. Meanwhile, Arkansas passed a very good equal parenting presumption law in 2013, which judges intentionally and collectively overruled, until another, stronger bill was passed into law in 2021. Educating judges, attorneys, family therapists, court employees, and the general public might have gone a long way in making sure the original law was enforced.

This is where I call on national efforts to take a broad and long view to support equal parenting in a community's DNA—its courts, its legal community, its mental health practitioners, educating and supporting the general population—to ensure access to a presumption of equal parenting, not just focused on equal parenting laws. I would like to see an equal parenting war room, populated by professional political strategists who could identify the best opportunities to launch campaigns, with broader support of judiciary education and thoughtful, culture-changing public service campaigns. Then, once laws are passed, there is continued support to ensure they are enacted and followed with the goal of an equal parenting norm, not just laws, which are irrelevant if they are not followed. A long-term strategic plan would be attractive to affluent donors and well funded.

Continue to Reform Child Support

One pleasantly surprising thing I learned in writing this book is how little child support is used and how it is largely improving to be less punitive to dads and more supportive of helping the whole family through parenting classes, workforce development, and arrears management. Overall, there is recognition of the connection between reasonable child support requirements and father involvement, paired with more recognition of the importance of dads. Still, there is much work to do.

Let's listen to what child support clients (mostly moms) are telling us with their plummeting enrollment and end child support as we know it. Let's embrace the reality that women are no longer universal financial victims and accept that most dads do want to pay, even when they can't afford to. Moms recognize that their co-parents do or want to pay, don't want the government in their business, and otherwise are not up for chasing after small sums of support at the expense of a compromised relationship between their kid and his dad. Let's listen to the national reports that find success in lowering family poverty comes from good government programs—not robbing poor dads to pay poor moms.

Child support administrators look to the co-parenting apps that are mushrooming on the market as a private sector answer to this new way of sharing expenses, such as health insurance, camp, childcare, diapers, and extracurricular activities. As parents get along better, they can devise creative ways to share expenses, including a joint bank account and credit card for all the endless clothes and school supplies and field trip fees that kids accrue. Some like for one parent to administer that task and send their co-parent a monthly tally that is settled by Venmo.

I support David Kilgore, director of the California Department of Child Support Services, who told me he'd like to see a tiered system in which no one is required to participate in the state program but can choose to run payments through the state if they like and that could ramp up for cases in which a parent chooses not to participate with the kids and state enforcement is appropriate. In all scenarios, the recipient has more power as to whether she wants to seek child support payments, wage garnishment, and arrears enforcement. Increasingly, she doesn't.

Today, more and more states are decoupling their child support programs from federal welfare and passing some of what the dad pays directly to the child as opposed to withholding those funds to replenish welfare outlay.

We can look to Colorado as a model for moving child support in the right direction. Since 2017, 100 percent of all support paid to a mom who receives Temporary Assistance for Needy

Families or other cash welfare goes directly to her—something every state could implement. Further, over the past decade, Colorado has dramatically changed the tenor of its programming, away from enforcement and toward delivery of services designed to support parents and help them better engage with their children, whether they live with the children or not. This includes social service work that helps with job training, housing, applying for benefits, and managing support arrears. These programs have been linked to higher support payments and more father involvement.

In a *New York Times* article, director of the Colorado Office of Economic Security Ki'i Powell said, "Historically, the child support system was built on a philosophy that people had the ability, but not the desire, to pay. That's why it was punitive. Over the last five years in Colorado, we've been flipping that on its head. What would a system look like if it were acknowledging that actually most noncustodial parents have the desire to pay, but not the ability?"

Give Men Reproductive Rights Too

If we really want to stem gender inequality, we must reinstate and protect reproductive rights. And not just for women.

Modern feminism has been rooted in first passing and then defending a woman's guaranteed right to decide whether she wants to bring her pregnancy to term. Without this right, a woman loses agency over her body, her time, her energy, her family, her career trajectory, and her financial future. Devastatingly, in most U.S. states, we now must focus on finding workarounds to the fact that that right is denied.

Planned Parenthood and mainstream feminism failed us with their misguided messaging of "My body, my choice," which has largely ignored the fact that most women who abort are not ambitious white college students who just want to succeed professionally but women who are already mothers and feel they cannot afford another baby. Further, mainstream feminism failed us all, including our children, by ignoring men's reproductive rights. Today, men have no reproductive rights.

Don't get me wrong: a man cannot—nor should he ever—have any say over whether a woman carries a fetus to term or aborts. But a man should also not ever be forced to be a father—or to abdicate his role of father—against his will.

Typically, the argument I hear in response to this suggestion is "If a man doesn't want to be a father, he should keep it in his pants!"

It infantilizes women to suggest that only men's pants need to be held accountable for unwanted pregnancies. The urge to have—and enjoy—sex is genderless. The responsibility that comes with sex is also genderless. And the human right to easy access to reproductive health care, i.e., safe abortions, should also be genderless.

Women, in our feminist ideal, are to be ensured the right to choose not to be parents if we are not ready, can't afford it, or just plain do not want to—without further judgment or penalty. Legally and morally, men should also be protected by those same rights. Men, just as women, are penalized financially when they become parents against their will. Like for women, studies find that reproductive rights for men better secure their family's financial security: men whose partners had abortions are more likely to graduate from college and earn more, and like their female partners, they typically already have children whose financial interests they are concerned about when a new pregnancy occurs.

When men have agency over their parenthood, they are better dads and co-parents. A study published in 2016 found that fathers who did not expect to become fathers are less likely to live with their kids, be engaged parents, or feel positive about their roles as fathers. The children of unintended pregnancies tended to struggle emotionally, be less developed intellectually, and were raised by higher-conflict co-parents. This all means more care work and responsibility for the mothers and fathers who are more likely to be depressed.

I outlined in previous chapters how dads have an uphill battle to claim paternity, gain custody of their children, prevent the adoptions of their own kids, or battle the child support system for outcomes that validate their role—and rights—as fathers. Poor men and men of color are especially at a disadvantage here.

There is a solution, though, and it is straightforward:

1. When a woman finds she is pregnant, she has a window of sixty days to make an earnest attempt to get a written statement from the biological father of her child to commit to being engaged or

choose to terminate his parental rights. This agreement either commits or absolves him from any parenting rights or responsibilities, including financially. "Paper abortions" have been advocated for by legal scholars and social scientists for decades.

2. Require real, universal sex education in K-12 education.
3. Pass laws granting all parents paid family leave.

Granting all genders agency in deciding when to become a parent is central to ceasing gender wars. When men and women enjoy equal rights, they are more likely to bear equal time, money, and care responsibility for any children they may produce. And from a political perspective, enfolding men into the war on reproductive rights could be the silver bullet to ensuring access to abortion for women.

While this book is an argument for monumental changes, we are really at a tipping point for change. The momentum is there, and the public opinion and many thoughtful policies are moving gender and parenting in the right direction.

8

FAQs about 50/50 Parenting

When I talk about 50/50 parenting, I get a lot of "Yeah, buts" related to specific situations. Here are my answers to the most common questions about equal parenting.

But shouldn't the child spend more time with the better parent?

Children are not entitled to "good" parents. They are entitled to safety, love, and the parents they have. There is no evidence that more time with one parent, even if it can be determined that person is an objectively better parent, benefits the child or even influences the child more. However, there *is* evidence that equal parenting schedules benefit children.

Our current system is rooted in incentivizing parents to duke it out and prove they are the "better" parent—which leads to much trauma, expense, and undue drama for the whole family, while there is no evidence that lopsided schedules benefit anyone.

After all, think back to your own childhood and what memories, people, and experiences changed your life most. Were those influences correlated with sheer hours of time?

Today, my teenage daughter probably spends an hour per day with me but many more with her friends at school and hanging out. I may believe I am a better influence than those friends, but that doesn't mean that those hour calculations should be reversed, and a fifteen-year-old should spend ten hours daily with her mom. That would be bananas. Instead, I accept that my child is not mine to control in that way. She is her own person entitled to many influences and experiences. All I can do is my best to influence her, give her a good home, some guidance, love, a vegetable, and a stern word here and there, and hope for the best.

What about when he only wants equal time so he doesn't have to pay as much child support? Or What if she's advocating for equal parenting time only so she will get more child support?

I am lumping these two common arguments against a presumption of equal parenting into one item, because the nut of them is the same, and I believe, based on my own anecdotal observations, both men and women leverage child custody in family and divorce court for their own financial benefit.

Our twenty-first-century family court system has put a financial price on children. As appalling as that may seem at first glance, children have long been considered chattel—boys were valuable for inheritance purposes (keeping land and wealth in the family) and as workers, girls for marrying off to provide heirs—up until as recently as the twentieth century, when marriage for the first time became borne primarily out of love instead of economic survival. Child labor laws, a rise in the middle class, universal education, and other advancements meant that children became a protected class rather than a source of cheap labor or economic security by way of inheritance. It is only our modern notion that child-rearing is a spiritual endeavor, one designed to cultivate the miracle of life into the fullest expression of its magical self, that makes us bristle at the suggestion that children are financially valuable to their parents.

But they are.

Based on my numerous conversations with women who respond to my email newsletters and comment on my blog, many who are angling for more parenting time have higher child support and/or alimony as a significant motivator. I have sympathy for these women: this is the game they have been taught to play. It's likely what their attorney, family, and friends urge them to do and what their own conceptions of life as a single mother make to seem inevitable. These are all very real and human feelings.

In some cases, having more custody means a mom can stay in

the family home and not have to face the very terrifying prospect of getting a job or a better job or advancing her career enough to support herself without a spouse. It is hard to blame her for trying to maintain the status quo.

I also have sympathy for fathers who really don't care to have their kids more than a few days per month but are financially strapped and argue for 50/50 time-sharing to reduce their child support obligations (but don't have plans to actually show up 50 percent of the time).

If a dad chooses not to spend time with his kid, that is a symptom of the chronic sexism that has told men they are not important as fathers and that their presence in their child's life is not meaningful. These are the men who were not engaged parents at any time of their child's life. Perhaps they did not have a say in whether the child was brought to term or were never in a serious relationship with their kid's mother or otherwise did not bond deeply with the child because of a lack of time, opportunity, or a trusting relationship with the mom.

It is easy to say that money doesn't matter when it comes to the love you have for your child, but it matters enormously. For dads who struggle to pay child support—especially low-income men of color—back child support can mean loss of a driver's license, garnished wages, and even jail time in some states. Barely getting by because of unaffordable child support means that you may not have stable housing or that you have to rely on gig work or other jobs that come with unstable and inconsistent hours—both of which are hugely detrimental to a regular custody schedule.

But the story is not just that girls won and boys lost. The story is complicated and nuanced. While men struggle to gain equity in private life, with equal access to their children and equal flexibility in carrying the burden of breadwinning and leading, women still struggle to close the damn pay gap.

As previously discussed, it's not as simple as straight-up sexism that prevents the wage gap from closing. It's also the giant discrepancy in parenting responsibility and the tough decisions that women make under the pressure or necessity to care for others.

The caretaking cleave that prevents the wage gap from closing can be fixed by equal caregiving by fathers—including single dads who never lived with their kids' moms.

As such, it is time to dismiss any argument against a 50/50 parenting schedule under any premise of financial gain or loss. In 2023, men and women are capable of and have the opportunity to work and earn equally, given equal access to childcare. This is where equal rights and equal responsibility meet—with 50/50 shared parenting, both parents are now equally responsible for paying their own rent, securing childcare, and taking on the time, logistics, and emotional labor of child-rearing.

If I agree to an equal parenting schedule, I will receive less child support. What if I can't afford that?

Child support is supposed to be for the children—not to subsidize your lifestyle. In reality, it doesn't work that way, and even the best-intentioned father advocates, including researchers from the University of Colorado, authors of a 217-page report on the net result of child support, conclude that child support may have helped lift women and children out of poverty, but it drove hundreds of low-income dads *into* poverty.

Here's a quote from that report:

> Since its establishment in 1975, child support has achieved tremendous scale and accomplishment. In FY 2020, it served 13.8 million children and collected $34.9 billion. Child support payments are credited with raising 790,000 children and 593,000 adults out of poverty. Among poor custodial families who receive child support, it comprises 41 percent of income, and among deeply poor families, child support comprises 65 percent of family income.
>
> However, the reduction in poverty for the one million recipients of child support has been coupled with the impoverishment of 200,000 low-income fathers and their new families due to the burden of paying child support to their prior families. One-fourth of noncustodial fathers are estimated to live in poverty, with an income of less than $12,760 for noncustodial fathers living alone.

When men go into child support debt, the results can be lost driver's or professional licenses, which can hurt their ability to work (less money for you) or be involved with the kids. In some states, men can be sent to jail for unpaid support (less money for you) and come out with insurmountable debt (still less money for you). Plus, this money becomes a source of tension for you, for him, for your co-parenting relationship—and the kids suffer.

Child support debt has been shown to be an enormous stressor in men's lives, and the elimination of the debt and its associated stress contributed to more work opportunities, improved credit scores, more secure housing status, and feelings of control over the finances. Men also reported improved relationships with their children, their co-parents, and the child support system.

A 2021 study found that fathers' child support arrears but not other types of parental household debt are associated with worse socioemotional outcomes among children who do not live with their dads. I think the real question here is can you afford the *costs* of more child support?

Who pays when one parent can't afford activities or a big bill?

Basics like health expenses, childcare, clothes, and school supplies should be split equally. After all, should one parent die or otherwise fall off the face of the earth (hypothetically), the remaining parent would face 100 percent of these expenses. Equal rights mean equal responsibility—including for basic financial obligations.

If parents disagree about expensive camps or music lessons, then the pro-expense parent should pay—especially if their income is greater. Many parents find a way to split these differences in an equitable way, with the higher-earning parent paying more, whether through their own negotiations or with the help of a therapist, mediator, or, worst-case scenario, a judge.

My kids' dad refuses to do his share of the physical and logistical childcare, which costs me time away from my business. What can I do?

We are in the middle of a revolution, and things will not be equal today. Doing your best to model a better, fairer family by way of nudging your kids' other parent to do the right thing and bringing up the issue in negotiations with attorneys and in front of court employees are tiny stitches in a larger tapestry of a better reality for everyone—moms, dads, and kids.

In the short term, I will share this strategy that a mom posted in my Facebook group. Frustrated during her marriage with the burden of taking on nearly all the scheduling and driving to school, activities, and doctor appointments for their four kids (two of them who had high medical needs), Carrie wrote into her divorce agreement a true 50/50 schedule and an even split in childcare costs, including this clause: "Each parent logs hours spent each year on transporting kids around, at $20 per hour. At the end of the year, the sum is tallied, and the difference is paid to the other parent. If the logistical labor is equal, no money changes hands."

In the first year after Carrie's divorce, the sum of the value of the hours she spent chauffeuring the kids was close to $1,000—a total that sent the dad reeling (even though he was only responsible for paying his share, which was $500). "He was so mad, accusing me of charging him to be a parent," Carrie said. But he paid it.

The next year? He did his share of parenting, and they each spent the exact same number of hours driving the kids around town.

What if one parent has more money than the other? Shouldn't the state aim to make the households equal?

It's true that income disparity can breed resentment, bitterness, and jealousy between parents—not to mention a sense of entitlement. But there is no study that I know of that shows that equal home size or discretionary income has any effect on child well-being in separated families, as long as a child has a reasonably comfortable and safe place to sleep at both homes.

For low-income families, the answer to poverty is more government support, which, thankfully, is working. The answer is *not* strapping poor men with unreasonable child support payments.

For middle- and upper-class families, the idea that one parent owes the other support to equalize homes is simply sexist and keeps women locked into the dependent, caretaker role—the very essence of any financial gender gap.

The argument in favor of child support to equalize standards of living is moot, in part because people of all classes overwhelmingly date, marry, and have babies with people of similar education levels. Thankfully, the pay gap between spouses is fading. Also, more and more women are becoming their home's breadwinner by way of true equality as well as the rise of single-parent households. While male doctors used to marry female nurses, today, doctors are more likely to marry other doctors (or similarly educated peers), nurses have children with nurses, retail workers couple with similar income partners, etc. The likelihood of a child growing up between two homes headed by parents with dramatically different earning potentials is slim.

One trend that bucks this fact is Black women, who tend to be higher educated and have higher incomes than their Black male peers. In 2015, the Brookings Institution reported 41 percent of white women had husbands who had similar educations, while only 32 percent of married Black women could say the same. About 48 percent of white women reported having husbands with lower education levels, while nearly 60 percent of Black women had married someone with less education under their belt. Brookings estimates these discrepancies could mean Black households earn about $25,000 less each year.

This discrepancy is important, as Black men face the biggest obstacles to work, earning, saving, and getting out of poverty than any other U.S. demographic yet face fallout from the broken child support system far more than any other part of our society. Nonetheless, as discussed earlier, poor Black dads are eager to contribute financially to their kids, especially in ways outside the government's child support system.

A focus on children and a sense of grace and kindness can go a long way—and often do. I have heard many stories of co-parents who, no matter how they did or do feel about one another, take turns caring for the kids—and sometimes the other parent—financially and logistically when one gets sick, loses a job, steps away to care for an ill parent, or is faced with other crises of life. One mom I know, Susan, divorced when her husband transitioned to being a woman, which was personally devastating for her but really struck the whole family in the heart when the now-female ex retreated from the children. Within a few years of the breakup, the ex was diagnosed with lung cancer, and Susan moved her back into her home to nurse her until her passing, which created space for some healing and forgiving moments for the whole family.

What if the dad has a big corporate job and travels all the time?

Why does the father get the freedom to squeeze his parenting duties around his career, presumptively leaving any of his unmet parenting responsibilities to the child's mother?

It is often assumed more money makes for better parenting, especially for men whose value as a parent has been tied to breadwinning. This means that professional opportunities trump parenting responsibilities, and the parent with the higher income or more prestigious job is entitled to take opportunities that take them away from their children, because more money, the argument goes, is always more important than parenting time.

Throughout history and still today in many parts of the world, true financial necessity has required one or both parents to be away from their children. War, extreme weather, and dire economic hardship often leave relocation as one of the few options for survival. But for the most part, parents in the United States, Canada, and western Europe thankfully do not need to relocate to avoid starvation or violent death.

In the real world, life is not perfect. There are times when parents are deployed, have to travel extensively for work, or have another reason why they can only spend a minimal amount of time caring for their children. In a culture that defaults to 50/50 parenting, co-parenting relationships become more amicable, or at least functional, because they must continue to collaborate on their children's upbringing. An equally shared responsibility facilitates more flexibility between mothers and fathers to equitably accommodate the needs of one another as well as their children and not view any request for flexibility as an opportunity to pounce on a costly and punitive legal battle to re-right the ship.

That said, a culture that presumes equal parenting time and equal parenting responsibility means there is an expectation that both parents have to build their lives around their children. In this example, we cannot assume that any one parent's career must be worked around but rather that each parent is responsible for coordinating childcare or making professional and financial sacrifices in order to take responsibility for the kids. It becomes unacceptable for a dad to shrug his shoulders and dump the kids with his co-parent because he has to travel for work. He has to figure out who can care for them while he's away or negotiate for a job with less required travel. Again, we are challenging these assumptions for the sake of all, including the gender norms that thus far have given men permission/pressured them to abandon their childcare responsibilities in the name of breadwinning.

What if one parent lives too far away to house the kids equally?

Why is it OK for one parent to move far from their parenting responsibilities? If I, as the primary, majority-time parent of my kids, picked up and moved out of the country, leaving them with a neighbor without making any arrangement, that would be considered child abandonment, and I would be criminally charged as such. We don't charge fathers with abandonment when they move away from their children because, as a society, we don't believe they are important as parents. However, we do believe they are financially responsible and are happy to send them to jail or face other legal penalties for not paying child support that they may or may not be able to afford.

I argue we change laws to make it unacceptable for parents to abandon their kids physically and help parents understand how valuable both of their regular, active involvement is to their children.

If this applies to you, please consider a way to live close enough to your kids that they can spend equal time at your houses. Remember that the closer it is to 50/50, the better it is for kids. Yes, it would be inconvenient to move, but it's also inconvenient to experience the outcomes that become statistically more likely to happen when kids aren't parented equally. Even though culture does the most to reinforce a presumption of 50/50 parenting, it's worth it to pass laws that require it so that kids don't have to experience growing up without one of their parents when that parent is alive and well.

What if I want to move two hours away from my ex to live with my new husband/be near my parents?

If you're planning on bringing the kids with you, you are kidnapping your children. That is illegal and unethical. If you're planning to leave your kids with their other parent, you are abandoning your children. They need you. Please find a way to stay. It will be so worth it—now and in decades to come.

How is a man supposed to build a career if he has his kids 50 percent of the time?!

Mari, thirty-three, has two kids with two different men. One is in jail for embezzlement. The other lives in the town next to hers and sees their child occasionally despite a custody order that the visits amount to about 30 percent of the time and her urging for 50/50 time-sharing. Mari enjoys a close relationship with her siblings and their families and welcomes their support in caring for and loving her kids while she continues to grow her career in the construction industry, date, and generally have a full life. But she learned that even the most caring of loved ones can be unconsciously sexist.

One evening while enjoying a family dinner, Mari's brother-in-law and sister asked her about her dating life. Mari shared some ups and downs and funny stories and then lamented, "It's tough to find what I'm looking for, especially since I won't get involved with a man unless he has a 50/50 custody schedule or at least has fought hard for one."

The brother-in-law became incredulous. "That is unreasonable!" he said. "How can someone build a career and have to take care of his kids half the time?!"

"I didn't even say anything," Mari recalled later. "I just looked at him. You could see the cogs turning, looking at me with my kids 100 percent of the time, with 100 percent financial responsibility for them, and I am able to build my career, even though he knows it's hard. I could see his attitude change right there in that minute."

That is one of my favorite stories of all time, not only because it illustrates how powerful social change can and does happen organically, in everyday interactions between everyday citizens taking common yet radical action. But it also illustrates how we are all such complicated and nuanced people, each of us plagued by unconscious bigotry rooted in long-standing norms—without us even having a clue that its powerful presence holds all of us back. Here, the loving and supportive relative pooh-poohed equal parenting schedules because he couldn't personally imagine succeeding professionally while also being so responsible for his kids—a notion informed by his assumption that it is a man's job to be the breadwinner. A wonderful person with horrifying presumptions that were undone in one silent exchange.

This interaction is loaded with yet more layers.

In social justice movements, there is often expressed a mantra that for one unrepresented group to have more of the pie, others do not necessarily have to get less pie. In other words, there is no reason for privileged white people to fight against social programs that give people of color more access to good schools or good jobs because there is no threat to those white people's schools or jobs.

Related to custody, in order for men to have more access to and more meaningful relationships with their children, mothers have to have less time with their children. Though—again!—less time with our kids does not mean we have less of a bond or less of a relationship with our children. And by some measures, a mother with more time to earn, relax, recharge, exercise, and enjoy the support of an equal parent is a better mom who is more emotionally and energetically available to her kids, not to mention has more for the other parts of her life. If we measure parenting and personal success only in hours, we limit ourselves. Taken holistically, sharing parenting time means more love, energy, and cooperation for everyone involved.

For women and men to work and earn and have public

power in business, government, and our communities in equal measure, men must have less earning and less power. The pie simply is not infinite—at least in the short term. Eventually, it is possible, with equality at home, for men and women to occupy the public sphere in equal measure, as those jobs and admissions seats and public offices expand, just as has happened through-out modern history.

What if he doesn't want to parent 50 percent of the time?

It is very true that many men do not want to parent any more than a minority number of hours each week, and their children often see it. Shared parenting activists bristle when I say this, but it is true, and I have seen it in people I know personally and from many, many moms, some of whom have asked judges to make him parent more. (A typical response from the judge is "I can't make a person parent if they don't want to," to which millions of primary-time single moms silently scream, "No one asked me if I wanted to be a full-time single mom! Make him step up!") This story is also one that is complicated and human and rooted in old, sexist models that linger on. After all, if men have been raised to understand that parenting is inferior women's work and that their worth is as a breadwinner—and they feel they are mediocre parents at best—why would they step up into the role of equal parent? Especially if they are not experienced in daily parenting and they believe, like most people do, that kids fare best with but one primary parent?

I challenge my fellow activists to start implementing language into legislative bills to use the terms enjoyed in other countries: "equal care" and "equal responsibility" in addition to protections over time and rights.

I'm not used to having my kids half the time. They stress me out, and I don't do everything as good as their mom. Can't I let her take the lead on this?

Many men come to parenthood with the assumption that they are not the primary caregiver. This does not mean that they do not love their children, are not devoted to them, are a bad dad, or are a lousy person. This just means that these men are a product of our time—a human on a journey that was largely informed by a culture that tells all of us that mothers are the superior parent.

Whether you lived with or were married to your kids' mom or are currently on an unequal parenting schedule, most dads spend minority time with their children, which makes it harder to parent when you do spend time with them. Kids are inherently stressful and often irritating. Little ones need constant attention, medium-sized ones are weird and can be hard to discipline and entertain, and the big ones can be moody, bratty, or worse. You love them, you're committed to them, but they can suck.

On top of it, you may believe that their mom is a good parent and she has a better grip on the kids' needs. She has all their schedules down pat, knows what foods they like and dislike, has the bedtime routine on lockdown, and has all the doctors/ coaches/teachers/friends' parents organized on her phone. Plus, when you were a couple, she may have let you know regularly that you weren't doing it right. The criticisms were real, they hurt, and you likely accepted them as truth.

Now some advocates, your new girlfriend, a judge, or your own desire or even guilt is asking you to reconsider this every-other-weekend schedule. But can you handle it? Do you want it? Shouldn't she just do it since she's better at it? Wouldn't that be better for the kids? *Do you have to?*

As for the notion that "you can't make a person parent," I argue that you *absolutely can* make a person parent. Many of us have taken on far, far more of the parenting duties than are fair or just or reasonable because the other parent refuses to do their share.

Here is what I want dads to know about equally shared parenting time.

In these pages, I have laid out how important it is for you to be not only involved but *equally* involved. Your child is entitled to a meaningful relationship with you, just *as you are entitled to a meaningful relationship with them*. Adherence to bedtime routine or deep connections to your kids' friends are important but not as important as them knowing that you want to, can, and do show up equally.

Once you have the kids equal time and take on daily routines and school pickups and get to know their teachers and friends and classmates, all the parenting becomes easier. More time, especially more daily time, requires you to establish routines—your own routine. Many dads report feeling more confident as a dad after their divorce. Without having to negotiate with or answer to their spouse, these men can step into being the dads they are capable of being. They also have to take responsibility for the inevitable parenting mistakes we all make. In other words, they grow and evolve and rise to the occasion.

I often remind my kids that parenting is the dumbest job in the world: you are handed this enormous responsibility of raising a human with zero qualifications or training, and as soon as you start to figure out one parenthood stage, you are faced with another. The only difference between men and women in this wacky endeavor is that one half of us grow up assuming we have the inherent ability to figure it all out, while the other half of the population is raised to think that they don't.

It is your responsibility to care for your kids equally. Countless fathers around the globe are currently fighting to spend quality sums of time with their children but are denied this right because of vintage, sexist norms. Most of us agree that men and women should have equal rights to their children and have the right to spend equal time with them. With rights comes responsibility. A call for an equal parenting presumption is rooted in equal sums of equal rights *and* equal responsibility. In fact, in some parts of the world, family courts use terms like "care sharing" and "responsibility sharing" instead of the parenting *rights*-centric terms used in the United States: custody, parenting time, and visitation.

There is also a larger responsibility at play. By stepping into an equal parenting role, you are changing the world. Your kids will grow up to understand the importance of fathers and equality between men and women. People in your community will see you and understand that this parenting schedule is normal, possible, and positive. And you can do it by taking care of your kids with what will likely be just a couple more days each week.

When we were married, I did most of the parenting work, so I should be rewarded with more parenting time, right?

Parenting is not a community soccer league in which you put in hours and get a participation trophy. Parenting is hard and unfair and heartbreaking. It is also not about you. The research is there: parenting time split equally is what is best for children. While it can be a difficult transition from having your time and identity tied to being a mom and hard to see what life can be like for your whole family after this change, rest assured that an equal schedule is very much the place you want to land. Instead of fighting for more time in court or pushing back against a judge's orders, save yourself the time, energy, and upset. Work on accepting that you are no longer the primary parent. You, your kids, and your kids' other parent will be better for it.

**When we were a couple, I was home more and
spent more time with the kids. Wouldn't a 50/50
schedule be too traumatic of a change?**

To put into context why less time with you and more time with
their dad in his house will *not* be a traumatic change, remember that childhood—like the rest of life—is full of transitions and
changes, large and small. Tiny children in day care transition
from one room and set of caretakers to another every morning
and afternoon and continue to swap out classrooms and teachers
every year for the rest of their educations. Families move, grandparents pass, pets die, and kids continue to thrive at every stage.
Throughout history, the species has survived despite plague, war,
natural disasters, mass rapes, and systematic abuse. Yet orphaned,
abandoned, traumatized, and abused children did survive and ultimately thrive—usually because of some informal care from adults.

What empowers children to overcome hardship and heartbreak isn't sleeping in the same bed every night; it's having a
safety net of loving adults to catch them. What could be more
loving than having two equally involved parents—plus each parent's network of family, neighbors, and friends?

**Won't my child feel rejected if we move from
majority time with me to 50 percent with her dad?**

I have heard this genuine concern from mothers many times.
Worries in this vein include "Today, our custody agreement

includes the kids staying with me the majority time. If I push for or even readily agree to 50/50, I worry my kids will feel like I'm pushing them away or otherwise rejecting them." Or "All the other divorced families we know have an every-other-weekend schedule. Won't my kids feel like I'm a bad mom who doesn't want them as much as the other moms?"

A single-mom girlfriend and I were discussing my equal parenting advocacy work and her current time-sharing arrangement: her daughter stayed with her the majority of time, though she saw her dad frequently for overnights, both on weekends and during the week, as both parents lived in the same New York City neighborhood. My friend was sharing the typical struggles of parenting—she had little personal time, and she could use some extra hours to invest in her career, working out, and her new boyfriend. She knows me well enough that I didn't even have to suggest an easy solution: encouraging or even demanding more parenting time with the girl's father. Or really, in her case, allowing it, as her ex was pushing for just that.

"But won't Celia feel like I'm rejecting her?" was her honest worry. "We're so close. It's been primarily the two of us for all of her twelve years."

On a practical note, I pointed out that the girl already spent something like 40 percent of her time with her dad, and she and her ex had recently agreed that Celia would spend afternoons at her paternal grandmother's home after school most days. Celia also spent lots of time with her maternal grandparents, often spending the night with them, as they lived in the same apartment building. I pointed out that Celia had an abundance of family love and care. And all the time she spent with other family members—including her dad—combined with the hours she spent at school and sports were far fewer than 50 percent of her waking hours with her mom. In other words, the girl already had close relationships and lots of time with other people other than her mom, so the risk of feeling rejected by her mother, while understandable, was not in play.

Those practical (math-based!) points punctured the presumptions about the superiority of maternal care, which landed with my friend. Soon after, she and her kid's dad moved to a 50/50 schedule.

What will people think of me as a mother if I agree to give her up 50/50 of the time?

My friend Tyler, who lives in a rural town in Michigan, went through a very difficult custody battle with his son's mother, even though they co-parented very amicably and equally for the first three years of the kid's life. Then, when child support disagreements arose, Tyler found himself embroiled in a nasty family court battle in which he was accused of neglect and abuse. "One day after yet another family court appearance, I took my son's mother aside and asked her what the heck this was really about," he told me. "She said, 'Don't you see? What will people think about me as a mother if I don't have him the majority of time?'"

While Tyler was shocked and you may be too, it is important to hear where this mother is coming from and how subjected to sexist norms she is. This mom, who clearly had proven her capacity to co-parent amicably with her son's dad, found herself subject to the scrutiny of her community because she had challenged gender-typical norms by giving up mother-martyr status. Until it was too much and she acquiesced.

Many moms—single or otherwise—derive enormous pride from their role as mother. And most of us, no matter our marital status or parenting schedule, are proud of our kids and want the world to know about these miracles we helped to create, whether we can rightfully take credit for their accomplishments or not.

Depending on where you live, your family culture, where you worship, or any number of other pressures, a mother who willingly gives up a minute of time with her children is considered the lesser mother—a pressure men simply do not face. Yet. Despite all the progress we have made toward gender equality, we see these pressures express themselves in the helicopter parenting movement, in the pressure for mothers to homeschool their kids and of course to give up or downscale their careers— all in the name of spending more time with the damn kids. And I do say the *damn kids* because I know that the vast majority of you reading this find your kids exhausting, mind-numbing, and superbly annoying a lot of the time. Let us liberate each other from this pressure to derive our identities and cultural worth from a relentless activity that may not bring us much joy and cripples other parts of our lives: incessant parenting.

All the back-and-forth between homes is too much for kids.

First, it is nearly always annoying, if not really upsetting, for kids to go back and forth between parents' homes. We can't minimize that, but we can put it into perspective.

Second, a week-on, week-off schedule is far less chaotic than typical divorced family schedules. My kids go to their dad's Friday after school, then my house the following Friday after school—just one switch per week. A typical every-other-weekend, Wednesday dinner requires far more switch-offs.

Here is the most traditional separated family schedule, with the number of back-and-forths, during a four-week period:

Week 1
Wednesday dinner with dad
     (pick up and drop off from mom's house)
Friday pickup
Sunday drop-off

Week 2
Wednesday dinner with dad

Week 3
Wednesday dinner with dad
     (pick up and drop off from mom's house)

Friday pickup

Sunday drop-off

Week 4

Wednesday dinner with dad

    (pick up and drop off from mom's house)

Total handoffs: 12

Here is the most common 50/50 schedule, in which kids go to the other parent's house after school Friday:

Week 1

Change house Friday

Week 2

Change house Friday

Week 3

Change house Friday

Week 4

Change house Friday

Total handoffs: 4

Winner? Math.

It is too hard on the kids. They don't have a real home.

_____

Kids may not feel like they can settle into one home when they share their time between two homes, and this can be hard. I worry about this for my kids and other kids, and here is where I land:

+ You can spend your whole childhood—heck, your whole *life*—in a place and never feel at home.

+ It is possible to feel at home in more than one house. People can feel at home in their own house plus that of a loving relative or a second, summer home. As an adult, you may feel at home in your primary home as well as your parents' home.

+ When kids do feel unsettled by a weekly back-and-forth, that upset is less disruptive than the alternative: living primarily with one parent while losing the second one mostly or entirely.

+ There are many, many benefits to children who are raised in a separated family where care time and love are equal: the benefit of learning from two different ways of life, a larger orbit of friends, family, love, and family customs and traditions. I often think about how my own children benefit from having stepparents on both sides and their unique talents, love, and spheres. What better gift than to expose children to as many different ways to live? For example, at our house, we belong to a liberal church, and at their dad's house, they do not attend church. However, my daughter sometimes attends a conservative church with her friends. As a parent, I hope to expose her to many different experiences so she can find her own meaningful path in life, and I welcome the different experiences she can only get outside one parent's home.

It's so hard to bring all the stuff back and forth. Doesn't one primary home make it easier on kids?

It can be hard on kids to be living between two places, and the daily rhythm of life can get muddled when your viola or hockey gear or essay always seems to be at the other house. This is primarily about parents working together to come up with common-sense solutions.

Some practical advice on this topic includes acquiring multiples and duplicates of as many things as you can: diapers, pajamas, car seats, socks, underwear and clothes, electronics chargers, sports gear, and art and school supplies.

Another important part of easing this particular type of stress is for parents to live close to each other. This brings up big, ethical issues about parents' rights to live where they want, pursue professional opportunities, and be near a new lover, but if we agree now that the priority is to successfully parent these shared kids, living as close together as possible (though on the same street may be asking too much for many exes!) is an incredible benefit to all parties involved. Not only are parents not spending so much time shuttling kids in the car but that inevitable last-minute exchange of the dress pants for the honors ceremony becomes less of a trigger, which reduces conflict with the co-parents and children alike. Life is just so much easier on all levels when you live within a walk or short bike or car ride.

The other important way co-parenting can reduce the everyday friction of raising kids between two homes is to reject current parenting trends.

First of all, I urge you to downgrade any economic expectations you may have had when parenting. The realities are that most people in the United States live with consumer debt while also housing far more items than they need or can even use, as evidenced by our overflowing landfills, the rise of Facebook Marketplace, and mini storage facilities mushrooming around the country. We shop too much, buy too much stuff, and cannot afford the stuff we buy. Divorced and separated families are poorer than other families. It is always more expensive to maintain two houses than one.

Be the change you want to see: buy your kids only what they need, and reject the urge to indulge them in new and fancy products—especially when kids are little and cycling through clothes and toys monthly.

Second, resist the pressure to helicopter parent, and lean into free-range parenting. My friend Lenore Skenazy has been working on this issue for fifteen years, wrote the book, hosted the TV show, and now runs the nonprofit Let Grow to promote more free play and more independence and help parents and educators understand that the world is safe to let our kids do what decades of social science and millennia of history have proven out: kids need independence, free play, and time away from adults in order to grow up healthy and well-rounded. They don't need more stuff.

Though it is a wise and simple investment to duplicate items in order to minimize the stress of having something your kid needs at the other parents' house, there's a limit to everything. Better to buy four pairs of pants instead of two than to splurge on every high-tech gadget your kid could ever want.

This fits into an argument for equal parenting for separated moms and dads by first freeing us from the notion that kids need maximum time with their parents and also asserting that, starting at even age four or five, kids can become responsible for their belongings at each parent's house, move between the homes alone to fetch a needed homework assignment (given they live within a reasonable walk or bike ride), and otherwise be empowered to be independent on these practical matters. This is good for the kids, good for co-parenting tensions, and good for parents!

AFTERWORD

I recently spoke with Pam, a stay-at-home mom who fought hard for majority time with her kids until her attorney informed her that despite her surgeon husband's previous apathy toward the children and that yes, he was probably fighting for 50/50 to punish her, judges in their community were mostly ordering equal schedules. Her attorney also shared the research with her that demonstrates that kids fare better with equally shared parenting. Reluctantly, she agreed to 50/50. Five years later, she wouldn't have it any other way but equal.

"People in my town come up to me all the time and tell me that they wish they had what we had, that we are so amazing," Pam told me, adding how great all four of her kids were doing, how she was happily remarried, and how her ex stunned her in becoming the involved father they all deserved.

Choosing a 50/50 parenting schedule is likely not only a change from anything you've considered but also a change from any culture you have known. Just as divorce or a breakup promises something better than your relationship, so too does equal parenting—an antidote for the deep struggles that face children, men, women, and our communities when we stick to old models. Often, the change is only a matter of moving around a few days each month, but it can create a seismic shift in how each member of the family sees and trusts one another, manages their time, and takes on responsibilities. A 50/50 schedule is activism. It is being the change you want to see, and it is a powerful way we really, truly can care for one another.

ACKNOWLEDGMENTS

The 50/50 Solution exists in gratitude to so many.

To Helena and Lucas, who I hope will be proud of their mom and enjoy a future world abundant in equality, love, and family. Thanks for being so cool and inspiring. To the shared parenting activists and researchers who have done so much already and generously shared your expertise with me, a tiny sampling of which includes National Parenting Organization and its leaders Don Hubin, Matt Hale, Ashley-Nicole Russell, and Ginger Gentile, and in memory of Greg Wood; Terry Brennan, Linda Nielsen, Jennifer Harman, Bill Fabricius, and Ed Kruk. There are so many others. Special thanks to Kate Hanley—you know this book would not exist without you! To agent Wendy Sherman and editor Anna Michels— you took a chance on a big idea, and that is everything. To the very bestest friend ever, Kirsten Searer. To have one such friend in a lifetime is an extraordinary gift. And to the many laughs, words of support, love, meals, tears, and kindness of

Acknowledgments

Jennifer Light, Cynthia Ramnarance, Trae Bodge, Heather Ernst, Jessica Pooley, Betsy and Kris Smith, Josh, Susan, Jac, Cindy Johnson, Emmanuel, and Alero. To the old feminists and the new feminists. And especially to Mitch.

NOTES

Introduction: Equal Rights, Equal Responsibility

Timothy Grall, "Custodial Mothers and Fathers and Their Child Support: 2017," United States Census Bureau, May 2020, https://www.census.gov/content/dam/Census/library/publications/2020/demo/p60-269.pdf.

Grall, "Custodial Mothers and Fathers."

William V. Fabricius et al., "Father-Child Relationships: The Missing Link between Parenting Time and Children's Mental and Physical Health," in *Parenting Plan Evaluations: Applied Research for the Family Court*, ed. Leslie Drozd, Michael Saini, and Nancy Olesen, 2nd ed. (New York: Oxford University Press, 2016), 74–84, https://doi.org/10.1093/med:psych/9780199396580.003.0004.

Claudia Goldin, in discussion with the author, Sept. 1, 2021.

Chapter 1: The Cult of Motherhood and Gender Gaps

Margaret Mead, "Some Theoretical Considerations on the Problem of Mother-Child Separation," *American Journal of Orthopsychiatry*, 1954, 24: 471–483, https://doi.org/10.1111/j.1939-0025.1954.tb06122.x.

Linda Nielsen, in discussion with the author, May 4, 2022.

Darcy Lockman, "Don't Be Grateful That Dad Does His Share," *The Atlantic*, May 7, 2019, https://www.theatlantic.com/ideas/archive/2019/05/mothers-shouldnt-be-grateful-their-husbands-help/588787/; American Time Use

Survey, Bureau of Labor Statistics, "Table A-7A. Time spent in primary activities by married mothers and fathers by employment status of self and spouse, average for the combined years 2011–15, own household child under age 18." Retrieved July 31, 2023, from https://www.bls.gov/tus/tables/a7_1115.pdf.

Laura M. Vowels et al., "Systematic Review and Theoretical Comparison of Children's Outcomes in Post-Separation Living Arrangements," PLoS One 18(6): e0288112 (June 2023): https://doi.org/10.1371/journal.pone.0288112.

Joanna R. Pepin and David A. Cotter, "Trending towards Traditionalism? Changes in Youths' Gender Ideology," Council on Contemporary Families, April 6, 2017, https://thesocietypages.org/ccf/2017/04/06/trending-towards-traditionalism-changes-in-youths-gender-ideology/.

Claire Cain Miller, "Young Men Embrace Gender Equality, but They Still Don't Vacuum," New York Times, February 11, 2020, https://www.nytimes.com/2020/02/11/upshot/gender-roles-housework.html.

"American Time Use Survey—2021 results," Bureau of Labor Statistics, U.S. Department of Labor, June 23, 2022, https://www.bls.gov/news.release/pdf/atus.pdf.

Rachel Minkin and Juliana Menasce Horowitz, "Parenting in America Today: Gender and Parenting," Pew Research Center, January 24, 2023, https://www.pewresearch.org/social-trends/2023/01/24/gender-and-parenting/.

Darcy Lockman, All the Rage: Mothers, Fathers, and the Myth of Equal Partnership (New York: Harper Collins, 2019), 123.

Francesca Donner, "The Household Work Men and Women Do, and Why," New York Times, February 12, 2020, https://www.nytimes.com/2020/02/12/us/the-household-work-men-and-women-do-and-why.html.

Joanna Syrda, "Gendered Housework: Spousal Relative Income, Parenthood and Traditional Gender Identity Norms," Work, Employment and Society 37, no. 3 (June 2023): 794–813, https://doi.org/10.1177/09500170211069780.

Paola Scommegna, "Married Women with Children and Male Partners Do More Housework Than Single Moms," Population Reference Bureau, May 8, 2020, https://www.prb.org/resources/married-women-with-children-and-male-partners-do-more-housework-than-single-moms/.

Minkin and Horowitz, "Gender and Parenting."

Mary Mark Ockerbloom, ed., "Caroline Norton (1808–1877)," A Celebration of Women Writers, accessed February 27, 2023, https://digital.library.upenn.edu/women/norton/nc-biography.html#section4.

John Wroath, Until They Are Seven: The Origin of Women's Legal Rights (Sherfield on Loddon, England: Waterside Press, 1998), 99.

Mary Ann Mason, *From Father's Property to Children's Rights: The History of Child Custody in the United States* (New York: Columbia University Press, 1994), 53.

Mason, *From Father's Property*, 169.

Inge Bretherton, "The Origins of Attachment Theory: John Bowlby and Mary Ainsworth," *Developmental Psychology* 28, no. 5 (1992): 759–75, https://psycnet.apa.org/doi/10.1037/0012–1649.28.5.759.

John Bowlby, "The Influence of Early Environment in the Development of Neurosis and Neurotic Character," *International Journal of Psycho-Analysis* 21 (1940): 154–78, https://psycnet.apa.org/record/1940-04574-001.

John Bowlby, *Child Care and the Growth of Love* (Harmondsworth, UK: Penguin Books, 1953), 53.

Marga Vicedo, *The Nature and Nurture of Love: From Imprinting to Attachment in Cold War America* (Chicago and London: University of Chicago Press, 2013), 73.

John Bowlby, "Should Mothers of Young Children Work?," *Ladies Home Journal*, November 1958.

John Bowlby, "The Nature of the Child's Tie to His Mother," *International Journal of Psycho-Analysis* 39, no. 5 (September–October 1958): 350–73, https://pubmed.ncbi.nlm.nih.gov/13610508/.

Robbie Duschinsky, Monica Greco, and Judith Solomon, "The Politics of Attachment: Lines of Flight with Bowlby, Deleuze and Guattari," *Theory, Culture & Society* 32, no. 7–8 (December 2015): 173–95, https://doi.org/10.1177/0263276415605577.

Nikki Graff, "Most Americans Say Children Are Better Off with a Parent at Home," Pew Research Center, October 10, 2016, https://www.pewresearch.org/short-reads/2016/10/10/most-americans-say-children-are-better-off-with-a-parent-at-home/; Megan Leonhardt, "Americans Don't Assume Moms Will Stay Home with Their Kids, but the Gender Pay Gap, Motherhood Penalty, and Childcare Crisis Makes It Hard for Them to Keep Working," *Fortune*, March 26, 2023, https://fortune.com/2023/03/26/americans-dont-assume-moms-will-stay-home-with-their-kids-anymore/.

"The Mom Gig," *Redbook*, June 6, 2016, https://www.redbookmag.com/life/mom-kids/a43578/stay-at-home-mom-survey/.

Kathleen L. McGinn, Mayra Ruiz Castro, and Elizabeth Long Lingo, "Learning from Mum: Cross-National Evidence Linking Maternal Employment and Adult Children's Outcomes," *Work, Employment and Society* 33, no. 3 (June 2019): 374–400, https://doi.org/10.1177/0950017018760167.

Kathleen McGinn, in discussion with the author, Aug. 30, 2016.

Notes

"Modern Parenthood," Pew Research Center, March 14, 2013, http://www
.pewsocialtrends.org/2013/03/14/modern-parenthood-roles-of-moms-and
-dads-converge-as-they-balance-work-and-family/.

"Occupations of Women in the Labor Force Since 1920," Women's Bureau,
U.S. Department of Labor, accessed February 13, 2023, https://www.dol.gov
/agencies/wb/data/occupations-decades-100; "Labor Force Participation
Rate of Women by Age," Women's Bureau, U.S. Department of Labor, accessed
February 13, 2023, https://www.dol.gov/agencies/wb/data/lfp/women-by-age.

Stephanie Coontz, "The American Family," *Life*, May 31, 1997, https://www
.stephaniecoontz.com/node/350.

"Total Fall Enrollment in Degree-Granting Postsecondary Institutions, by
Attendance Status, Sex of Student, and Control of Institution: Selected Years,
1947 through 2030," National Center for Education Statistics, accessed
February 13, 2023, https://nces.ed.gov/programs/digest/d21/tables/dt21
_303.10.asp.

"Quantifying America's Gender Pay Gap by Race/Ethnicity," National Partnership
for Women and Families, April 2023, https://www.nationalpartnership.org
/our-work/resources/economic-justice/fair-pay/quantifying-americas
-gender-wage-gap.pdf.

Ana Hernández Kent and Lowell R. Rickets, "Gender Wealth Gap: Families
Headed by Women Have Lower Wealth," January 12, 2021, https://www
.stlouisfed.org/en/publications/in-the-balance/2021/gender-wealth-gap
-families-women-lower-wealth.

"Q1 2023 Key Findings Reveal Progress in Gender Diversity on U.S. Corporate
Boards, but More Work Is Needed for Equitable Inclusion," 50–50 Women
on Boards, https://5050wob.com/wp-content/uploads/2023/05/5050WOB
-Q1–23-Infographic-FINAL.pdf.

Rebecca Leppert and Drew Desilver, "118th Congress Has a Record Number of
Women," Pew Research Center, January 3, 2023,https://www.pewresearch.org
/short-reads/2023/01/03/118th-congress-has-a-record-number-of-women/.

Emily A. Kuhl, "Gender Pay Gap Contributes to Increased Rates of Depression
and Anxiety among Women," American Psychiatric Association Foundation
Center for Workplace Mental Health, updated December 2016, https://
workplacementalhealth.org/Mental-Health-Topics/Depression/gender-pay
-gap-contributes-to-increased-rates-of-d.

Carolina Aragão, "Gender Pay Gap in U.S. Hasn't Changed Much in Two
Decades," Pew Research Center, March 1, 2023, https://www.pewresearch
.org/short-reads/2023/03/01/gender-pay-gap-facts/.

Jessica Grose, "Male Executives Don't Feel Guilt, See Work-Life Balance as a Woman's Problem," Slate, March 5, 2014, https://slate.com/human-interest /2014/03/harvard-business-review-study-on-work-life-balance-male -executives-see-family-issues-as-a-women-s-problem.html.

Yuan-Chiao Lu, Regine Walker, Patrick Richard, and Mustafa Younis. "Inequalities in Poverty and Income between Single Mothers and Fathers," *International Journal of Environmental Research and Public Health* 17, no. 1 (2020): 135.

Kids Count Data Center, "Children in Single-Parent Families by Race and Ethnicity in the United States," The Annie E. Casey Foundation, January 2023, https://datacenter.aecf.org/data/tables/107-children-in-single-parent -families-by-race-and-ethnicity#detailed/1/any/false/2048,1729,37,871,870 ,573,869,36,868,867/10,11,9,12,1,185,13/432,431.

"Characteristics of Public School Teachers," National Center for Education Statistics, updated May 2023, https://nces.ed.gov/programs/coe/indicator /clr.

"Fast Facts: Mothers in the Workforce," American Association of University Women, accessed February 13, 2023, https://www.aauw.org/resources /article/fast-facts-working-moms/.

Amanada Barroso and Anna Brown, "Gender Pay Gap in U.S. Held Steady in 2020," Pew Research Center, May 25, 2021, https://web.archive.org/web /20210525160426/https://www.pewresearch.org/fact-tank/2021/05/25 /gender-pay-gap-facts/.

Katherine Schaeffer, "Working Moms in the U.S. Have Faced Challenges on Multiple Fronts during the Pandemic," Pew Research Center, May 6, 2022, https://www.pewresearch.org/fact-tank/2022/05/06/working-moms-in-the -u-s-have-faced-challenges-on-multiple-fronts-during-the-pandemic/.

Jill E. Yavorsky, Lisa A. Keister, and Yue Qian, "Gender in the One Percent," *Contexts* 19, no. 1 (Winter 2020): 12–17, https://doi.org/10.1177/1536504220902196.

Sreedhari D. Desai, Dolly Chugh, and Arthur Brief, "The Organizational Implications of a Traditional Marriage: Can a Domestic Traditionalist by Night Be an Organizational Egalitarian by Day?," UNC Kenan-Flagler Research Paper No. 2013–19, March 12, 2012, https://doi.org/10.2139/ssrn .2018259.

Jill Filipovic (@JillFilipovic), "More mothers at home makes for worse, more sexist men who see," Twitter, April 12, 2022, 8:53 AM, https://twitter.com /JillFilipovic/status/1513862962297163781.

Daniel Fernandez-Kranz and Natalia Nollenberger, "The Impact of Equal Parenting Time Laws on Family Outcomes and Risky Behavior by Teenagers:

Evidence from Spain," *Journal of Economic Behavior & Organization* 195 (March 2022): 303–25, https://doi.org/10.1016/j.jebo.2022.01.001.

Caroline Norton, *Observations on the Natural Claim of the Mother to the Custody of Her Infant Children as Affected by the Common Law Right of the Father* (London: James Ridgway and Sons, 1837), https://www.google.com/books/edition /Observations_on_the_natural_claim_of_the/xSz8Ks3uqBAC?hl=en& gbpv=1&printsec=frontcover.

Nielsen, discussion.

Jodi Pawluski, in discussion with the author, May 22, 2023.

Nielsen, discussion.

Sarah M. Allen and Alan J. Hawkins, "Maternal Gatekeeping: Mothers' Beliefs and Behaviors That Inhibit Greater Father Involvement in Family Work," *Journal of Marriage and Family* 61, no. 1 (February 1999): 199–212, https:// doi.org/10.2307/353894.

Xinghua Wang et al., "Linking Maternal Gatekeeping to Child Outcomes in Dual-Earner Families in China: The Mediating Role of Father Involvement," *Early Child Development and Care* 191, no. 2 (2021): 187–97, https://doi.org/10.1080 /03004430.2019.1611568; Yi-Chan Tu, Jen-Chun Chang, and Tsai-Feng Kao, "A Study on the Relationships between Maternal Gatekeeping and Paternal Involvement in Taiwan," *Procedia—Social and Behavioral Sciences* 122 (March 2014): 319–28, https://doi.org/10.1016/j.sbspro.2014.01.1347.

Edward Kruk, "The Disengaged Noncustodial Father: Implications for Social Work Practice with the Divorced Family," *Social Work* 39, no. 1 (January 1994): 15–25, https://www.jstor.org/stable/ 23717019.

Chapter 2: Beyond the Male Breadwinner

Kevin Bremond, in discussion with the author, January 23, 2023.

Michael Rosenfeld, "Who Wants the Breakup? Gender and Breakup in Heterosexual Couples," presented August 22, 2015, at the American Sociological Association's Annual Meeting in Chicago.

Grall, "Custodial Mothers and Fathers."

Augustine J. Kposowa, "Marital Status and Suicide in the National Longitudinal Mortality Study," *Journal of Epidemiology & Community Health* 54, no. 4 (2000): 254–61, https://doi.org/10.1136/jech.54.4.254.

Augustine J. Kposowa, "Divorce and Suicide Risk," *Journal of Epidemiology & Community Health* 57, no. 12 (2003): 993. http://dx.doi.org/10.1136/jech.57.12.993.

E. Ann Carson, "Prisoners in 2021—Statistical Tables." U.S. Department of Justice, December 2022, https://bjs.ojp.gov/sites/g/files/xyckuh236/files/media/document/p21st.pdf.

Elizabeth Arias et al., "Provisional Life Expectancy Estimates for 2021," National Vital Statistics System, August 2022, https://www.cdc.gov/nchs/data/vsrr/vsrr023.pdf.

Jonathan Rothwell, "Scarred Boys, Idle Men: Family Adversity, Poor Health, and Male Labor Force Participation," Institute for Family Studies, January 17, 2023, https://ifstudies.org/blog/scarred-boys-idle-men-family-adversity-poor-health-and-male-labor-force-participation.

Grall, "Custodial Mothers and Fathers."

"Mental Illness," National Institute of Mental Health, updated March 2023, https://www.nimh.nih.gov/health/statistics/mental-illness.

"Men's Mental Health: 40 Percent of Men Won't Talk about Their Mental Health," Priory, accessed August 31, 2022, https://www.priorygroup.com/blog/40-of-men-wont-talk-to-anyone-about-their-mental-health.

"Suicide," National Institute of Mental Health, updated May 2023, https://www.nimh.nih.gov/health/statistics/suicide.

Fatih Guvenen, Greg Kaplan, Jae Song, and Justin Weidner. "Lifetime Earnings in the United States over Six Decades," *American Economic Journal: Applied Economics* 14, no. 4 (2022): 446–479.

Rakesh Kochhar, "Women Make Gains in the Workplace amid a Rising Demand for Skilled Workers," Pew Research Center, January 30, 2020, https://www.pewresearch.org/social-trends/2020/01/30/womens-lead-in-skills-and-education-is-helping-narrow-the-gender-wage-gap/.

Kelly Field, "The Problem Nobody's Talking About," *Chronicle of Higher Education*, June 14, 2022, https://www.chronicle.com/article/the-problem-nobodys-talking-about.

Daniel A. Cox, "The State of American Friendship: Change, Challenges, and Loss," Survey Center on American Life, June 8, 2021, https://www.americansurveycenter.org/research/the-state-of-american-friendship-change-challenges-and-loss/.

Kenneth D. Kochanek, Robert N. Anderson, and Elizabeth Arias, "Changes in Life Expectancy at Birth, 2010–2018," National Center for Health Statistics, January 30, 2020, https://www.cdc.gov/nchs/data/hestat/life-expectancy/life-expectancy-2018.htm.

José Manuel Aburto et al., "Quantifying Impacts of the COVID-19 Pandemic through Life-Expectancy Losses: A Population-Level Study of 29 Countries,"

International Journal of Epidemiology 51, no. 1 (February 2022): 63–74, https://doi.org/10.1093/ije/dyab207.

Anne Case and Angus Deaton, "Rising Morbidity and Mortality in Midlife Among White Non-Hispanic Americans in the 21st Century," *Proceedings of the National Academy of Sciences* 112, no. 49 (November 2, 2015): 15078–15083, https://doi.org/10.1073/pnas.1518393112.

"Male Supremacy," Southern Poverty Law Center, accessed on July 19, 2023 from https://www.splcenter.org/fighting-hate/extremist-files/ideology/male-supremacy.

Daniel De Visé, "Most Young Men Are Single. Most Young Women Are Not," *Hill*, February 22, 2023, https://thehill.com/blogs/blog-briefing-room/3868557-most-young-men-are-single-most-young-women-are-not/; Karen Benjamin Guzzo, "Childbearing Desires, Intentions, and Attitudes among Childless Adults 40–49," National Center for Family and Marriage Research, 2022, https://doi.org/10.25035/ncfmr/fp-22-11.

Laura Bates, "Men Going Their Own Way: The Rise of a Toxic Male Separatist Movement," *Guardian*, August 26, 2020, https://www.theguardian.com/lifeandstyle/2020/aug/26/men-going-their-own-way-the-toxic-male-separatist-movement-that-is-now-mainstream.

Lydia R. Anderson, Paul F. Hemez, and Rose M. Kreider, "Living Arrangements of Children: 2019," United States Census Bureau, February 2022, https://www.census.gov/content/dam/Census/library/publications/2022/demo/p70-174.pdf.

Fabricius et al., "Father-Child Relationships."

Leah Wang, "Both Sides of the Bars: How Mass Incarceration Punishes Families," Prison Policy Initiative, August 11, 2002, https://www.prisonpolicy.org/blog/2022/08/11/parental_incarceration/.

"Parenting in America: Satisfaction, Time and Support," Pew Research Center, December 17, 2015, https://www.pewresearch.org/social-trends/2015/12/17/2-satisfaction-time-and-support/#parenting-matters-to-overall-identity.

Gretchen Livingston, "Most Dads Say They Spend Too Little Time with Their Children; About a Quarter Live Apart from Them," Pew Research Center, January 8, 2018, https://www.pewresearch.org/fact-tank/2018/01/08/most-dads-say-they-spend-too-little-time-with-their-children-about-a-quarter-live-apart-from-them/.

"Parenting in America."

Jordan Shapiro, *Father Figure: How to Be a Feminist Dad* (New York, Little, Brown Spark, 2021), x.

Bremond, discussion.

Kim Parker and Renee Stepler, "Americans See Men as the Financial Providers, Even as Women's Contributions Grow," Pew Research Center, September 20, 2017, https://www.pewresearch.org/fact-tank/2017/09/20/americans -see-men-as-the-financial-providers-even-as-womens-contributions-grow/.

Sanford L. Braver and William A. Griffin, "Engaging Fathers in the Post-Divorce Family," *Marriage & Family Review* 29, no. 4 (2000): 247–67, https://doi.org /10.1300/J002v29n04_02.

Malin Bergström, in discussion with author, July 3, 2022.

Bremond, discussion.

Erol Ricketts, "The Origin of Black Female-Headed Families," *Focus* 12, no. 1 (Spring/Summer 1989): 32–36, https://www.irp.wisc.edu/publications/focus /pdfs/foc121e.pdf.

Jason L. Riley, "An Alternative Black History Month," *Wall Street Journal*, February 10, 2016, https://www.wsj.com/articles/an-alternative-black-history-month-1455063609.

Gretchen Livingston and Kim Parker, "A Tale of Two Fathers," Pew Research Center, June 15, 2011, https://www.pewresearch.org/social-trends/2011/06 /15/chapter-1-living-arrangements-and-father-involvement/.

Joyce A. Martin et al., "Births: Final Data for 2018," *National Vital Statistics Reports* 68, no. 13 (November 27, 2019), https://www.cdc.gov/nchs/data/nvsr/nvsr68 /nvsr68_13–508.pdf.

Jason L. Riley, "Still Right on the Black Family after All These Years," *Wall Street Journal*, February 10, 2015, https://www.wsj.com/articles/jason-l-riley-still -right-on-the-black-family-after-all-these-years-1423613625.

Bremond, discussion.

Juju Chang et al., "A Father's Fight to Win Back His Daughter Secretly Put up for Adoption," ABC News, September 15, 2015, https://abcnews.go.com/US /fathers-fight-win-back-daughter-secretly-put-adoption/story?id=33237316.

Torsten Dahlén et al., "The Frequency of Misattributed Paternity in Sweden Is Low and Decreasing: A Nationwide Cohort Study," *Journal of Internal Medicine* 291, no. 1 (January 2022): 95–100, https://doi.org/10.1111/joim .13351; Mark A. Bellis et al., "Measuring Paternal Discrepancy and Its Public Health Consequences," *Journal of Epidemiology and Community Health* 59, no. 9 (2005): 749–54, https://doi.org/10.1136/jech.2005.036517.

Karin Modig et al., "Payback Time? Influence of Having Children on Mortality in Old Age," *Journal of Epidemiology and Community Health* 71, no. 5 (2017): 424–30, https://doi.org/10.1136/jech-2016–207857.

Craig F. Garfield, Anthony Isacco, and Wendy D. Bartlo, "Men's Health and Fatherhood in the Urban Midwestern United States," *International Journal of Men's Health* 9, no. 3 (2010): 161–74, https://doi.org/10.3149/jmh.0903.161.

Shelley J. Correll, Stephen Benard, and In Paik, "Getting a Job: Is There a Motherhood Penalty?," *American Journal of Sociology* 112, no. 5 (March 2007): 1297–338, https://doi.org/10.1086/511799.

Jamie J. Ladge and Beth K. Humberd, "Impossible Standards and Unlikely Trade-Offs: Can Fathers Be Competent Parents and Professionals?," in *Engaged Fatherhood for Men, Families and Gender Equality*, ed. Marc Grau Grau, Mireia las Heras Maestro, and Hannah Riley Bowles (Cham, Switzerland: Springer, 2022), 183–96, https://doi.org/10.1007/978-3-030-75645-1_10.

Jamie J. Ladge et al., "Updating the Organizational Man: Fathers in the Workplace," *Academy of Management Perspectives* 29, no. 1 (February 2015): 152–71, https://doi.org/10.5465/amp.2013.0078.

Sharin Baldwin et al., "Mental Health and Wellbeing during the Transition to Fatherhood: A Systematic Review of First-Time Fathers' Experiences," *JBI Database of Systematic Reviews and Implementation Reports* 16, no. 11 (November 2018): 2118–91, https://doi.org/10.11124/JBISRIR-2017–003773.

Chien-Chung Huang and Lynn A. Warner, "Relationship Characteristics and Depression among Fathers with Newborns," *Social Service Review* 79, no. 1 (March 2005): 95–118, https://doi.org/10.1086/426719.

Janella Street, in discussion with the author, January 30, 2023.

William J. Chopik and Robin S. Edelstein, "Retrospective Memories of Parental Care and Health from Mid to Late Life," *Health Psychology* 38, no. 1 (2019): 84–93, https://doi.org/10.1037/hea0000694.

Kruk, "Disengaged Noncustodial Father."

Nicholas Zill, "Facts about Custodial and Non-Custodial Fathers in the U.S.," Institute for Family Studies, June 16, 2020, https://ifstudies.org/blog/facts-about-custodial-and-non-custodial-fathers-in-the-us.

Calvina Z. Ellerbe, Jerrett B. Jones, and Marcia J. Carlson, "Race/Ethnic Differences in Nonresident Fathers' Involvement after a Nonmarital Birth," *Social Science Quarterly* 99, no. 3 (September 2018): 1158–82, https://doi.org/10.1111/ssqu.12482.

Jay Fagan, "The Myth of Low-Income Black Fathers' Absence from the Lives of Adolescents," *Journal of Family Issues* (January 2023), https://doi.org/10.1177/0192513X221150987.

Anna Machin, *The Life of Dad: The Making of a Modern Father* (London: Simon & Schuster, 2018), 5.

Mónica Sobral et al., "Neurobiological Correlates of Fatherhood during the Postpartum Period: A Scoping Review," *Frontiers in Psychology* 13 (2022): 745767, https://doi.org/10.3389/fpsyg.2022.745767.

Machin, *The Life of Dad*, 39.

Pilyoung Kim et al., "Neural Plasticity in Fathers of Human Infants," *Social Neuroscience* 9, no. 5 (2014): 522–35, https://doi.org/10.1080/17470919.2014.933713.

Katherine R. Wilson and Margot R. Prior, "Father Involvement: The Importance of Paternal Solo Care," *Early Child Development and Care* 180, no. 10 (2010): 1391–405, https://doi.org/10.1080/03004430903172335.

Geoffrey L. Brown et al., "Associations between Father Involvement and Father-Child Attachment Security: Variations Based on Timing and Type of Involvement," *Journal of Family Psychology* 32, no. 8 (2018): 1015–24, https://doi.org/10.1037/fam0000472.

Chapter 3: Shared Parenting *Is* in the Best Interest of the Child

"Is Shared Parenting a Good Idea in High Conflict Divorces? Interview with Dr. William Fabricius," National Parents Organization, February 17, 2021, YouTube video, 25:25, https://www.youtube.com/watch?v=SRm8blv6O0Y.

Laura M. Vowels et al., "Systematic Review and Theoretical Comparison of Children's Outcomes in Post-Separation Living Arrangements," *PLoS One* 18(6): e0288112 (June 2023): https://doi.org/10.1371/journal.pone.0288112.

Linda Nielsen, "Joint versus Sole Physical Custody: Outcomes for Children Independent of Family Income or Parental Conflict," *Journal of Child Custody* 15, no. 1 (2018): 34–54, https://doi.org/10.1080/15379418.2017.1422414.

Nielsen, discussion.

Nielsen, discussion.

Lars-Erik Malmberg et al., "The Influence of Mothers' and Fathers' Sensitivity in the First Year of Life on Children's Cognitive Outcomes at 18 and 36 Months," *Child: Care, Health and Development* 42, no. 1 (January 2016): 1–7, https://doi.org/10.1111/cch.12294.

Natasha J. Cabrera, Jacqueline D. Shannon, and Catherine Tamis-LeMonda, "Fathers' Influence on Their Children's Cognitive and Emotional Development: From Toddlers to Pre-K," *Applied Development Science* 11, no. 4 (2007): 208–13, https://doi.org/10.1080/10888690701762100.

Malmberg, et al., "Influence of Mothers' and Fathers' Sensitivity."

María Cristina Richaud de Minzi, "Loneliness and Depression in Middle and Late Childhood: The Relationship to Attachment and Parental Styles," *Journal of Genetic Psychology: Research and Theory on Human Development* 167, no. 2 (2006): 189–210, https://doi.org/10.3200/GNTP.167.2.189–210.

Machin, *Life of Dad*, 166.

Va. Code Ann. § 20–124.3 (2020), https://law.lis.virginia.gov/vacode/title20/chapter6.1/section20–124.3/.

William Fabricius, in discussion with the author, May 12, 2021.

Sara McLanahan, Laura Tach, and Daniel Schneider, "The Causal Effects of Father Absence," *Annual Review of Sociology* 39 (July 2013): 399–427, https://doi.org/10.1146/annurev-soc-071312–145704.

Sanford L. Braver, Ira M. Ellman, and William V. Fabricius, "Relocation of Children after Divorce and Children's Best Interests: New Evidence and Legal Considerations," *Journal of Family Psychology* 17, no. 2 (June 2003): 206–19, https://doi.org/10.1037/0893–3200.17.2.206.

"Moving with Children after Separation or Divorce," Michigan Legal Help, accessed February 16, 2023, https://michiganlegalhelp.org/self-help-tools/family/moving-children-after-separation-or-divorce; "The 2022 Florida Statutes (Including Special Session A)," Online Sunshine, accessed February 16, 2023, http://www.leg.state.fl.us/statutes/index.cfm?App_mode=Display_Statute&URL=0000–0099/0061/Sections/0061.13001.html.

Debrina Washington, "Child Custody Relocation Rules and Considerations," Verywell Family, April 9, 2021, https://www.verywellfamily.com/child-custody-relocation-rules-2997618.

Matthew M. Stevenson et al., "Associations between Parental Relocation following Separation in Childhood and Maladjustment in Adolescence and Young Adulthood," *Psychology, Public Policy, and Law* 24, no. 3 (August 2018): 365–78, https://doi.org/10.1037/law0000172.

"Fast Facts: Preventing Adverse Childhood Experiences," Centers for Disease Control and Prevention, updated June 29, 2023, https://www.cdc.gov/violenceprevention/aces/fastfact.html.

William V. Fabricius and Linda J. Luecken, "Postdivorce Living Arrangements, Parent Conflict, and Long-Term Physical Health Correlates for Children of Divorce," *Journal of Family Psychology* 21, no. 2 (June 2007): 195–205, https://doi.org/10.1037/0893–3200.21.2.195.

Takashi X. Fujisawa et al., "Oxytocin Receptor DNA Methylation and Alterations of Brain Volumes in Maltreated Children," *Neuropsychopharmacology* 44, no. 12 (November 2019): 2045–53, https://doi.org/10.1038/s41386-019-0414-8.

Felicitas Auersperg et al., "Long-Term Effects of Parental Divorce on Mental Health—A Meta-Analysis," *Journal of Psychiatric Research* 119 (December 2019): 107–15, https://doi.org/10.1016/j.jpsychires.2019.09.011.

Joan B. Kelly, "Children's Living Arrangements following Separation and Divorce: Insights from Empirical and Clinical Research," *Family Process* 46, no. 1 (March 2007): 35–52, https://doi.org/10.1111/j.1545–5300.2006.00190.x.

Nielsen, "Joint versus Sole Physical Custody."

Laura M. Vowels et al., "Systematic Review and Theoretical Comparison of Children's Outcomes in Post-Separation Living Arrangements," PLoS One 18(6): e0288112 (June 2023): https://doi.org/10.1371/journal.pone.0288112.

Nielsen, "Joint versus Sole Physical Custody."

Kim Bastaits and Inge Pasteels, "Is Joint Physical Custody in the Best Interests of the Child? Parent-Child Relationships and Custodial Arrangements," *Journal of Social and Personal Relationships* 36, no. 11–12 (November-December 2019): 3752–72, https://doi.org/10.1177/0265407519838071.

Marsha Kline Pruett et al., "Supporting Father Involvement after Separation and Divorce," in Drozd, Saini, and Olesen, *Parenting Plan Evaluations*, 85–117, https://doi.org/10.1093/med:psych/9780199396580.003.0005.

Kimberlee D'Ardenne, "ASU Psychology Research Leads to International Conversation about Custody Laws," Arizona State University, March 2, 2020, https://news.asu.edu/20200302-asu-psychology-research-leads-international-conversation-about-custody-laws.

Seth Gershenson et al., "The Long-Run Impacts of Same-Race Teachers," *American Economic Journal: Economic Policy* 14, no. 4 (November 2022): 300–342, https://doi.org/10.1257/pol.20190573.

Sarah C. Gomillion and Tracy A. Giuliano, "The Influence of Media Role Models on Gay, Lesbian, and Bisexual Identity," *Journal of Homosexuality* 58, no. 3 (2011): 330–54, https://doi.org/10.1080/00918369.2011.546729.

Lisa A. Serbin, Kimberly K. Powlishta, and Judith Gulko, "The Development of Sex Typing in Middle Childhood," *Monographs of the Society for Research in Child Development* 58, no. 2 (1993): 1–95, https://doi.org/10.2307/1166118.

Alyssa Croft et al., "The Second Shift Reflected in the Second Generation: Do Parents' Gender Roles at Home Predict Children's Aspirations?," *Psychological Science* 25, no. 7 (July 2014): 1418–28, https://doi.org/10.1177/0956797614533968.

Margaretha E. de Looze et al., "The Happiest Kids on Earth: Gender Equality and Adolescent Life Satisfaction in Europe and North America," *Journal of Youth and Adolescence* 47, no. 5 (May 2018): 1073–85, https://doi.org/10

.1007/s10964-017-0756-7; Liz Plank, "Why the Patriarchy Is Killing Men," *Washington Post*, September 13, 2019, https://www.washingtonpost.com /outlook/why-the-patriarchy-is-killing-men/2019/09/12/2490fa7e-d3ea -11e9–86ac-0f250cc91758_story.html.

Malin Bergström et al., "Preschool Children Living in Joint Physical Custody Arrangements Show Less Psychological Symptoms Than Those Living Mostly or Only with One Parent," *Acta Paediatrica* 107, no. 2 (February 2018): 294–300, https://doi.org/10.1111/apa.14004.

William V. Fabricius and Go Woon Suh, "Should Infants and Toddlers Have Frequent Overnight Parenting Time with Fathers? The Policy Debate and New Data," *Psychology, Public Policy, and Law* 23, no. 1 (November 2016): 68–84, http://doi.org/10.1037/law0000108.

Fabricius and Suh, "Should Infants and Toddlers."

Fabricius and Suh, "Should Infants and Toddlers."

Linda Nielsen, "10 Surprising Findings on Shared Parenting after Divorce or Separation," Institute for Family Studies, June 20, 2017, https://ifstudies .org/blog/10-surprising-findings-on-shared-parenting-after-divorce-or -separation; Linda Nielsen, "Re-Examining the Research on Parental Conflict, Coparenting, and Custody Arrangements," *Psychology, Public Policy, and Law* 23, no. 2 (May 2017): 211–31, https://doi.org/10.1037/law0000109.

"Is Shared Parenting a Good Idea in High Conflict Divorces? Interview with Dr. William Fabricius," National Parents Organization, February 17, 2021, YouTube video, 34:46, https://www.youtube.com/watch?v= SRm8blv6O0Y.

Malin Bergström et al., "Living in Two Homes: A Swedish National Survey of Wellbeing in 12 and 15 Year Olds with Joint Physical Custody," *BMC Public Health* 13 (2013): 868, https://doi.org/10.1186/1471-2458-13-868.

Bergström, discussion.

"Is Shared Parenting a Good Idea."

"Is Shared Parenting a Good Idea."

Eleana Armao and Lida Anagnostaki, "Attachment Parenting and Shared Residence" (oral presentation, 6th International Conference on Shared Parenting, Athens, Greece, May 5, 2023), https://athens-2023.org/.

Nielsen, discussion.

Lenore Skenazy, in discussion with the author, October 26, 2022.

Max Roser, "Mortality in the Past: Every Second Child Died," Our World in Data, April 11, 2023, https://ourworldindata.org/child-mortality-in-the-past.

Katharine Olson, "Plague, Famine, and Sudden Death: 10 Dangers of the

Medieval Period," History Extra, July 10, 2020, https://www.historyextra.com /period/medieval/why-did-people-die-danger-medieval-period-life-expectancy/.

Skenazy, discussion.

Jessica Grose, "Parenting Was Never Meant to Be This Isolating," *New York Times*, October 7, 2020, https://www.nytimes.com/2020/10/07/parenting/childcare -history-family.html.

Christine Gross-Loh, *Parenting Without Borders: Surprising Lessons Parents Around the World Can Teach Us* (New York: Avery, 2013), 462.

Barbara Rogoff, *The Cultural Nature of Human Development* (New York: Oxford University Press, 2003), 122–24.

Ariana C. Vasquez et al., "Parent Autonomy Support, Academic Achievement, and Psychosocial Functioning: A Meta-Analysis of Research," *Educational Psychology Review* 28 (September 2016): 605–44, https://doi.org/10.1007 /s10648-015-9329-z.

William Stixrud and Ned Johnson, *The Self-Driven Child: The Science and Sense of Giving Your Kids More Control over Their Lives* (New York: Viking Penguin, 2018), 12.

Laurence van Hansijck de Jonge, "Helicopter Parenting: The Consequences," International School Parent, accessed February 18, 2023, https://www .internationalschoolparent.com/articles/helicopter-parenting-the -consequences/.

Holly H. Schiffrin et al., "Helping or Hovering? The Effects of Helicopter Parenting on College Students' Well-Being," *Psychological Science* 23 (April 2014): 548–57, https://doi.org/10.1007/s10826-013-9716-3.

Skenazy, discussion.

Melissa A. Milkie, Kei M. Nomaguchi, and Kathleen E. Denny, "Does the Amount of Time Mothers Spend with Children or Adolescents Matter?," *Journal of Marriage and Family* 77, no. 2 (April 2015): 355–72, https://doi.org/10.1111 /jomf.12170.

Melissa Milkie, in discussion with the author, Jan. 11, 2023.

Chapter 4: Money Always Matters

Janella Street, discussion.

Felicia R. Lee, "Influential Study on Divorce's Impact Is Said to Be Flawed," *New York Times*, May 9, 1996, https://www.nytimes.com/1996/05/09/garden /influential-study-on-divorce-s-impact-is-said-to-be-flawed.html.

Felicia R. Lee, "Influential Study on Divorce's Impact Is Said to Be Flawed," *New*

York Times, May 9, 1996, https://www.nytimes.com/1996/05/09/garden /influential-study-on-divorce-s-impact-is-said-to-be-flawed.html.

"Retirement Security: Women Still Face Challenges," U.S. Government Accountability Office, July 25, 2012, https://www.gao.gov/products/gao-12-699.

Nicole Kapelle and Janeen Baxter, "Marital Dissolution and Personal Wealth: Examining Gendered Trends across the Dissolution Process," *Journal of Marriage and Family* 83 (2021): 243–259, https://doi.org/10.1111/jomf.12707.

Mia Hakovirta, Daniel R. Meyer, and Christine Skinner, "Does Paying Child Support Impoverish Fathers in the United States, Finland, and the United Kingdom?," *Children and Youth Services Review* 106 (November 2019): 104485, https://doi.org/10.1016/j.childyouth.2019.104485.

Maria Cancian, Daniel R. Meyer, and Robert G. Wood, "Final Impact Findings from the Child Support Noncustodial Parent Employment Demonstration (CSPED)," Institute for Research on Poverty, March 2019, https://www.irp .wisc.edu/wp/wp-content/uploads/2019/07/CSPED-Final-Impact-Report -2019-Compliant.pdf.

Noah Zatz et al., "Get to Work or Go to Jail: Workplace Rights under Threat," UCLA Institute for Research on Labor and Employment, March 2016, https://irle.ucla.edu/wp-content/uploads/2016/03/Get-To-Work-or-Go -To-Jail-Workplace-Rights-Under-Threat.pdf.

Samantha Melamed, "Sheriffs Target 'Deadbeat Dads' with Midnight Raids, Debtor's Prison. But Does It Help the Kids?," *Philadelphia Inquirer,* September 11, 2018, https://www.inquirer.com/philly/news/child-support-arrests -deadbeat-dads-pennsylvania-20180911.html.

Elaine Sorensen et al., "Examining Child Support Arrears in California: The Collectability Study," Urban Institute, March 2003, http://webarchive.urban .org/UploadedPDF/411838_california_child_support.pdf.

Hakovirta, Meyer, and Skinner, "Does Paying Child Support."

Grall, "Custodial Mothers and Fathers."

Deadbeat Parents Punishment Act of 1998, 18 U.S.C. § 228 (2011).

Eli Hager, "These Single Moms Are Forced to Choose: Reveal Their Sexual Histories or Forfeit Welfare," ProPublica, September 17, 2021, https://www .propublica.org/article/to-get-public-assistance-these-single-mothers-are -forced-to-share-intimate-details-about-their-families.

Hager, "Single Moms Are Forced"; "FY 2020 Preliminary Annual Report and Tables," Office of Child Support Services, U.S. Department of Health and Human Services, June 17, 2021, https://www.acf.hhs.gov/css/policy-guidance /fy-2020-preliminary-annual-report-and-data.

Kenya Rahmaan, in discussion with the author, Feb. 4, 2021.

Jane C. Venohr, "Differences in State Child Support Guidelines Amounts: Guidelines Models, Economic Basis, and Other Issues," *Journal of the American Academy of Matrimonial Lawyers* 29, no. 2 (2017): 377–408, https://aaml.org /wp-content/uploads/MAT205_7.pdf.

Kimberly J. Turner and Maureen R. Waller, "Indebted Relationships: Child Support Arrears and Nonresident Fathers' Involvement with Children," *Family Relations* 79, no. 1 (February 2017): 24–43, https://doi.org/10.1111 /jomf.12361.

Jennifer B. Kane, Timothy J. Nelson, and Kathryn Edin, "How Much In-Kind Support Do Low-Income Nonresident Fathers Provide? A Mixed-Method Analysis," *Family Relations* 77, no. 3 (June 2015): 591–611, https://doi.org/10 .1111/jomf.12188.

Jill Rosen, "Many 'Deadbeat Dads' Support Children through Gifts, no Cash, Study Shows," Johns Hopkins Hub, June 15, 2015, https://hub.jhu.edu/2015 /06/15/how-low-income-dads-provide/.

Gina Azito Thompson, Diana Azevedo-McCaffrey, and Da'shon Carr, "Increases in TANF Cash Benefit Levels Are Critical to Help Families Meet Rising Costs," Center on Budget and Policy Priorities, updated February 3, 2023, https:// www.cbpp.org/research/family-income-support/states-must-continue -recent-momentum-to-further-improve-tanf-benefit.

"Rent Determination," Cuyahoga Metropolitan Housing Authority, accessed February 21, 2023, https://www.cmha.net/hcvp/rentdetermination.

Robert Greenstein, "Targeting, Universalism, and Other Factors Affecting Social Programs' Political Strength," Brookings Institution, June 28, 2022, https:// www.brookings.edu/research/targeting-universalism-and-other-factors -affecting-social-programs-political-strength/.

Jason DeParle, "Expanded Safety Net Drives Sharp Drop in Child Poverty," *New York Times*, September 11, 2022, https://www.nytimes.com/2022/09/11/us /politics/child-poverty-analysis-safety-net.html.

Susan Guthrie, in discussion with the author, November 16, 2022.

Wendy Wang, "The Happiness Penalty for Breadwinning Moms," Institute for Family Studies, June 4, 2019, https://ifstudies.org/blog/the-happiness -penalty-for-breadwinning-moms.

"FY 2002 and FY 2003 Annual Report to Congress," Office of Child Support Enforcement, U.S. Department of Health and Human Services, December 1, 2003, https://www.acf.hhs.gov/css/report/fy-2002-and-fy-2003-annual -report-congress; "Preliminary Report FY 2021," Office of Child Support

Enforcement, U.S. Department of Health and Human Services, 2021, https://
www.acf.hhs.gov/sites/default/files/documents/ocse/fy_2021_preliminary
_report.pdf.

Grall, "Custodial Mothers and Fathers."

Chapter 5: A Deeper Look at Domestic Violence Postdivorce

Leigh Goodmark, in discussion with the author, Aug. 30, 2022.

Edward Kruk, "Arguments for an Equal Parental Responsibility Presumption
in Contested Child Custody," *American Journal of Family Therapy* 40, no. 1
(2012): 33–55, https://doi.org/10.1080/01926187.2011.575344.

Megan O'Matz, "He Beat Her Repeatedly. Family Court Tried to Give Him
Joint Custody of Their Children," ProPublica, September 16, 2021, https://
www.propublica.org/article/he-beat-her-repeatedly-family-court-tried-to
-give-him-joint-custody-of-their-children; Barry Goldstein and Veronica
York, "'Shared Parenting' Places Ideology over Children," Center for Judicial
Excellence, August 16, 2022, https://centerforjudicialexcellence.org/2022/08
/16/shared-parenting-places-ideology-over-children/.

Adiel Kaplan, Kate Snow, and Eric Salzman, "Jacqueline Franchetti Says She
Did What She Was Supposed to Do. So Why Did Her Daughter Die?,"
NBC News, May 13, 2021, https://www.nbcnews.com/news/us-news
/jacqueline-says-she-did-everything-she-was-supposed-do-so-n1266982;
Tom Giglio, "Guest Opinion: 'Kayden's Law' Needed to Protect Children in
Family Court," *Bucks County Courier Times*, November 13, 2021, https://www
.buckscountycouriertimes.com/story/opinion/2021/11/13/advocate-kaydens
-law-childrens-safety-family-court/6390111001/.

Jeffrey Kluger, "Domestic Violence Is a Pandemic within the COVID-19 Pandemic,"
Time, February 3, 2021, https://time.com/5928539/domestic-violence-covid-19/.

Hallie Jackson, "Domestic Violence Cases Surge amid Covid-19 Crisis," MSNBC
.com, April 15, 2020, https://www.msnbc.com/hallie-jackson/watch
/domestic-violence-cases-surge-amid-covid-19-crisis-82070085551.

"New Analysis Shows 8% Increase in U.S. Domestic Violence Incidents Following
Pandemic Stay-at-Home Orders," Council on Criminal Justice, accessed
February 22, 2023, https://counciloncj.org/new-analysis-shows-8-increase-in
-u-s-domestic-violence-incidents-following-pandemic-stay-at-home-orders/.

Amy J. Frontz, "National Snapshot of Trends in the National Domestic Violence Hotline's Contact Data before and during the COVID-19 Pandemic," Officer of Inspector General, U.S. Department of Health and Human Services, April 2022, https://oig.hhs.gov/oas/reports/region9/92106000.pdf.

Stephen J. Dubner, "Did Domestic Violence Really Spike during the Pandemic?," June 1, 2022, in *Freakonomics Radio*, produced by Zack Lapinski, podcast, 54:17, https://freakonomics.com/podcast/did-domestic-violence-really-spike-during-the-pandemic/.

Denise A. Hines, "Extent and Implications of the Presentation of False Facts by Domestic Violence Agencies in the United States," *Partner Abuse* 5, no. 1 (January 2014): 69–82, https://doi.org/10.1891/1946-6560.5.1.69.

Louis Jacobson, "How Much Have Domestic Violence Rates Fallen Since the Violence Against Women Act Passed?," PolitiFact, February 22, 2019, https://www.politifact.com/factchecks/2019/feb/22/joe-biden/how-much-have-domestic-violence-rates-fallen-viole/.

Jacobson, "Domestic Violence Rates."

Leigh Goodmark, "Stop Treating Domestic Violence Differently from Other Crimes," *New York Times*, July 23, 2019, https://www.nytimes.com/2019/07/23/opinion/domestic-violence-criminal-justice-reform-too.html.

Shannan Catalano, "Intimate Partner Violence, 1993–2010," Bureau of Justice Statistics, U.S. Department of Justice, revised September 29, 2015, https://bjs.ojp.gov/content/pub/pdf/ipv9310.pdf; Jennifer L. Truman and Lynn Langton, "Criminal Victimization, 2014," Bureau of Justice Statistics, U.S. Department of Justice, revised September 29, 2015, https://bjs.ojp.gov/content/pub/pdf/cv14.pdf; Jennifer L. Truman and Rachel E. Morgan, "Criminal Victimization, 2015," Bureau of Justice Statistics, U.S. Department of Justice, revised March 22, 2018, https://bjs.ojp.gov/content/pub/pdf/cv15.pdf; Rachel E. Morgan and Alexandra Thompson, "Criminal Victimization, 2020," Bureau of Justice Statistics, U.S. Department of Justice, October 2021, https://bjs.ojp.gov/sites/g/files/xyckuh236/files/media/document/cv20.pdf.

"Overview of the Office on Violence Against Women FY 2022 Request," Office on Violence Against Women, U.S. Department of Justice, May 2021, https://www.ojp.gov/sites/g/files/xyckuh241/files/media/document/ovwfactsheet.pdf.

"Child Maltreatment Databank Indicator," ChildTrends, May 7, 2018, https://www.childtrends.org/publications/child-maltreatment-databank-indicator.

Robert Sege and Allison Stephens, "Child Physical Abuse Did Not Increase during the Pandemic," *JAMA Pediatrics* 176, no. 4 (2022): 338–40, https://doi.org/10.1001/jamapediatrics.2021.5476.

Brenda Patoine, "Child Abuse Actually Decreased during COVID. Here's Why," TuftsNow, February 14, 2022, https://now.tufts.edu/2022/02/14/child-abuse -actually-decreased-during-covid-heres-why.

"Shared Parenting and Child Abuse and Neglect: An Ohio Study," National Parents Organization, accessed July 8, 2023, https://static1.squarespace .com/static/5e28a95cdc8bed16729b93de/t/63fd03169713e651626d8254 /1677525782296/Shared+Parenting+and+Child+Abuse+and+Neglect+ -+An+Ohio+Study.docx.pdf.

"Violent or Graphic Content Policies," YouTube Help, retrieved July 20, 2023 from https://support.google.com/youtube/answer/2802008?hl=en.

Denise Hines, in discussion with the author, January 16, 2023.

Jennifer O'Mahony, "Women: Hitting Your Man Is Not Cute; It's Abuse," Telegraph, March 15, 2013, https://www.telegraph.co.uk/women/womens -life/9930142/Women-hitting-your-man-is-not-cute-its-abuse.html.

Natalia Milano, "Why I Stopped Slapping My Boyfriend in the Face," Medium, February 15, 2016, https://medium.com/@natalia.milano/why-i-stopped -slapping-my-boyfriend-in-the-face-61d16a7f618c.

Sharon G. Smith et al., "The National Intimate Partner and Sexual Violence Survey: 2015 Data Brief—Updated Release," National Center for Injury Prevention and Control, November 2018, https://www.cdc.gov/violenceprevention/pdf /2015data-brief508.pdf.

Erica L. Smith, "Just the Stats: Female Murder Victims and Victim-Offender Relationship, 2021," Bureau of Justice Statistics, U.S. Department of Justice, December 2022, https://bjs.ojp.gov/female-murder-victims-and-victim -offender-relationship-2021.

"Child Maltreatment 2019: Summary of Key Findings," Children's Bureau, U.S. Department of Health and Human Services, April 2021, https://www .childwelfare.gov/pubpdfs/canstats.pdf.

"Foster Care Statistics 2019," Children's Bureau, U.S. Department of Health and Human Services, March 2021, https://www.childwelfare.gov/pubPDFs/foster .pdf.

Deborah H. Siegel and Susan Livingston Smith, "Openness in Adoption: From Secrecy and Stigma to Knowledge and Connections," Evan B. Donaldson Adoption Institute, March 2012, https://www.adoptionstar.com/openness -in-adoptionfrom-secrecy-and-stigma-to-knowledge-and-connections/.

Mikel L. Walters, Jieru Chen, and Matthew J. Breiding, "The National Intimate Partner and Sexual Violence Survey (NISVS): 2010 Findings on Victimization by Sexual Orientation," National Center for Injury Prevention and Control, January 2013, https://www.cdc.gov/violenceprevention/pdf /nisvs_sofindings.pdf.

Luca Rollè et al., "When Intimate Partner Violence Meets Same Sex Couples: A Review of Same Sex Intimate Partner Violence," *Frontiers in Psychology* 9 (2018): 1506, https://doi.org/10.3389/fpsyg.2018.01506.

Larissa MacFarquhar, "The Radical Transformation of a Battered Women's Shelter," *New Yorker*, August 12, 2019, https://www.newyorker.com/magazine /2019/08/19/the-radical-transformations-of-a-battered-womens-shelter.

Matthew R. Durose et al., "Family Violence Statistics Including Statistics on Strangers and Acquaintances," Bureau of Justice Statistics, U.S. Department of Justice, June 2005, https://bjs.ojp.gov/content/pub/pdf/fvs02.pdf.

Leigh Goodmark, discussion.

Leigh Goodmark, discussion.

Lawrence W. Sherman and Heather M. Harris, "Increased Death Rates of Domestic Violence Victims from Arresting vs. Warning Suspects in the Milwaukee Domestic Violence Experiment (MilDVE)," *Journal of Experimental Criminology* 11 (2015): 1–20, https://doi.org/10.1007/s11292-014-9203-x.

Ashley-Nicole Russell, in discussion with the author, January 25, 2023.

"Child Maltreatment 2019."

Mary I. Sanchez-Rodriguez, "Gender Differences in Child Maltreatment: Child Sexual and Physical Abuse" (honors thesis, Grand Valley State University, 2021), https://scholarworks.gvsu.edu/honorsprojects/828.

Denise Hines, discussion.

Leigh Goodmark, discussion.

Jennifer J. Harman, Sadie Leder-Elder, and Zeynep Biringen, "Prevalence of Parental Alienation Drawn from a Representative Poll," *Children and Youth Services Review* 66 (July 2016): 62–66, https://doi.org/10.1016/j.childyouth .2016.04.021.

Caitlyn Bentley and Mandy Matthewson, "The Not-Forgotten Child: Alienated Adult Children's Experience of Parental Alienation," *American Journal of Family Therapy* 48, no. 5 (2020): 509–29, https://doi.org/10.1080/01926187 .2020.1775531.

Jennifer J. Harman et al., "Gender Differences in the Use of Parental Alienating Behaviors," *Journal of Family Violence* 35 (2019): 459–69, https://doi.org/10 .1007/s10896-019-00097-5.

Jennifer J. Harman et al., "Developmental Psychology and the Scientific Status of Parental Alienation," *Developmental Psychology* 58, no. 10 (October 2022): 1887–911, https://doi.org/10.1037/dev0001404.

Sadie Ruben, "With $500,000 Grant Law Professor to Lead Research on Domestic Violence," *GW Hatchet*, updated November 5, 2014, https://www.gwhatchet.com/2014/10/30/with-500000-grant-law-professor-to-lead-research-on-domestic-violence/.

Joan S. Meier et al., "Child Custody Outcomes in Cases Involving Parental Alienation and Abuse Allegations," GWU Law School Public Law Research Paper No. 2019-56, 2019, https://scholarship.law.gwu.edu/cgi/viewcontent.cgi?article=2712&context=faculty_publications.

Jennifer Harman, in discussion with the author, October 4, 2022.

Jennifer J. Harman and Demosthenes Lorandos, "Allegations of Family Violence in Court: How Parental Alienation Affects Judicial Outcomes," *Psychology, Public Policy, and Law* 27, no. 2 (May 2021): 187–208, https://doi.org/10.1037/law0000301.

Joan S. Meier et al., "Harman and Lorandos' False Critique of Meier et al.'s Family Court Study," *Journal of Family Trauma, Child Custody & Child Development* 19, no. 2 (2022): 119–38, https://doi.org/10.1080/26904586.2022.2086659.

SCImago Journal & Country Rank, accessed July 8, 2023, https://www.scimagojr.com/journalsearch.php.

Jennifer J. Harman, William Bernet, and Joseph Harman, "Parental Alienation: The Blossoming of a Field of Study," *Current Directions in Psychological Science* 28, no. 2 (April 2019): 212–17, https://doi.org/10.1177/0963721419827271.

Joan Meier, email message to the author, January 31, 2023.

William Bernet, "Recurrent Misinformation Regarding Parental Alienation Theory," *American Journal of Family Therapy* 51, no. 4 (2023): 334–55, https://doi.org/10.1080/01926187.2021.1972494.

"(February 10, 2022) S.3263 Violence Against Women Act Reauthorization Act of 2022. Title XV—Keeping Children Safe from Family Violence." https://www.congress.gov/bill/117th-congress/senate-bill/3623/text.

Harman, discussion.

Elizabeth Randol, "Opposition to SB 78 P.N. 73 (Baker)—'Kayden's Law,'" ACLU Pennsylvania, February 22, 2021, https://www.aclupa.org/en/legislation/sb-78-child-custody-proceedings-kaydens-law.

Harman, discussion.

Greg Varner, "GW Law's Joan Meier Is Installed in Newly Endowed Professorship Supporting Family Violence Survivors," *GW Today*, April 1, 2022, https://gwtoday.gwu.edu/gw-laws-joan-meier-installed-newly-endowed-professorship-supporting-family-violence-survivors.

Matt Hale, "Kentucky's Popular Joint-Custody Law Shows Why It's the Most Effective at Helping Families," *Courier Journal* (Louisville, KY), August 30, 2019, https://www.courier-journal.com/story/opinion/2019/08/30/kentuckys-joint-custody-law-leads-decline-family-court-cases/2158216001/.

Hale, "Kentucky's Popular Joint-Custody Law."

Fernandez-Kranz and Nollenberger, "Impact of Equal Parenting Time Laws."

William V. Fabricius et al., "What Happens When There Is Presumptive 50/50 Parenting Time? An Evaluation of Arizona's New Child Custody Statute," *Journal of Divorce & Remarriage* 59, no. 5 (2018): 414–28, https://doi.org/10.1080/10502556.2018.1454196.

Denise Hines, discussion.

Chapter 6: The Future Is Now

Justin Pfaff, in discussion with the author, January 3, 2023.

Gretchen Livingston, "The Changing Profile of Unmarried Parents," Pew Research Center, April 25, 2018, https://www.pewresearch.org/social-trends/2018/04/25/the-changing-profile-of-unmarried-parents/.

Livingston, "Changing Profile of Unmarried Parents."

"Here's Why Millennials Are Ditching Engagement Rings," Wabii Branding, July 6, 2019, https://wabiibranding.com/heres-why-millennials-are-ditching-engagement-rings/?doing_wp_cron=1688841625.5603530406951904296875.

Emma Johnson, "Single Moms with 50/50 Co-Parenting Schedules Earn More, Survey of 2,279 Finds," *Wealthy Single Mommy* (blog), updated June 20, 2023, https://www.wealthysinglemommy.com/survey/.

Siegel and Smith, "Openness in Adoption."

"CBS News Poll: Two-Thirds of Americans Say Separating Children, Parents at Border Unacceptable," CBS News, June 18, 2018, https://www.cbsnews.com/news/two-thirds-of-americans-say-separating-children-parents-at-border-unacceptable/.

Justin McCarthy, "Same-Sex Marriage Support Inches Up to New High of 71 Percent," Gallup, June 1, 2022, https://news.gallup.com/poll/393197/same-sex-marriage-support-inches-new-high.aspx.

Richard Reeves, in discussion with the author, December 8, 2022.

Julie Johnson, in discussion with the author, October 5, 2020.

Erin K. Holmes, Braquel R. Egginton, Alan J. Hawkins, Nathan L. Robbins, and Kevin Shafer, "Do Responsible Fatherhood Programs Work? A Comprehensive Meta-Analytic Study," *Family Relations*, 69 (2020): 967–982, https://doi.org/10.1111/fare.12435.

"Shared Parenting Polling: A National Consensus," National Parents Organization, accessed February 23, 2023, https://static1.squarespace .com/static/5e28a95cdc8bed16729b93de/t/6033f1dc5b2baf3663ac1d83 /1614016988674/NPO+Nationwide+Polling+Report.pdf.

Mary Kuhlman, "Poll Shows New Shared Parenting Law Popular among Kentuckians; Joint Custody Is the Legal Presumption," *Northern Kentucky Tribune*, September 6, 2018, https://www.nkytribune.com/2018/09 /poll-shows-new-shared-parenting-law-popular-among-kentuckians-joint -custody-is-the-legal-presumption/.

"U.S. Custody Dispute Statistics," Father's Rights Movement, accessed February 23, 2023, https://tfrm.org/statistics/.

"FY 2002 and FY 2003 Annual Report to Congress," Office of Child Support Enforcement, U.S. Department of Health and Human Services, December 1, 2003, https://www.acf.hhs.gov/css/report/fy-2002-and-fy-2003-annual -report-congress; "Preliminary Report FY 2021," Office of Child Support Enforcement, U.S. Department of Health and Human Services, 2021, https:// www.acf.hhs.gov/sites/default/files/documents/ocse/fy_2021_preliminary _report.pdf.

Grall, "Custodial Mothers and Fathers."

"Preliminary Report FY 2021."

"403.270 Custodial Issues—Best Interests of Child Shall Determine—Rebuttable Presumption that Join Custody and Equally Shared Parenting Time Is in Child's Best Interests—De Facto Custodian." https://apps.legislature.ky.gov /law/statutes/statute.aspx?id=51299.

"Child Support and Incarceration," National Conference of State Legislatures, updated February 1, 2022, https://www.ncsl.org/human-services/child -support-and-incarceration#anchor8476.

"Ensuring Families Receive All Child Support Payments," Aspen Institute, February 2023, https://ascend-resources.aspeninstitute.org/resources/child -support-policy-fact-sheet-paying-support-to-families/.

Elaine Sorenson, "Exploring Trends in the Percent of Orders for Zero Dollars," Office of Child Support Enforcement, U.S. Department of Health and Human Services, April 2018, https://www.acf.hhs.gov/sites/default/files/documents /ocse/story_behind_the_numbers_cases_with_zero_dollar_orders.pdf.

Noam Scheiber, "An Expensive Law Degree, and No Place to Use It," *New York*

Times, June 19, 2016, https://www.nytimes.com/2016/06/19/business
/dealbook/an-expensive-law-degree-and-no-place-to-use-it.html.

Ashley-Nicole Russell, discussion.

Susan Guthrie, discussion.

Chapter 7: Solutions

Malin Bergström, discussion.

Kevin Bremond, discussion.

"The Maternal, Infant, and Early Childhood Home Visiting Program,"
Administration for Children & Families, May 2023, https://mchb.hrsa.gov
/sites/default/files/mchb/about-us/program-brief.pdf.

Erin Holmes et al., "Do Responsible Fatherhood Programs Work? A
Comprehensive Meta-Analytic Study," Fatherhood Research & Practice
Network, December 2018, https://www.frpn.org/asset/frpn-grantee-report
-do-responsible-fatherhood-programs-work-comprehensive-meta-analytic
-study.

Kevin Bremond, discussion.

Arizona State University, "ASU Psychology Research Leads to International
Conversation about Custody Laws," ASU News, March 2, 2020, https://
news.asu.edu/20200302-asu-psychology-research-leads-international
-conversation-about-custody-laws.

Courtney E. Martin, "Child Support vs. Deadbeat States," *New York Times*,
September 10, 2019, https://www.nytimes.com/2019/09/10/opinion/child
-support-states.html.

Bethany G. Everett et al., "Male Abortion Beneficiaries: Exploring the Long-
Term Educational and Economic Associations of Abortion among Men Who
Report Teen Pregnancy," *Journal of Adolescent Health* 65, no. 4 (October 2019):
520–26, https://doi.org/10.1016/j.jadohealth.2019.05.001.

Laura Duberstein Lindberg, Kathryn Kost, and Isaac Maddow-Zimet, "The Role
of Men's Childbearing Intentions in Father Involvement," *Journal of Marriage
and the Family* 79, no. 1 (February 2017): 44–59, https://doi.org/10.1111/jomf
.12377.

Jacinta Bronte-Tinkew et al., "Male Pregnancy Intendedness and Children's
Mental Proficiency and Attachment Security during Toddlerhood," *Journal of
Marriage and Family* 71, no. 4 (November 2009): 1001–25, http://www.jstor
.org/stable/27752515; Jacinta Bronte-Tinkew et al., "Pregnancy Intentions

during the Transition to Parenthood and Links to Coparenting for First-Time Fathers of Infants," *Parenting* 9, no. 1–2 (2009): 1–35, https://doi.org/10.1080/15295190802656729.

Chapter 8: FAQs about 50/50 Parenting

Jessica Pearson and Rachel Wildfeuer, "Policies and Programs Affecting Fathers: A State-by-State Report," Fatherhood Research & Practice Network, October 2022, https://www.frpn.org/asset/policies-and-programs-affecting-fathers-state-state-report-combined-pdf.

Hyunjoon Um, "The Role of Child Support Debt on the Development of Mental Health Problems among Noncustodial Fathers," Columbia University School of Social Sciences, Working Paper No. 19–05-FF, cited in Vicki Turetsky and Maureen R. Waller, "Piling on Debt: The Intersections between Child Support Arrears and Legal Financial Obligations," *UCLA Criminal Justice Law Review* 4, no. 1 (2020): 129n65, https://escholarship.org/uc/item/7vd043jw; Heather Hahn et al., "Relief from Government-Owed Child Support Debt and Its Effects on Parents and Children," Urban Institute, August 20, 2019, https://www.urban.org/research/publication/relief-government-owed-child-support-debt-and-its-effects-parents-and-children.

Lenna Nepomnyaschy et al., "Parental Debt and Child Well-Being: What Type of Debt Matters for Child Outcomes?," *Russell Sage Foundation Journal of the Social Sciences* 7, no. 3 (August 2021): 122–51, https://doi.org/10.7758/rsf.2021.7.3.06.

Claire Cain Miller and Quoctrung Bui, "Equality in Marriages Grows, and So Does Class Divide," *New York Times*, February 27, 2016, https://www.nytimes.com/2016/02/23/upshot/rise-in-marriages-of-equals-and-in-division-by-class.html.

Richard V. Reeves and Edward Rodrigue, "Single Black Female BA Seeks Educated Husband: Race, Assortative Mating and Inequality," Brookings Institution, April 9, 2015, https://www.brookings.edu/research/single-black-female-ba-seeks-educated-husband-race-assortative-mating-and-inequality/.

ABOUT THE AUTHOR

Emma Johnson is a journalist, entrepreneur, and activist. Founder of Wealthysinglemommy.com and Moms for Shared Parenting, her books, interviews, and writing on gender equality have been featured in hundreds of news outlets, including the *New York Times*, the *Wall Street Journal*, *Elle*, and CNBC. She has spoken about equal parenting to audiences at Google and the United Nations Summit for Gender Equality. Emma lives in Richmond, Virginia, with her son and daughter.